☆、Marquis Yongchun Ma
Xichun Street in Kyoto
Apart from four and a
at both ends, only the (
However, this family has

In the past, the ancestors of the Chen family had fought with the founding emperor and made immortal military achievements. They were named Yongchun Hou by the emperor and the title was inherited from generation to generation. However, after the old emperor passed away and the new emperor came, the head of the Chen family also changed, and the Chen family was no longer as glorious as before.

The reason was that after the founding of the country, it was a prosperous era for a long period of time and there had been no wars for many years. The descendants of the Chen family either neglected training or did not inherit their ancestors' martial arts skills. In the third year of Taiwu, the old man of the Chen family was sent by the new emperor to the desert to attack the Mongolian soldiers. As a result, the old man of the Chen family returned in defeat.

The new emperor was furious and almost took away the Chen family's title. In the end, it was only after the officials pleaded for mercy that he dismissed them from their posts. The Chen family never recovered from that defeat and it was not until more than 20 years later that they gradually got better.

At this time, the crabapple trees in front of Yongchun Hou Mansion were full of pink flowers. Another year had passed, and in the blink of an eye it was early summer.

In Ci Xin Garden, Madam Chen was talking with her eldest aunt Chen Linzhi, the eldest lady Zhang, her eldest grandson's wife Cao Xiangmei, and the second lady Chen Ning'an.

Chen Ning'an is very beautiful and her manners are often praised as dignified and graceful.

Zhang looked at her daughter lovingly, nodded and smiled, "It would be nice to invite them to be our guests. I miss Madam Wu too. When they moved to Suzhou, I thought I would never see her again."

"Yeah, I think so too," Chen Linzhi said while looking at Chen Ning'an with a smile, "The second young lady of the Wu family is about the same age as you, I think you two will get along well."

As they were talking, the second wife, Jiang, and the third, fourth, and fifth girls arrived.

The four of them came together to pay their respects.

Chen Linzhi smiled and said, "It's been a long time since we last met. My nieces have become more and more likable."

But his eyes stayed on the face of the fourth girl, Chen Ningyu.

There are many beauties in Kyoto, too many

to count with two hands, but her fourth niece is probably among the top three. It is quite rare, as the looks of the couples in the first and second wives are not much different, but only the second wife has such a stunning beauty.

The lady asked them to sit down and sighed, "Fortunately, I have these lovely girls. I feel comfortable just looking at them and don't think about those bad things often!"

Chen Linzhi knew her mother was upset about her sister, so she joked, "Just now I heard from Mother Ji that Ning Yu often played mahjong with you and lost a lot of money to you? Mom, you are so mean, bullying your granddaughter."

Chen Ningyu smiled and said, "Aunt, losing to grandma is a happy thing. Losing to others is a big loss. Besides, grandma doesn't bully people. She won my money and gave me delicious food."

The lady couldn't help but burst out laughing: "Oh, you are good at making up stories. I am just like an old woman who uses food to trick children into giving her money. This girl!"

Everyone laughed.

"But mother, don't let Ning Yu play this next time." Jiang sat on the chair closest to Chen Linzhi, slightly dissatisfied, "After all, she is a girl. If it gets out, people will think she is a gambler, wouldn't that make her a laughing stock? Girls should be like Ning An."

Chen Ningan said modestly: "Second Aunt, don't say that. I can't learn it because I'm stupid. I'm not like Fourth Sister, who can learn it right away."

Jiang raised her eyebrows.

The lady didn't take it seriously: "It's just a family joke, how can it spread? It's just to entertain me." She took a sip of tea, "You guys come now, I'll tell you about the matter. In a few days, we will invite the Wu family to come as guests. You and your sister-in-law will take care of it together, so that everything can be done more thoroughly."

Jiang had also heard her husband mention it, and said with a smile, "It's a happy event for old friends to meet, but my daughter-in-law doesn't know the Wu family at all."

She was not like the first lady, Madam Zhang, who was originally born in the capital. Even though she had lived here for many years, she didn't recognize the ladies who had lived here before.

"Mr. Wu has traveled all over the country and served as an official in various places, but his hometown is in the capital, and he got married there as well." Zhang listed all the details. "Mrs. Wu and I are old friends. She likes to eat candied fruits and always brings them with her wherever she goes. We all jokingly call her the Candied Fruit Girl. It's been many years."

Chen Linzhi said, "She loves to eat it now, so she should be called Mrs. Preserved

Fruit."

Jiang curled her lips. Mrs. Wu had a very good relationship with Chen Linzhi, but Zhang just spoke as if she was her close friend. She had just married into the family at that time, so why was she pretending to be so familiar?

"It's a rare visit from my aunt, so she must stay here for dinner." She quickly laughed, "It's a pity that Ji He and Ji Wan were not brought along. Li Er often said it was lonely and he missed his two cousins."

When talking about her two sons, Zhang sighed: "They are poor students. My husband is very strict with them. He usually doesn't let them go out to play. He said that if they don't pass the imperial examination, they can't relax for a day."

The lady frowned disapprovingly and said, "Why are you pushing so hard? The Zhang family still has to rely on Ji He and Ji Wan to support the family. Besides, Ji He is just a kid, but Ji Wan doesn't look like a good student. I think it would be better for him to come to our house and learn martial arts from his uncle. He might have a future."

She felt that it was more likely that Zhang Jiwan would become a military general.

But Zhang was unwilling to let her son go. Being a military commander was not an easy thing. Learning martial arts was hard, and going to the battlefield was likely to cost you your head. Even managing public security in the capital was risky. She would rather her son study, but she did not object to the lady's opinion: "Let him try first. Ji Wan is a very naughty child. I only feel sorry for Ji He."

Chen Ningyu had been listening, thinking of how Zhang Jiwan had never been at peace since he came to the Chen family. During the New Year, he had even knocked over her teacup. She said that she had learned kung fu from a street performer, and that she could catch the teacup with both hands, but two out of three broke into pieces.

The teacup was a complete set, sky blue in color, and as beautiful as jade. She was so angry at that time!

Zhang Jiwan was afraid that she would go and complain and be beaten by his father, so he swore to heaven that he would compensate her in the future.

This guy, at least, is better behaved than a naughty kid. He knows he is wrong. For the sake of her relatives, she did not argue with him. However, it seems that the compensation might be wasted.

After sitting for a while, the lady asked them to leave, as she had something private to say to Chen Linzhi.

Jiang took her three daughters back to Xingfangyuan.

As the name suggests, this yard is full of apricot trees. Unfortunately, Jiang didn't like these trees. She glanced at Chen Ningyu and then shifted her gaze to Chen

Ninghua's face.

"When someone from the Wu family comes, you must not lose your manners." She warned them in a serious tone, "Although Madam Wu is an old friend of your aunt and was raised by your madam, you haven't seen her for many years. You still have to be tactful."

All three girls said yes.

Jiang asked them to go, and only Chen Ningrou stayed.

That was her biological daughter, unlike Chen Ningyu and Chen Ninghua, one was born to her husband's ex-wife and the other was a concubine's daughter.

Chen Ningrou held Jiang's arm affectionately, blinked her eyes and said, "I saw my eldest aunt coming, and I was afraid that she would matchmake my second sister again."

Chen Ningrou had an oval face and round eyes, and was very cute. Jiang looked at her and said angrily, "Little clever girl, you know all this."

"He must have taken a fancy to the young master of the Wu family. I don't know what kind of person he is. How does he compare to the young master Li from last time?"

Chen Ningrou thought of something funny and chuckled, "What if he takes a fancy to Fourth Sister again? Wouldn't the eldest aunt be furious again?"

When the young master of the Wu family was fifteen years old, he went to Beijing for the imperial examination and came to visit the family. She and Zhang had both met him and had a good impression of him. However, after these years, who knows what he is like? There is nothing to be said about his fate. Jiang immediately frowned and said, "Girls should not talk about these things. If others know about it, they will think you are frivolous. You just don't listen!"

"My daughter has heard this many times, and it has long been engraved in my heart. Don't worry, mother." Chen Ningrou said perfunctorily, thinking that she was just asking out of curiosity, what was the big deal.

Jiang pulled her into the house and asked the maid to bring her favorite snacks, saying, "Don't just say that Ning Yu is good at pleasing the Madam. The Madam was upset and wanted to play cards to relieve her boredom. She accompanied her for so many days and only stopped after she made her happy. You just keep telling me that the Madam has some good things in her hands. Let's see if she will give them to you."

Chen Ningrou said awkwardly, "I'm making a headband for grandma. It will be ready in a few days."

Jiang sighed.

Her daughter is smart but she lacks patience. Fortunately, she has her husband to protect her and she also likes her. Otherwise, it would be a real worry!

At this moment, Chen Ningyu also entered

the courtyard where she lived, Furong Garden.

To match the name, she ordered people to plant a lot of hibiscus flowers here two years ago. By last year, they had already taken root and bloomed, but this year it is still too early for them to bloom.

"Tell them to add some more fertilizer later. I think the branches and leaves are not growing fast enough." Hibiscus flowers can usually grow very tall, and when they form a cluster, the flowers bloom, which is quite stunning.

Chen Ningyu walked into the house, drank a few sips of cold tea, and asked her maid Gu Qiu to bring the sewing basket.

"It's hot today, why don't you take a rest?" Gu Qiu took it as he said and said with concern, "There's no rush. Second Master's birthday is still a long way off."

"It's just to kill time." Chen Ningyu took out a shoe pattern and brown cotton thread. "Besides, it's good to make one more pair. Dad likes the shoes I make."

In this world, her biological mother is gone, and the person closest to her is only her father. Fortunately, her father is not a fool, so there is no such situation as "if there is a stepmother, there must be a stepfather". He still loves her very much.

In return, she was very attentive to her father.

Gu Qiu stopped persuading her and picked up the silk fan to fan her.

Chen Ningyu had just finished threading the needle when Bai Tao came in and asked mysteriously, "Miss, do you know who the young master of the Wu family who will be coming tomorrow is?"

☆, Between sisters-in-law

Chen Ningyu had expected Chen Linzhi to come early on, and it must be related to these things. It was because Chen Linzhi particularly liked to be a matchmaker. Since she had not given birth to a daughter, she was very concerned about the life-long affairs of her nieces. Whenever there was a suitable one, she could not wait. Chen Ningrong, the eldest daughter of the Chen family, was married because of her.

Of course, she married well. Her husband's family was a prominent family in Kyoto. The master of the Lin family was the right vice minister of the Ministry of Works and concurrently the governor of Jiangxi. The young master of the Lin family was still young and was serving as the magistrate of Luoning County in Luoyang, which was considered as an experience, and Chen Ningrong also followed him.

Chen Ningyu looked up and asked, "Did your mother tell you this again?"

Bai Tao scratched her head and chuckled, "This maid is also doing this for the young lady's own good."

Bai Tao's biological mother, Liu Pozi,

works in the Lady Dowager's Courtyard. She has come to ask for credit several times, but she just wants her daughter to be valued by Chen Ningyu. All parents in the world have the same idea.

Chen Ningyu ignored her, poked the needle into the sole of her shoe, and said to Danqiu, "Go to the kitchen later and tell them to steam some sweet-scented osmanthus fish and stew some skirt at noon."

She was no longer a child, and she did not need her elders to arrange meals for her. She could order dishes on her own. Although the Yongchun Marquis Mansion was not as prominent as before, the personal expenses in the mansion were much better than those of ordinary families.

Not to mention, Chen Ningyu is different from other girls. Even if she eats delicacies from land and sea every day, it is nothing.

Bai Tao was a little dazed. She originally wanted to tell Chen Ningyu that the young master of the Wu family was the one who rescued the emperor in Tong County last time.

Speaking of saving the emperor, it was because the emperor of this dynasty occasionally liked to go on tours incognito, and he did not bring many people with him. Not long ago, he was on a tour to Tong County near the capital. I don't know if it was because he showed off his wealth that he attracted bandits, but he was attacked on the way. Fortunately, someone came to his rescue.

That person is the young master of the Wu family.

Saving the emperor's life is a great achievement.

But my own girl didn't even want to understand.

Gu Qiu frowned and said, "Why don't you leave? Don't disturb the girl from doing needlework."

Bai Tao had no choice but to leave unhappily.

In fact, Chen Ningyu did not have no ideas, but she felt that whether Mr. Wu was good or bad was meaningless to her, and it was not her turn. Besides, she was not in a hurry. If possible, she really wanted to live in the mansion until she was twenty years old.

Nowadays, although she has no biological mother, she lives a very comfortable life. She has endless money, her grandmother likes her, her father loves her, she can eat whatever she wants every day, and her stepmother is apparently doing well too, so she can be said to be worry-free.

But what if you get married?

There may be days of chaos and trouble soon. The more powerful the family, the more likely it is to be so. Wasn't the lady unhappy about her little daughter's affairs a few days ago?

Her younger daughter, Chen Linru, the

second aunt of the Chen family, married into the Xu family nine years ago. Xu Ke was also a capable man. At the age of 32, he had already become a fourth-rank official. He was currently the Left Censor-in-Chief of the Censorate. This marriage was a good one no matter how you looked at it.

But the annoying thing is that Xu Ke is the only son in the family, while Chen Linru has not given birth to a son in all these years of marriage, but three daughters.

Old Madam Xu was not happy about this and wanted to take a concubine for her son. She wanted a girl with a bad record, who was her distant niece.

This matter made the old lady very angry. She was afraid that her daughter would be wronged, but she could not object. People were counting on Chen Linru to have children, but she didn't have a son and was getting older. What reason did she have to stop it?

What's more, Xu Ke has always been a good person, how could she not allow people to take concubines? Even if it was normal, taking one was nothing, let alone this situation.

The old lady had no choice but to agree, but she still fought for Chen Linru and firmly disagreed with the candidate that Old Madam Xu liked. Old Madam Xu was also annoyed, so she simply became a hands-off boss and let the old lady choose one herself and send it to the Xu Mansion.

Chen Ningyu sighed.

In this world, it is really not easy for anyone to live. She was a good young man in her previous life, but she lost her life because of an unexpected disaster. But no matter what, she still has to live well in this life and try to live comfortably.

The premise is that you cannot marry into a family with so many troubles.

However, she was not sure whether things could go as she wished, so she could only do her best.

In the evening, Chen Xiu came back. He was the assistant commander of the Beijing Guard Command, in charge of ten guard posts. He was very busy every day and often had to go on patrols. In such summer, he was basically drenched in sweat.

Jiang hurriedly asked the servants to prepare water for him to bathe, and ordered the kitchen to bring some cold soup to cool him down.

Chen Xiu changed into clean clothes and felt better after drinking the soup.

Only then did Jiang chat with him for a while.

When he heard that the Wu family was going to be invited over, Chen Xiu said, "We should invite them. When they were in Kyoto, we often went to their house. I didn't expect that we would be separated for so long. The last time I ran into Brother Wu in the government office, I didn't even recognize him."

Time makes people grow old, and he couldn't help but sigh.

Jiang comforted him, "This time, even if Mr. Wu is transferred out again, it seems that Mrs. Wu will not follow him. The child has grown up and needs to settle down here."

"Yes, they are from Kyoto after all."

Jiang leaned over and asked with a smile, "I heard from Madam Tai today that the two families are really close friends. Were you also very familiar with Mr. Wu when you were young?"

Chen Xiu shook his head: "Brother Wu is about the same age as my elder brother. In fact, he was closer to my elder brother. I was still young at that time, so he didn't play with me very much."

Jiang nodded: "No wonder the eldest sister-in-law is so happy."

The master of the Wu family was directly promoted to the position of Left Vice Minister of the Ministry of Personnel, and he was a childhood playmate of the master of the Chen family, Chen Xing, the Marquis of Yongchun. If the two young people are suitable, this marriage will most likely be successful.

Zhang's two daughters really have a smooth life!

Jiang pursed her lips and said, "In fact, it's time for our Ning Hua to talk about her. She is only three months younger than Ning An."

Chen Xiu glanced at her and said calmly, "Why are you saying this suddenly? Even if Ning Hua wants to get married, she has to wait until Ning An is married." He paused, "But if there is a suitable one, you can keep an eye out for it first."

Jiang smiled and said, "Yes, that's what I meant. Aunt Su told me the same thing last time..."

"What?" Chen Xiu frowned, a hint of anger on his face, "Who is she to bring up this?"

"She will give birth to Ning Hua." Jiang pleaded for Aunt Su.

Chen Xiu snorted, "She's really pushing it too far. If she dares to say one more word next time, she'll be confined to her house. Ning Hua, don't let her go to see her!"

Jiang looked embarrassed, but still nodded.

As a result, Aunt Su was put under house arrest the next day and her monthly salary for three months was withheld.

When going to pay respects to the lady dowager, Chen Ningyu saw that Chen Ninghua's eyes were a little red, but he still forced a smile and did not look very sad.

No one noticed it, only Chen Ningrou asked her with concern: "What's wrong with Third Sister? Are you crying?"

Chen Ninghua hurriedly shook his head: "The wind blew sand in when I came here."

Chen Ningrou snorted slightly.

Chen Ninghua lowered his head and clenched the hem of his clothes with his hands.

The lady said to Zhang, "This morning the farm just sent some wild animals. Ask the kitchen to prepare them and cook something fresh. The Wu family may get tired of eating other food."

Jiang clapped her hands and said, "Game is indeed suitable. Madam is very thoughtful. The chef at home always makes delicious food. We have invited the Jin family, the Dai family, and the Li family to come before, and everyone praised the venison!"

Zhang's face suddenly turned bad, and she glared at Chen Ningyu fiercely.

What did she do but still get blamed? Jiang was really going to bring hatred upon her. Chen Ningyu pretended not to know. Anyway, she did not seduce the young master of the Li family, so she had a clear conscience.

As for the conflict between the Zhang and Jiang families, that has a long history.

It was just because one of them came from a wealthy family and the other from a small one, they disliked each other. In addition, Jiang's husband was not Marquis Yongchun, so the two of them were not harmonious.

Whenever she had the chance, Jiang would always stab Zhang.

I don't know if it's really that good after getting stabbed. Chen Ningyu was speechless. The lady-in-waiting was also unhappy with what Jiang said. You know, the incident with the Li family was quite a blow to Zhang. After all, she was the one who chose him, and then she was stabbed in the back.

She was extremely angry.

Of course, this cannot be blamed on Chen Ningyu.

The lady still had great faith in Chen Ningyu's character. She could only say that the young master of the Li family was a lecher who went limp when he saw a beautiful woman.

It's actually better to know about this kind of person in advance, which is not a bad thing.

It's better than marrying Chen Ning'an. Then why not let Mr. Li take a concubine when he sees a beauty?

The old lady looked at Jiang with displeasure, but did not get angry. The two daughters-in-law had been fighting for a long time. As long as it was not a big deal, she would not take sides. As people, living together, there were always conflicts. There were times when Jiang was angered by Zhang.

The lady changed the subject: "The girls are grown up now. I think we can make two more dresses for each of them this season so that they won't be so shabby when they go to other people's houses to enjoy the flowers."

"It's good that the madam loves them. I'll ask someone to bring fabrics for them to choose from later." Zhang came from a scholarly family and usually didn't argue with Jiang in public. Her expression turned from gloomy to bright.

Jiang was very happy and joked, "Madam, please be kind to us and give me, my sister-in-law, and Xiang Mei one more set each."

Zhang was not so generous and had to cooperate with her: "I am old, I can make do with anything."

The lady smiled and said, "As for age, I'm here. How dare you say I'm old? Forget it, forget it. Just give me one more set. My eldest daughter-in-law, you've worked hard for many years. One more set is also my thought."

This was the attitude of a lady-in-waiting. Zhang would never refuse and agreed with a smile.

Although Jiang Shi was a little embarrassed, she didn't say much. She didn't dare to really offend the lady.

☆, Sisters

"Let's all go sit in my room. When the fabrics are delivered, we can choose together." Chen Ningrou suggested, looking at Chen Ningan with a smile, "We sisters don't have many opportunities to get together." She looked at Cao Xiangmei again, "Sister-in-law, come too."

Cao Xiangmei had a gentle personality and agreed immediately.

Chen Ning'an didn't like Jiang, but Chen Ningrou was on good terms with her, so it was difficult for her to refuse. She told her maid Shizhu, "Bring me the green mountain tea in my room."

Chen Ningyu's eyes lit up: "Is it wild tea from the mountains of Fujian? We are in for a treat!"

Chen Ningrou asked curiously, "What wild tea? How come I don't know about it?"

"My uncle brought it back when he returned to Beijing to report on his work. There very little wild tea, so I didn't give it to my sisters. Only my grandmother got some, and I have some here too. It's a good time to take it out and let you taste it now."

Chen Ning'an has loved tea since she was a child. Her grandmother's family loves her and always sends her good tea whenever they get it.

The smile on Chen Ningrou's face faded a little.

Thinking about her grandmother's family, it would be good if she didn't take advantage of them. How could she be as blessed as Chen Ningrou! Her father was a marquis, and her mother was from a wealthy family. Not only did she exude nobility, but her manners were also dignified. She was truly a lady from a noble family.

When she thought of this, Chen Ninghua felt even more bitter.

Cao Xiangmei asked Chen Ningyu: "How do you know about this tea?"

"I drank it at my aunt's house once. I heard it was Bishan tea." Chen Ningyu recalled the taste and praised it, "It's bitter but sweet, very fragrant, and it makes me feel clearer after drinking it."

Chen Ningrou didn't even have a smile on her face at this moment.

Chen Ning'an has his maternal grandparents, and Chen Ningyu has a wealthy aunt. Anyway, she has nothing!

"I can't tell good tea from bad tea. Don't waste Second Sister's things." Chen Ningrou didn't show any anger. She just looked at Chen Ninghua and smiled slightly. "Third Sister can taste some, but she's not like Second Sister, who often has good ones."

Chen Ninghua's face suddenly turned red.

She did love elegance, and was proficient in playing the piano, chess, calligraphy, painting, drinking tea, and composing poetry, and had some talent. But when she heard those words just now, her heart felt as if it was pricked by a needle.

"Such good tea, let alone us, I heard that there is very little in the palace, so it is a blessing to be able to drink it." Seeing that Chen Ninghua was embarrassed, Chen Ningyu helped her out.

Cao Xiangmei wiped her face with a handkerchief and said with a smile, "Stop talking here. It's so hot. Let's go quickly."

Several people went to Chen Ningrou.

There is no shortage of courtyards in the Yongchun Marquis Mansion. Several girls each have a private courtyard, but it is not very large, with only three main rooms and an ear room on each side. There are about seven or eight maids and servants in total.

Chen Ningrou named her yard Jinxiu Garden herself, so it is full of colorful flowers and various flowers and trees.

Entering the main room, she asked the maid to bring fruits and vegetables, and asked them to sit down one by one.

"The decoration here is exquisite and it looks very comfortable." Chen Ning'an likes to praise people whenever he meets them.

Chen Ningrou naturally liked to hear nice words, and said with a smile: "How can I not keep my own place clean? But it's not as good as my second sister's. If I could learn her flower arrangement skills, that would be beautiful."

"You yourself don't love it. Isn't that what Master Liang taught you? You were just dozing off there. Do you regret it now?"

Master Liang was a female teacher who was invited to teach the girls in the mansion a few years ago. She was versatile and capable. Unfortunately, Chen Ningyu only studied with her for one year because Master Liang left the capital because of her husband's family affairs.

Looking back, Chen Ningrou was indeed the least diligent one. She smiled and said, "That's right. You were the one who made Master Liang unhappy every time. You were really naughty back then. You are not like a grown-up girl now."

Chen Ningrou giggled: "It's the same if I learn from the sisters anyway."

While they were eating fruits, the housekeeper asked someone to bring some fabrics. They were all silk cotton for summer wear, very light and thin, and could be made into dresses, which were very cool.

The colors are also very rich, including lotus red, crabapple red, parrot green, lilac, bean green, light blue, grass white, etc. The patterns are mostly twined branches, scattered flowers, auspicious grass or no patterns.

Chen Ning'an is the oldest here and should be the first to be challenged, but she has always been humble and called the other three to join her.

Chen Ningrou didn't hesitate and picked two items. When she saw Chen Ninghua was hesitating, she reached out and took one of the emerald green ones with floral patterns for her, saying with a smile, "Since you can't make up your mind, why don't you wear this one? Otherwise, you'll be dazzled by the choices and end up choosing something that doesn't fit you."

Chen Ninghua looks like Aunt Su, with an oval face and big eyes. She is also very good-looking, but her skin is not white enough, and she would look bad in dark green.

"I..." Chen Ninghua wanted to refuse.

Unexpectedly, Chen Ningrou turned around and told the housekeeper that Chen Ninghua wanted the material.

Chen Ninghua was so angry that his eyes turned red. He could no longer bear it and left without saying a word.

"What's wrong with third sister?" Chen Ningrou was curious.

Chen Ning'an frowned slightly. This was their second room's business and she didn't want to say anything more. But it seemed inappropriate to be a spectator and she felt a little embarrassed.

Chen Ningyu sighed. Chen Ningrou had really gone too far today. "Fifth sister, these materials should have been chosen by Third Sister herself. Although Fifth Sister means well, she should also ask Third Sister's opinion, right?"

"Third sister didn't say it herself, so how can I make the decision for her?" Chen Ningrou pouted, "Third sister is really overthinking. We sisters should be honest. If I don't like it, I will naturally not take it. She didn't say it clearly."

Chen Ningyu really didn't know what to say to such a girl, so he stopped talking and picked out two items by himself, one was a lilac-colored one with a pattern of broken crabapple branches, and the other was a lake-colored one with a pattern of curling grass.

Chen Ningan nodded and said with a smile: "Fourth sister looks the most beautiful in these."

When Chen Ningrou heard this, her eyes

darkened.

Ever since she was born, she has been used to set off Chen Ningyu. Although the two have the same father but different mothers, they are both legitimate daughters. When talking about the second branch of the Chen family, they will inevitably be mentioned in the same breath.

But Chen Ningyu was so beautiful, her skin was as lustrous as jade, her eyes were as charming as brown gems, and with just a smile she could captivate a man's soul. Even her voice was clear and pleasant.

She pinched her fingernails in her palms, pursed her lips tightly and said, "Yes, Fourth Sister is really beautiful. No wonder those gentlemen couldn't walk when they saw Fourth Sister."

Chen Ningyu's face darkened slightly.

Chen Ning'an felt uncomfortable when she thought about that incident, but she didn't say anything, as if she still cared about it. But that kind of young man was so unbearable, so she didn't want to marry him!

"Fifth sister, you must never say that again." She warned seriously, "No matter how beautiful Fourth Sister is, not everyone can see her!"

Chen Ningrou didn't expect that she would actually speak for Chen Ningyu, and she was stunned for a moment.

"Fifth sister is young and naive, so sometimes she naturally doesn't understand the importance of things." Chen Ningyu let go of the material in her hand and smiled, "Second sister taught you today, did you listen to her?"

Facing the gazes of the two, Chen Ningrou could not remain stubborn and could only lower her head and say, "I was wrong just now. I hope the sisters won't blame me."

Chen Ning'an was no longer interested at this time and soon said goodbye and left.

Naturally, Chen Ningyu would not stay there. She just asked the housekeeper to pick out some suitable materials and send them to Chen Ninghua for selection.

The housekeeper later told Zhang, who said disdainfully: "I've long seen that girl's character is the same as her mother's, not worthy of being in public!"

"Should I tell the Madam?" the housekeeper asked ingratiatingly.

"Forget it, just think that I am targeting you on purpose. Time will tell, and Madam Tai will know." Zhang paused, turned the mutton-fat jade bracelet on her wrist and said thoughtfully, "The fourth girl is well-educated. Even though she doesn't have a mother to teach her, she is not worse than Ning An."

The housekeeper didn't know how to respond for a moment.

In terms of appearance, the fourth girl is the best in the mansion. In terms of character, she is not bad either, so she is more outstanding than the second girl. As a mother, Zhang is naturally a little unhappy.

The housekeeper managed to utter something: "Beauty is a disaster. A good family would never look for someone with such appearance."

Zhang's expression eased a little.

Chen Ninghua returned to the yard and cried bitterly.

The next day, her eyes were swollen like walnuts. When she went to pay her respects, Chen Zheng was at home on his day off. Jiang said with a fake smile, "Ning Hua is really kind-hearted. It's a pity that Aunt Su loves you well."

Chen Xiu's face immediately turned stern and he hated Chen Ninghua even more.

In fact, Chen Ningyu didn't know why Chen Xiu disliked Chen Ninghua so much. In her impression, Chen Xiu, as a father, had hardly ever shown any concern for Chen Ninghua.

But he treated her, Chen Ningrou, differently.

Seeing that Jiang was gloating over other's misfortune, Chen Ningyu could not help Chen Ninghua. She wanted to tell him about the conflict yesterday. In fact, it was just a trivial matter. Chen Ninghua's big reaction was too petty in the eyes of Chen Xiu, who didn't like her in the first place. What's more, Jiang would definitely help her at that time, and it would be bad if she said it.

On the next holiday, the Wu family, who were mysterious in the eyes of many people, were finally coming. Taking this opportunity, the two aunts of the Chen family also returned to their parents' home with their husbands and children to accompany them.

Gu Qiu combed Chen Ningyu's hair into a double bun and was about to put a colorful pearl hairpin on her head, but Chen Ningyu picked up an inconspicuous white jade hairpin and put it on.

"That's all." She stood up, not dressed too formally.

Gu Qiu had no choice but to give up.

Danqiu came in and said with a smile, "I heard that Madam Wu loves to eat candied fruits, so Madam Tai has prepared a lot of them, all kinds of them. The guests will be here soon."

Chen Ningyu said: "Then let's go."

In such weather, even with servants serving her, she couldn't let go of the fan. She turned around and took the fan before going out.

☆, Years of Friendship

There are already quite a few people at the Madam's place.

Eldest aunt Chen Linzhi was showing off her eldest son Zhang Jihe, saying that he had written an article last time, which won high praise from Master Wang, who read it to all the students in public and ordered them to learn from Zhang Jihe.

It is not without reason that she is so proud. Master Wang is a famous scholar. Many of the students who have been praised by him over the years have become pillars of the court, such as the current Langzhong of the Ministry of Works, Mr. Liu, and Mr. Zhang, the Inspector of Zhejiang. In fact, there are quite a few such people.

But Zhang Jihe's face turned red and he even felt a little angry.

He didn't like this.

While everyone was praising him, Chen Ningan said with a smile: "Master Wang's teaching is indeed extraordinary, but we can't praise our cousin like this, it won't be good if he becomes proud."

Zhang Jihe breathed a sigh of relief immediately.

"Pride brings harm, humility brings benefit, that's the truth." The lady nodded, "Ji He has studied with Master Wang for so many years, so it's only natural that he can write good articles."

"But Ji He is also smart. Other brothers may not be as quick to understand as he is." Zhang said and stopped. "I think they will be here soon."

At this time, the people from the Wu family had just arrived at the Marquis' Mansion.

Mrs. Wu came down from the second gate and looked up to see the Chinese toon trees on both sides of the path. They were already thirty or four feet tall. She couldn't help but sigh, "When I left the capital, the trees were only this tall, right?"

She gestured a little before reaching her waist.

Chen Linzhi came up a few steps and said with a smile: "Big sister, do you still remember?"

"How could I not remember? I came here quite often back then. Originally there was a osmanthus tree planted here, but your eldest brother didn't like the fragrance, so I had it replaced." Madam Wu sighed, "It's been so many years, Linzhi, look at you, you already have two sons."

"Big sister has three children, doesn't she?" Chen Linzhi looked at Wu Dairong and praised, "Look, she looks just like big sister when she was young. She is so beautiful."

Mrs. Wu smiled and said, "Your two sons are also promising. They are both studying under Mr. Wang."

"It's good enough if I don't embarrass my husband."

Chen Linzhi's husband, Zhang Zhijing, was a top scholar in the imperial examination. He was well-read and well-educated. The lady-in-waiting had to work very hard to marry Chen Linzhi to him.

Fortunately, Chen Linzhi knows how to behave and is able to bend and stretch. Not only can she please her parents-in-law and win over her husband, she also gave birth to two grandsons for the Zhang family. It is hard not to like her.

Mrs. Wu reminisced about the past with her. Chen Linzhi took the time to look at Mr. Wu again and again, thinking that he was even better than he was a few years ago, with an extraordinary temperament. No wonder they had never found a suitable daughter-in-law. When it comes to outstanding ladies, there are more in the capital.

Over there, Yongchun Hou Chen Xing and Chen Xiu were reminiscing about the old times with Mr. Wu, Wu Guang.

"Are you tired from the journey, old man?" Since the Wu family was invited, the old man of the Wu family naturally had to come as well. Chen Xiu heard that he was in poor health, so he asked.

"The old man really couldn't stand the running around. He has been sleeping these few days, but it's okay. Before he left, he told me that he would come next time when he is better. He said he couldn't even remember what you looked like." Wu Guang said as he looked at Chen Xing's legs and asked with concern, "Can the prescription I sent earlier help you?"

Yongchunhou Mansion was mediocre for many years until the Chen brothers grew up. Chen Xing was a general and had made some military achievements. Only last time he injured his leg in Shanxi, it was quite serious. The emperor sympathized with him and allowed him to recuperate at home, often giving him rewards. After two years, his leg was better, but he still walked with a limp on his right leg.

Fortunately, Chen Xing was open-minded by nature and didn't think it was a big deal. He smiled and said, "It's useful. Even the imperial physician said it's good. It shows that the famous doctors in Jiangnan are also very good."

Wu Guang was very happy. "When we first learned that you were injured, we were all very worried. But I was busy with official duties and couldn't spare the time. Now that I see that you are fine, I am relieved."

"Gong Yuan, don't worry. This injury is not a big deal for me." Chen Xing introduced his eldest son Chen Min and said with a smile, "I have seen your Jian'er several times, but you haven't seen my and my brother's children for many years."

The relationship between the Wu couple and the Yongchun Marquisate was deep. Even though they were not in the capital, they would always visit their son whenever he came to Beijing for the imperial examination. They had also been to the homes of the two aunts.

Therefore, they have all met Master Wu.

Wu Guang smiled and said, "I haven't seen it, but I knew it long ago. It must be good. The sons are brave and the daughters are beautiful!"

Chen Xing laughed: "Gong Yuan is getting better and better at speaking."

Chen Xiu teased: "Back then, it was hard

for me to ask Brother Wu to praise me."

"It's different. You are you, and those are your children."

The implication is that it is not easy for Wu Guang to praise other things.

Everyone laughed.

Chen Xing walked in front with his arm around Wu Guang's shoulder.

The group went to Ci Xin Garden and met the lady again.

The lady did cry with Mrs. Wu.

Back then, Madam Wu often came to the mansion. The lady-in-law had been good friends with her mother, Old Madam Zeng, since childhood. After Old Madam Zeng passed away, she treated Madam Wu as half a daughter and even wanted her to be her eldest daughter-in-law. Unfortunately, the two of them did not have such a fate.

Chen Ningyu was surprised that the relationship between the two families was so good, and she was very happy.

Who doesn't want true friends in their family?

This friendship is precious.

The lady had already asked people to bring out a lot of candied fruits, including ten-spice fruit, sugar-coated green plums, white sugar lotus seeds, tangerine cakes, etc.

Mrs. Wu saw it and laughed again and again: "Madam Tai really loves me. She still remembers me after all these years."

"I asked people to look everywhere in

Beijing a few days ago. They said you liked it, but I was afraid that the taste would be different from before, so I bought a lot. Speaking of the pain, it hurts more than it does me!" Chen Linzhi said with a smile.

The lady glanced at her sideways and said, "You have never been as well-behaved as Ya'er since you were a child."

Mrs. Wu's surname is Zeng and her given name is Ya.

Chen Linru chuckled: "Sister, don't you know that mother wishes she could switch with Sister Wu so that she can be her daughter?"

The lady laughed out loud: "Great, I can see that now."

Mrs. Wu was filled with warmth, and she pulled Chen Linzhi and Chen Linru aside and said, "Anyway, we are just like sisters, there is not much difference." She smiled at the old lady and said, "This candied fruit is really delicious, but did you buy it at the old Baiweiji store?"

The lady told her that many shops in the capital had been completely transformed.

The elders said that a few girls also gathered together and talked about interesting things so that others could get to know them and they could also get to know others.

As for the men, they naturally had to avoid suspicion. Besides, what they said was very different from what the women said, so they all followed Chen Xing out.

Chen Ningyu glanced at Zhang Jiwan at this time.

Zhang Jiwan, however, did not feel guilty and shook the purse hanging around her waist towards her.

Chen Ningyu was surprised. Could it be that this kid really intended to pay compensation?

As for her tea set, although it was not the top-grade Ru kiln porcelain, it was also pretty good. It cost at least thirty taels of silver. Of course, for a family like theirs, this amount of money was not much, but for Zhang Jiwan, it was a little unaffordable.

It was because Zhang Zhijing was a very strict father. Not only did he keep a close eye on their studies, he also controlled their finances. He said that boys with liberal finances would not know the sufferings of the world. As a result, the brothers Zhang Jihe and Zhang Jiwan lived a particularly hard life, and it was considered good if they could save twenty taels of silver a year.

Zhang Jiwan also liked to make friends and go out to spend money. When he had no money left, he would often go to Zhang Jihe to borrow some money.

I didn't expect that he would have money this time.

Chen Ningrou was joking with Wu Dairong: "Sister Wu and my third sister are quite similar. Look at the eyebrows and eyes.

They are both very pretty."

Chen Ninghua felt a little embarrassed and said quickly, "Miss Wu is much prettier than me."

"No way, Third Miss, don't be so modest. I can see that your every move and gesture is that of a lady from a noble family. Unlike me, mother always says that I am careless and don't act like a lady." Wu Dairong has a very easy-going personality.

Chen Ning'an smiled slightly: "My third sister is very decent." She changed the subject naturally, "I heard from my eldest aunt that you learned skills from a famous embroiderer in Suzhou. No wonder this purse looks so special."

Everyone's eyes were focused on Wu Dairong. As expected, they saw a purse with a white crane and lotus pattern on her waist. It was fresh and elegant. Both the color and stitching were impeccable and the embroidery was very good.

Wu Dairong was praised. She glanced at Madam Wu in the distance and whispered, "Don't say anything. I was forced to learn this by my mother. I really don't have even one-third of what my master has learned! If I really learned everything, that would be amazing!"

She is very natural and likable.

Everyone was talking happily, but no one mentioned Master Wu Jian.

However, Chen Ningyu knew that the Madam and Zhang would definitely be satisfied.

She also took a look at Wu Jian and found him to be very handsome and of calm temperament. He was a very good candidate for a son-in-law.

The two families had not met for the first time in many years, and the Wu family wanted to stay a little longer this time, so they did not leave even after lunch.

Because of the hot weather, no one went out to stroll around the garden. Several girls were chatting and laughing in Chen Ning'an's room. Chen Ning'an took out the green mountain tea and asked them to drink it. There was a maid behind them fanning them gently, which made them feel very comfortable.

Chen Linru's three daughters are still young. The oldest, Xu Hui, is only eight years old, so she is the only one who came with them. The other two stayed with their elders.

Chen Ninghua looked around and sighed inwardly. Compared with Chen Ningrou's place, this place was much more exquisite and noble. After all, she was the apple of the eye of both families. Chen Ning'an was different.

"We have talked a lot, why don't you say much, Fourth Miss?" Wu Dairong looked at Chen Ningyu with a smile. She had never seen such a beautiful girl even in Suzhou.

Chen Ningyu did not say much today. Hearing this, she smiled and said, "I just heard what Second Sister said because she and you got along so well. Besides, we can just sit together and have fun. I can't think of anything to say for the moment."

Wu Dairong smiled and nodded: "That's right, I've heard my mother always miss your family a long time ago. I feel happy to see you today. I'm sure my father and mother feel the same way."

"You are naturally happy like this, unlike me." Zhang Jiwan's voice came, deep and loud, "My father tells me that it is better here wherever I go. Second cousin, hurry up and bring me some tea." He winked at Chen Ningyu and patted his purse proudly.

Chen Ningyu was speechless. This kid just has no rules. Will he change even if he is scolded and beaten by his father? It's useless.

Chen Ning'an was also embarrassed. She didn't want Wu Dairong to see her cousin like this.

"Second cousin, how dare you barge into my boudoir? I'll get someone to tell my uncle!" Chen Ningrou was the first to reprimand him, glaring at him and scolding him, "My uncle will definitely beat you up, do you believe it? Isn't Sister Wu here?"

Hearing this, Zhang Jiwan was still afraid and said hurriedly: "Okay, okay, I'll leave now. Don't tell my father. Actually, I'm here to look for my fourth cousin."

Chen Ningyu knew that he was going to pay back the money. He glanced at him and saw that he was holding a cloth bag. He asked,

"Why are you in such a hurry now?"
"He's my father. He'll let us go back soon. I may not be able to come here again in the future." Zhang Jiwan urged her, "Come out quickly," and then left.
Fortunately, Zhang Jiwan was still young, otherwise people might gossip about her. Chen Ningyu thought about it and decided to go. After all, debts had to be repaid. Besides, she was quite curious about the money. Could it be that she had borrowed it from somewhere?

☆, Misunderstanding has come
As soon as Chen Ningyu went out, Zhang Jiwan pulled her to a pavilion quite far away.
He opened his purse and found several large-denomination banknotes and some small change inside.
Chen Ningyu was shocked: "How do you have so much money? Did your aunt give it to you?"
Maybe Chen Linzhi loved her son and gave it privately.
Zhang Jiwan curled her lips and said, "Mother listens to father the most. It would be strange if she gave it to me. I earned this myself. I didn't lie to you last time. I will compensate you if I say so. Is this enough?"
He took out thirty-five taels and gave them to her.

Chen Ningyu accepted it and still asked, "How do you make money? My aunt said you study all day long."

Zhang Jiwan chuckled, looked around mysteriously, and then said softly, "Fourth cousin, I'm only telling you this because I'm good to you. Don't tell my father and mother. Even my brother doesn't know."

He really liked talking to her, and every time he came back, he would always look for her. As for why, she didn't know, but considering they were relatives, Chen Ningyu treated him well. After all, although this boy was naughty, he had a generous personality and was not that annoying.

But to be honest, she didn't think she had such a good relationship with him.

Chen Ningyu nodded: "Go ahead."

If she did something bad, she would probably tell Chen Linzhi.

Zhang Jiwan crossed his legs and swayed them as he said, "I put money in a shop. At first, it was twenty taels of silver, and now it has tripled."

That meant buying shares. Chen Ningyu became even more curious and asked, "Since my aunt and uncle don't know, did you put it in another store? Whose store? Is the business so good that they gave you so much money?"

"Speaking of which, it was actually an accidental good deed. When I was studying at the academy, I met a student named Qiu.

He came from a poor family. His mother was ill and used up all the money in the family. He also failed the imperial examination several times and had no means of livelihood. So we funded him and asked him to open a small restaurant to make a living after learning skills." Zhang Jiwan laughed, "Guess what happened later? He opened a restaurant, and now it's always full of people every day."

Chen Ningyu was quite interested: "Which restaurant is it?"

"It's a very ordinary name, taken from his last name, Qiu Ji. His specialties are lion's head, three-piece duck, and soft-shelled long fish."

"They are all Huaiyang cuisine."

"Yes, the one who taught him cooking was from Huai'an."

"Then why doesn't my cousin know either?" They studied in the same academy.

Zhang Jiwan laughed out loud: "Don't you know my brother? He doesn't like to make friends with people, let alone close friends. Others only like to come to me. Anyway, the money was spent properly."

Chen Ningyu warned, "Please keep the money safe so that your uncle doesn't see it. I'm leaving now."

Zhang Jiwan then handed her the bag in his hand and said, "I have always smashed your things, which may not be bought with money. I will compensate you with this as well."

She was curious, so she opened it and found

that it was an egg white glaze pomegranate water decanter.

Zhang Jiwan explained: "Last time I saw the water jug in your study had a hole in it, and it was not elegant to leave it there. Although this water jug is not as good as yours, I liked it very much, so I bought it."

Seeing his sincere smile, Chen Ningyu accepted it. The water jug was not a valuable item and it was a token of her heart's love. Zhang Jiwan did not lie and he was indeed good to her.

"Next time you come, don't show off your skills to me. If you break the money again, you won't be able to pay me back. This money is hard-earned, so keep it well."

Chen Ningyu gave the water to Danqiu and told her to put it in the study.

Zhang Jiwan smiled and said yes.

The two of them went their separate ways.

As a result, when passing by a bamboo forest, Chen Ningyu met Chen Min, Chen Li, Zhang Jihe, and Wu Jian.

There was some distance between them, and she wanted to pretend she didn't see it and just walk past, but Chen Li called her.

Chen Li was born to Jiang and was the only legitimate son of the second wife.

Chen Ningyu had no choice but to come over to pay his respects.

"Why is Fourth Sister here? Are you here with them to appreciate the flowers?" Chen Min asked.

"No." Chen Ningyu replied, "My second cousin came over and said a few words to me just now."

Zhang Jihe sneered and said, "I was wondering where he had gone. Turns out he came to see you again without even saying hello. Aren't you afraid of being beaten by your father?"

She couldn't understand what these two brothers were thinking. Zhang Jiwan said he was on good terms with her, but Zhang Jihe seemed to always dislike her.

Chen Ningyu said: "I won't bother you anymore, goodbye."

Chen Li was still young, so he tried to persuade her to stay, "Fourth sister, we are going to watch Master Wu's sword dance, you should come too."

"I still have things to do. Your sisters are waiting for me to come back. Li'er, you also love these things. Follow Master Wu and learn from them." Chen Ningyu said gently, turned around and left.

Wu Jian discovered that she never even looked at him from beginning to end.

Of course he looked at her a few times, after all, she was a rare beauty, but he didn't have much thought about it. He was mature beyond his years and was not easily moved.

When Chen Ningyu returned, Chen Ningrou asked curiously, "Why did you take so long? What did your second cousin say to you?"

Chen Ningyu did not reveal the repayment.

Zhang Jiwan had made the compensation, so she had to keep it a secret. She smiled and said, "Nothing special. Just some ordinary words. She just said that her uncle blamed him."

Everyone knew that Zhang Jiwan was often scolded. Chen Ningrou snorted, "He deserves it!"

The Wu family stayed until the hour of You before leaving, and agreed that the two families should visit each other more often. By that time, Zhang was already very familiar with Mrs. Wu, and Mrs. Wu looked at Chen Ning'an with considerable satisfaction.

The lady was very happy. If it really came true, it would be a great joy.

At that time, she did not want Mrs. Wu to be her daughter-in-law, but now, her son has become her grandson-in-law, which can be regarded as a wish come true, not to mention that he is also an outstanding person.

Chen Linzhi promised: "Sister Wu praised Ning An to me many times."

Although the two families have not seen each other for many years, Mrs. Wu and Chen Linzhi have always kept in touch. Mrs. Wu said in the letter that she had not found a suitable daughter-in-law. Now that she says this, she must have this intention.

Zhang felt as if she had taken a reassurance pill.

The lady also asked Chen Xing and Chen Xiu

to take some time to visit Old Master Wu at the Wu family.

Chen Ningrou returned to the room, took off her shoes and lay on the beauty couch. Thinking of Wu Jian, her face turned slightly red. It was no wonder that they were all so satisfied with a man like him. Even though Chen Ningan thought highly of himself, he was probably moved.

The two sisters in the eldest wife's house really get whatever they want. I wonder what kind of husband she will be able to find in the future, but he must not be worse than the ones they have!

"I just met Yuelan, and she said that the second young master and his companions met the fourth young lady on the road." The maid Yingui came up and whispered.

Chen Ningrou suddenly perked up, sat up from the couch and asked, "Are you with my second cousin?"

"No, it's just the fourth girl."

Chen Ningrou sneered.

She put on her shoes and said, "I'm going to go see my brother."

The next day, everyone went to pay their respects to the old lady. The old lady had not yet gotten over the joy of meeting the Wu family, and mentioned the Wu family from time to time.

Jiang said, "Yesterday, Li'er saw Master Wu's swordsmanship and said it was beautiful."

The lady looked at Chen Li and asked with a

smile, "Is he more powerful than your father?"

Chen Li said seriously: "Brother Wu's swordsmanship is very powerful, but it is still a little worse than that of my father, so I just learned from my father."

He is serious.

Everyone couldn't help laughing.

Chen Li added: "It's a pity that we were the only ones who went to see it, and none of the sisters were there. I met the fourth sister on the way and wanted to ask her to go, but she refused."

The room was silent for a moment.

Chen Ningyu didn't expect Chen Li to say this, but it was the truth, and even if he mentioned it, it wouldn't matter: "I did encounter it, and I actually wanted to see it, but I wasn't familiar with Master Wu, so I didn't go."

She is very open.

Although the lady felt a little strange, she never thought about it in other ways.

Zhang's face looked extremely ugly.

Because they were all unaware of this, and Chen Ningyu's meeting halfway was just a matter of a moment, and they were all men that day, and they were not fussy by nature, so they would not mention it to other people when they returned. However, Chen Li was young, but he mentioned it to Yuelan, the maid who took care of him.

So Jiang's expression now is very complicated, and it is hard to tell whether she is gloating or embarrassed.

If this Chen Ningyu is not her nominal daughter, that would definitely be a good thing.

"Aren't you all staying at Ning'an's place? Why did you come out?" Jiang immediately made her attitude clear and said sternly, "I have reminded you many times not to lose your manners. You can hang out at any other time in your own place. Why do you have to come out at that time?"

She directly reprimanded Chen Ningyu to her face.

Chen Ningyu lowered her eyelids, looked at the bluestone slab on the ground, and said slowly: "Mother, how can this be considered as a breach of etiquette? If my second cousin hadn't come to see me, I wouldn't have gone out at all. If you don't believe me, ask them."

"Yes, mother, it was indeed my second cousin who came over, and that's why my fourth sister left." Chen Ninghua was the first one to testify for her.

"You and your cousin should also avoid suspicion!" Jiang stressed, "You are not children anymore. Besides, what can he say to you without telling you? Why do you have to go out?"

"Mother knows about my cousin." Chen Ningyu said calmly, "Since he came to me, I naturally have to say a few words. After all, Sister Wu is here too."

The lady said at this time: "Well, it's

just meeting Master Wu once, what's the big deal? The two families are so close, it shouldn't be like this."

Once she spoke, others naturally had to shut up.

But Chen Ningyu could sense Zhang's extreme anger.

Maybe the incident with the Li family really hurt her too much? But she felt that Mr. Wu should not be like Mr. Li. If so, the family tradition of the Wu family was too disappointing.

After everyone left, Chen Ningyu stayed behind.

The lady looked at her and said, "Why, do you have something to say?"

"Of course, other people don't believe me, but I have to explain to you, Grandmother." She said a little aggrievedly, "It's really my second cousin's fault! He broke my tea set last time, and I kept it a secret for him. Today he came to pay back the money, and he also asked me not to let my uncle know. I know he is often scolded, but I sympathize with him and didn't tell him. Grandmother, I really didn't mean to meet Mr. Wu. How could I not know what my aunt and my aunt were thinking?"

The lady laughed and poked her forehead with her finger: "You clever girl, how could you not know what I'm thinking? How could I doubt you, silly girl!"

Chen Ningyu was very happy. She went up to hug the lady's arm, put her head on it and said, "I know that grandma loves me the most!"

The lady sighed, "Don't blame your aunt."

Who told this granddaughter to be so worrying? She thought to herself that after the second and third granddaughters were married, she would have to get the fourth granddaughter married as well, only then would she feel at ease.

With such a look and the fact that she is about to get married, it always makes people a little worried.

☆、Princess Huiying's Mansion

After Zhang returned home, she almost dropped a vase but was stopped by her confidant, Mama Cai.

Madam Cai tried to persuade her, "I don't think the fourth young lady did it on purpose. Madam, calm down. After all, the Wu family is not the Li family. Given the relationship between our two families, how can we only look at appearance?"

Zhang sat down angrily and said through gritted teeth, "This damn girl might be targeting our Ning An!"

"How can she compare to the Second Young Miss?" Mother Cai said with a smile, "The Second Young Miss is your child with the Master."

Chen Ning'an's father is a marquis and his mother has an excellent family background. On the other hand, Chen Ningyu's biological mother is deceased and his father is not that prominent. No matter what, they are incomparable. Can being beautiful really make a living?

The Wu family is not such a stupid family. Their Master Wu has risen rapidly in the career and has a very broad vision.

Zhang felt better, drank a few sips of tea, rubbed her chest and said, "I was really angry just now. Now that you put it that way, it makes sense. Anyway, Madam Wu also likes Ning An, but she didn't mention the fourth girl."

"Yes, ma'am, don't worry."

But Jiang asked Chen Li on the way back: "Why did you suddenly mention your fourth sister?"

Chen Li tilted his head, looking confused.

Jiang frowned, thinking that he was just a child after all, he just said whatever he thought.

Chen Ningyu returned to the room and took another nap, not getting up until almost noon.

Danqiu picked the newly-bloomed lilacs and goldfinches in the yard and put them in a black-glazed carved flower vase. The flowers were purple and golden, and it was really lively.

But there is no beauty in it.

Chen Ningyu smiled as she looked at her. Danqiu, like her, had no talent for flower arrangement. But who cares? As long as there was some fragrance and beauty, it was just an embellishment.

Gu Qiu brought her some water to rinse her mouth.

After lunch, Chen Ningyu went to make shoes. She was usually very idle, but she was used to this kind of life. She embroidered flowers, read books, and the day passed like this.

At the beginning of May, Chen Ningyu's cousin sent someone to invite her to stay for a few days.

The lady did not refuse.

Chen Ningyu was also very happy. It was always a good thing to change places and get some fresh air. What's more, her cousin was the closest person to her besides her family, and she was very good to her.

She asked Gu Qiu to take out a few sets of clothes and take them over.

When she heard that she was going to her cousin's place, Chen Ningrou came over, fanning herself with a silk fan, and said, "Princess Huiying's mansion was where Princess Lanyu of the previous dynasty lived. It is said to be extremely magnificent, but I have never seen it once."

Chen Ningyu's cousin is Princess Huiying. She smiled and said, "My cousin didn't like the original one, so she rebuilt several parts a long time ago."

Chen Ningrou frowned slightly.

Princess Huiying was also their relative, but she had never invited them to visit her house. This time Chen Ningyu wanted to stay there again, but she was still unwilling to take her with her.

"Fourth sister, how long will you stay this time?" She put away her displeasure.

"I don't know, maybe six or seven days."

Chen Ningrou turned sideways, half covering her face, and asked with concern, "Is Mr. Fu feeling better?"

Chen Ningyu glanced at her, then turned and said, "It seems to be getting better, I'm not sure."

Chen Ningrou sighed, stopped talking, and left after a while.

When Chen Ningyu saw that the servants had finished taking care of the matter, he went to say goodbye to the lady.

The lady's face was slightly gloomy. "I asked someone to prepare some medicinal herbs. Although the princess's mansion has everything, these are rare in the capital. There are also some wild vegetables and fruits that have just been delivered from the farm. You can take them over and let them taste them."

Chen Ningyu responded.

"I don't know how Ezi is doing now. Come to think of it, I haven't seen her for ten years." The lady paused and said, "You can go. Your father will agree."

Chen Ningyu nodded without saying much. In fact, she really wanted to comfort the lady, but she knew that no matter what she said, it would be useless.

Because that was the fact. Princess Huiying Li Ezi had severed all ties with the Chen family and would no longer have any contact with anyone except her.

She sat in the carriage and sighed slightly. The princess's mansion was not far away, only three streets away, and we arrived there quickly.

She came down from the second gate, and Gu Qiu and Dan Qiu followed behind her, each carrying a bundle, but there was no maid.

A maid was already there to greet them.

Shi Lian ordered the maid to quickly take the bundle and the things in the car, and said with a smile: "The young lady is finally here. The princess has been waiting for a long time. She ordered the kitchen to stew Yunlin goose early in the morning, saying that you are slow."

"Sorry to have kept your aunt waiting for a long time. I'll be there right away." Chen Ningyu walked faster.

The eldest princess is impatient and quick-tempered, but Chen Ningyu does things slowly and methodically.

The princess's mansion covers a very large area. Princess Lan Yu of the previous dynasty was the emperor's most beloved daughter. The house she was given was magnificently built, with eight courtyards of different sizes, two gardens, and a large lake on the west side. It was surrounded by flowers and trees, and pavilions and terraces, just like the gardens in the south of the Yangtze River, full of poetic and picturesque beauty.

When Chen Ningyu lived here, that was her favorite place to go.

As soon as she stepped onto the corridors on both sides, a young man came towards her. He was wearing a lake-colored robe with a ruyi pattern and a square scarf of the same color on his head. He looked elegant and handsome.

When Chen Ningyu saw him, a happy smile appeared on his face and he called out, "Second cousin!"

Fu Chaoqing approached and pulled out a handkerchief from his sleeve and handed it to her: "Ayu, you are sweating, wipe it off."

Chen Ningyu tucked her forehead and asked with a smile, "Why did you come here? Do you think I'm late, just like your aunt? But it's still early before noon."

"It's noon? Are you here just to eat?"

"I heard they made Yunlin Goose!"

"I saw you enjoyed your meal last time, so I told mom about it." Fu Chaoqing wiped the sweat off his face and exhaled slightly, "It's really hot today."

Chen Ningyu said: "Let's go quickly."

"But there is plenty of ice in the house, you will be cool in a while."

When he smiled, he looked particularly gentle and handsome, making people feel comfortable all over. Chen Ningyu nodded and asked with a smile: "Is my eldest cousin home too?"

"No, he is not at home for many days a year." Speaking of his elder brother, Fu Chaoqing couldn't help but sigh.

"It's better than being idle. My cousin loves to move around. Now that he has joined the Jinyiwei, he will be busy."

Fu Chaoqing smiled: "Yes, I asked him if he was tired, and he didn't feel tired at all. It's just that he has too little time to spend with his sister-in-law, which is not good."

Chen Ningyu smiled and said, "Second cousin is really considerate. When he gets married in the future, he will definitely take good care of her."

Fu Chaoqing didn't say anything.

His eyes fell on her face, full of complexity.

Chen Ningyu's heart suddenly skipped a beat. It seemed like Fu Chaoqing started looking at her like this, a year ago, or two years ago?

She can't remember.

What she remembered most clearly was the first time she saw Fu Chaoqing. He was lying weakly on the bed, like a piece of jade that would break at the slightest touch. Although fragile, his brilliance could not be concealed.

Yes, Fu Chaoqing has a kind of noble and elegant air. He looks neither like the eldest princess nor like his father Fu Cheng. According to the lady, he looks more

like his grandmother, Concubine De.
He was also a good handwriter and painter. He was born intelligent and had a photographic memory. Unfortunately, he lost his health due to an accident, and his lady once sighed for him.
Chen Ningyu looked at him, thought of the past, and suddenly turned his head away.
The two of them said nothing more and walked forward in silence.
The princess was slightly surprised to see them coming together, then smiled and said, "It seems Qing'er misses you as much as I do, and can't wait to pick you up. Come, let me see how beautiful you are."
Chen Ningyu blushed slightly and said angrily, "Aunt, how dare I say beauty when you are here."
The eldest princess laughed out loud, "You're so sweet." She looked at her from left to right and said, "I haven't seen you for only half a year, and you've grown taller. Look at your face, you're like a fairy."
Chen Ningyu felt even more embarrassed.
This face has indeed brought her a lot of compliments, but she doesn't want others to mention it often. Of course, she still likes this face. Who doesn't want to look good?
"It seems that the Chen family has treated you well indeed." The eldest princess said seriously.
"Aunt, when I came here, the lady asked me

to bring a lot of things. She also missed you a lot."

The eldest princess said calmly, "Thank you for your concern."

In the past few years, she is always like this when talking about the Chen family. It's okay for Chen Ningyu, but many things cannot be forced.

"Cousin, I'm going to trouble you again." Chen Ningyu greeted Fu Chaoyun's wife, Yu.

Yu said hurriedly, "What are you talking about? Mother is so happy that you are here. It's not a bother at all. I have one more person to talk to. It's so nice."

The eldest princess sighed slightly: "It's a little quiet here."

Yu was anxious: "Mother, this is not what my daughter-in-law meant."

Yu was born timid. When Fu Chaoyun got married, Chen Ningyu actually didn't think of marrying her. But now that she thinks about it, it's only natural. The eldest princess has a strong personality. If she marries someone powerful, the family will be in turmoil. Therefore, Yu is the best choice.

She was beautiful, had a good temper, and was clear-headed. She was accommodating to the eldest princess in everything, so the two of them had never had any conflicts.

The princess looked at her and said with a smile, "What are you afraid of? I was just saying it casually."

Yu heaved a sigh of relief: "I'll go to the

kitchen and take a look."

"Let's go. It's time to eat later."

After Yu left, the princess asked Chen Ningyu to sit next to her, patted her hands and said, "I've been busy since the New Year, so I haven't asked you to come over."

"Aunt, I won't be able to come here often in the future. I'm not a child anymore."

The princess stared at her face and sighed, "Yes, you have grown up so fast. I still remember when you were little, you loved to follow me. You didn't want to leave when I came, and you cried and cried."

Ever since Chen Ningyu's mother passed away, the eldest princess often brought her here to live. Before she was eight years old, she spent one-third of her time here.

It's a pity that Chen Ningyu is not aware of so many things now. Her memory only starts from the age of nine.

☆, childhood sweetheart

Later, Anqing Hou Fu Cheng also came, and Chen Ningyu liked this uncle-in-law very much.

He is gentle and handsome, and relatively simple compared to many people in Kyoto. It doesn't require any scheming to get along with him.

Such a person is most suitable for the eldest princess.

"Ning Yu, it's good for you to come now. It's much cooler here than at the Chen family's. You can stay for a few more days to keep your aunt company and relieve her boredom." Fu Cheng expressed his welcome.

Chen Ningyu smiled and said yes.

Lunch was served quickly.

Fu Cheng asked: "Why didn't Chao Yun come back today?"

"It is said that the Northern Pacification Office has arrested officials from the Ministry of Justice and is busy with the trial." The eldest princess frowned, "I don't know why this child loves these things."

"It's always a good thing to be valued by the emperor." Fu Cheng said with a smile, "He can't be happy at home."

The princess pointed out a few items and left them for Fu Chaoyun: "Who knows, he might come back suddenly and eat some cold food without knowing right or wrong. There are extra ones in the kitchen, so keep them well."

The maid went to the kitchen and told her.

Chen Ningyu concentrated on eating the goose. The goose meat was tender and the soup was delicious. He ate until he was full and satisfied.

Such a delicacy is naturally complicated to make.

The whole goose needs to be rubbed with wine and honey first, and then steamed on bamboo sticks. One pound and eight ounces of mountain grass is used to burn in the stove. The temperature inside must be controlled very well. It cannot be turned over and can only be left to burn out. The lid of the pot must also be sealed, so that the steamed goose meat will be particularly delicious.

Chen Ningyu finished eating half of the goose leg very elegantly. When he looked up, he saw Fu Chaoqing looking at him with a smile in his eyes. It was hard to tell whether it was teasing or joy.

Her face couldn't help but turn slightly red.

It's always uncomfortable to be watched while eating.

"Mom, if Ayu really likes to eat this, why don't we bring our chef back to her." Fu Chaoqing spoke.

The eldest princess smiled and looked at Chen Ningyu: "Yu'er, do you want it?"

"Of course not. If the cook leaves with me, what can I expect next time I come? It will be boring." Chen Ningyu joked.

The eldest princess laughed: "You have no conscience. You are here just for food."

"Aunt, you know my true feelings. Look, you are smiling."

The princess became even happier: "Okay, okay, I'll keep the cook. Otherwise, if you don't come next time I invite you, I'll be very sad."

"How could that be, aunt? Even if there is no cook and the meals are simple, as long as you say the word, I will come even if it means going through fire and water." Chen Ningyu expressed his loyalty.

In addition to loving her, the eldest princess is also a big thigh, so she must hug her well.

Fu Cheng smiled and said, "When this child comes, it's always very lively."

The eldest princess glanced at him and said, "It's because you and Qing'er are both taciturn."

Normally, the two of them didn't talk much during meals, especially Fu Chaoqing. Only when Chen Ningyu came could one see his lively side.

Yu smiled and said, "It's because Ning Yu is so likable. I really hope she can live here forever."

The eldest princess sighed, "It's a pity that Yu'er's last name is Chen. Besides, girls always have to get married. If I had a daughter like this, I would be heartbroken."

There was a lot of regret in her tone. Like Chen Linzhi, she only gave birth to a son. She still hoped to have a daughter. Otherwise, how could she say that she had both a son and a daughter? She always felt that something was missing.

When it comes to getting married, Chen Ningyu is reluctant to make fun of herself.

In the afternoon, she chatted with the eldest princess for a while before leaving.

A special place was prepared for her to live in this mansion. Every time Chen Ningyu came back, she would stay here. Every blade of grass, every table and chair in the yard were designed according to her preferences, making it like another home.

Because she was sweating when she came here, she leaned on the bamboo couch after changing her clothes.

The servants brought ice and put it in a bronze tripod, and the room felt like spring.

When it comes to the luxury of Kyoto people, Princess Huiying must be one of them.

Gu Qiu brought some fruits and placed them next to her.

"It looks like the second young master is in much better health." Danqiu took out a silver knife, cut the fruits into small pieces and placed them on a white porcelain plate with peach patterns.

Chen Ningyu had just been talking to the eldest princess and had asked this question. The eldest princess looked relieved and it seemed that she was indeed well.

She nodded and said nothing.

He was afraid that if he said something good, Fu Chaoqing's health would deteriorate again one day.

Sometimes, fate always goes against what we expect. I just hope he can really get healthy.

She suddenly felt a little tired, so she lay down on the couch and took a short rest. Danqiu covered her with a thin blanket.

There are many osmanthus trees planted outside the house. They are quite old. Many birds are perched on them, chirping. She closed her eyes, dazed, as if she was back to the time when she was in school, and there were such trees and such bird calls on that road.

She didn't know how long she slept before she woke up.

She rubbed her eyes, her throat a little dry, and called Gu Qiu softly.

A cup of tea was suddenly handed to him, and Chen Ningyu realized that Fu Chaoqing was sitting on the chair opposite him.

He had changed into a new robe, this time it was moon-white, which made him look light and airy. His smile was also ethereal, as if it would disappear at any time.

Chen Ningyu sat up and asked with a smile, "When did my second cousin come?" while looking towards the door.

Gu Qiu and Dan Qiu just stood there, feeling somewhat helpless.

When Fu Chaoqing came, they wanted to stop him, but he sent them away with just one sentence, and they didn't even have the courage to stop him.

He sat there for some time, just looking at the sleeping Chen Ningyu.

"Not long." He didn't think it was abrupt, and his attitude was very natural. "You slept well, but are you tired?"

Chen Ningyu didn't know what to say.

The Chen family follows rules, but since she lived in the mansion, she was like a member of his family and was not restrained at ordinary times. She got off the couch and was about to show her jade feet, but quickly retracted them.

Fu Chaoqing smiled again and walked out the door: "Wash up first, I'll wait for you."

Gu Qiu and Dan Qiu came to serve her.

She had combed her hair before Fu Chaoqing came in again.

"Take this book and read it, so you won't be bored in your spare time." He put the book on the table and asked with his head tilted, "How long will you stay this time? It would be great if you can stay until the middle of the month, because the lotus flowers you love to see will be in bloom at that time."

When she gets older, she will stay here for three to five days at most. Chen Ningyu smiled and said, "Madam will miss you."

Fu Chaoqing raised his eyebrows: "If you want to stay, I will talk to the lady, she will definitely agree. In fact, if you are willing, even if you want to stay until June, why would they not agree?"

Chen Ningyu saw that his eyes were shining brightly, as if he wanted to lure people in to find out what was going on. She shook her head and said, "I've already told the Madam, it's not good to change it. Besides, I'm not just coming here this time, I'll come here often in the future, right?"

Fu Chaoqing's eyes flickered, he tilted his head to look out the window, and said calmly: "Forget it, it's up to you."

In the following days, she rarely saw him

and heard that he was often in the study.
That afternoon, she finally met Fu Chaoyun. He was full of heroic spirit, dressed in the uniform of a Jinyiwei, with an embroidered spring sword hanging from his waist, and had a tall and handsome figure.

"Ayu, you have been staying here for several days, but I have been busy. Please forgive me for my poor hospitality." He said happily.

"Cousin, don't apologize. I don't want to listen to your stories about fighting and killing. You've scared me so much that I couldn't sleep many times." She snorted.

Fu Chaoyun laughed: "Little girl, others can't hear it even if they want to, these are all secrets."

"You're lying. Do you think I'm stupid? If you talk nonsense about the secrets of the court, others will arrest you."

Fu Chengdu laughed: "You are just talking nonsense, kid. Your cousin Ning Yu is not ignorant. Who can you scare with what you read from chivalrous books?"

"Dad, why are you exposing me? It's boring!" Fu Chaoyun frowned, "But as a man, do you still want to be sad about the passing of time?"

"Yes, yes, you just love these. It's better that you don't stay at home. You will be happy if you don't see your mother for a year!" The eldest princess complained unhappily.

Fu Chaoyun hurriedly apologized: "Next time

I won't be so busy, I will definitely accompany mom every day." He patted Fu Chaoqing's shoulder and said, "You are always at home, why don't you take care of mom? What are you always saying about me?"

Fu Chaoqing said calmly: "I am not you."

"Hey, it doesn't matter if you are me or not. If mom is happy, she will naturally stop talking about me." Fu Chaoyun rolled up his sleeves. "But I happen to be free today. Let's go fishing. The fish in the pond are probably very fat. Ah Yu, don't you like fish? I'll catch some for you."

He threw a lot of fish in there a few years ago, all kinds of fish.

Fu Chaoqing said angrily: "Your fish have eaten up most of the koi in the pond."

"What's the point of koi? You can't eat them. My fish are better."

Fu Chaoqing raised his eyebrows: "Can't our family afford to buy fish? Ah Yu often comes here to admire the fish, but now the lake is dark, what else can we see?"

"It's just for fun."

Seeing that the two brothers refused to give in to each other, Chen Ningyu remembered that she had seen the two quarreling several times before. She privately asked Fu Chaoyun why he did so, after all, Fu Chaoqing was in poor health. But Fu Chaoyun said that if he gave in, Chaoqing would be even more unhappy.

Since then, Chen Ningyu realized that Fu Chaoyun was actually a truly good brother.

She smiled and said, "I love fishing and I also love watching fish. Let me see, why don't we divide the pond so that we can do both?"

"Okay, that's a good idea." Fu Chaoyun clapped his hands, "I'll let them do it tomorrow," and looked at his brother, "Xiao Lan, look, A-Yu isn't angry about the koi, why are you angry?"

Xiaolan is Fu Chaoqing's courtesy name, while Fu Chaoyun's courtesy name is Zixia.

Fu Chaoqing said nothing.

The princess laughed and said, "You are so grown up, but you still think you are just arguing when you were little. Yu'er, come here. I have something to tell you. Let them prepare the bait, and you can come out and play later."

Chen Ningyu followed the eldest princess.

However, she did not expect that the eldest princess actually gave her a lot of land deeds.

"Today I realized that you have grown up. You will have to get married in a few years. I have taken care of you for these years, and it is time for you to learn on your own."

Chen Ningyu's maternal grandfather, the Zhou family, was wealthy. In the early days, because the old man had a keen eye and used people properly, he made enough money for his descendants. Even in the capital, they had many shops and there were also many fertile fields in the subordinate counties.

After Chen Ningyu's mother passed away, the old lady also passed away soon after. As she had few descendants and no other relatives to inherit, she gave everything to Chen Ningyu.

But she was young at the time, so she was taken in by the eldest princess.

In this world, for Princess Yu, apart from her husband and son, Chen Ningyu is her closest person.

☆、Old memories

Chen Ningyu knew about this property, but she had not thought about taking it back now.

She looked at the eldest princess gratefully and said, "Thank you for your help, aunt. I know this is very troublesome, but now that you've handed it over to me, I don't know how to take care of it."

"It's not that difficult. These account books record everything clearly. I have driven away all the bad people in the farm and the shop, and the rest are relatively loyal and capable." The eldest princess smiled and opened the account book to show her. "Based on your understanding, it must be very easy. I have also removed some people. You can choose people to fill the vacant positions."

Then it must be returned to her. Chen Ningyu said, "If I don't understand something, can I ask my aunt?"

"What are you talking about, silly child? When will your aunt not see you?" The eldest princess said angrily, "But I see that you have little experience. When you get married in the future, you will know nothing. How can you manage the household?" Her eyes turned slightly cold. "I know she will not teach you much."

Chen Ningyu smiled and said, "There's always grandma."

"The lady is old too." The eldest princess's expression changed slightly.

Chen Ningyu sighed, "Yes, grandma is old. Her hair has turned a lot white in the past few years, and her body is not as strong as before. If the weather is a little cold, she will easily catch a cold."

The eldest princess pursed her lips and lowered her eyes.

Chen Ningyu added, "I'll catch some fish later and bring some back to grandma, okay?"

"If you want to take it, just take it. Chaoyun put a lot of mullets in the lake. We have pearl fruits now, and the mullet slices are the most delicious." The eldest princess' tone was still normal.

Chen Ningyu was very happy and said yes repeatedly.

She asked the eldest princess some more questions about the fields and shops, put away the deeds to the land, and went to the pond in the west.

Fu Chaoyun and Fu Chaoqing were already

sitting and fishing.

"Ayu, you are finally here. The bait is already on. Come over here and sit down." Fu Chaoyun patted the seat beside him and said, "Don't look around for a while. Be careful not to let the fish run away."

"What bait?" Chen Ningyu asked with a smile.

"It's better if you don't know." Fu Chaoyun laughed, "Don't be scared. That thing is dirty. When the bait is gone, I will put it on you again."

Chen Ningyu thanked him: "Please help me, cousin."

Fu Chaoyun said proudly: "It's a small matter."

As soon as she sat down, Yu came over quietly and asked her softly, "What would you like to eat tonight, Yu? I'll ask the kitchen to prepare it later."

"I don't really want to eat anything."

Yu went to ask Fu Chaoyun.

Chen Ningyu looked at her and smiled slightly. It was obvious that Yu had just changed into a bright dress and had made up her face a little bit, looking very pretty and charming.

Fu Chaoyun was very impatient: "Whatever, I'll eat anything."

He was in high spirits, his eyes fixed on the water, without even looking at Yu.

Yu's body stiffened for a moment, then she turned around and walked away slowly.

When Chen Ningyu saw this scene, she felt sad for Yu.

She knew that Fu Chaoyun would marry Yu only because of the eldest princess' choice. After all, his mind was not on women at all, so it didn't matter who he married.

"My sister-in-law helps my aunt take care of the household, and it's very hard. In fact, my cousin should spend more time with her." She began to persuade.

Fu Chaoyun disagreed: "Which wife is not like this? I am still very busy and it is rare for me to have a day off."

Chen Ningyu was silent.

Fu Chaoqing looked over and said, "Ayu, come here. The feng shui there is not good, and you can't catch any fish."

Fu Chaoyun's eyes widened. "When did you become a charlatan?"

"How could there not be one? I caught two." When Fu Chaoqing gets angry, he can make people jump up and down. "Even though you released the fish, it's a pity that they didn't catch you."

Fu Chaoyun said angrily: "Just wait and see who catches more fish in the end!"

Fu Chaoqing smiled faintly and asked Chen Ningyu to go again.

Chen Ningyu sat next to him.

A light breeze blew, and the faint scent of medicine on his body entered her nose.

"What fish did you catch?" she asked curiously.

"Look for yourself." He put the fish basket in front of her.

She leaned over and took a look, and almost

screamed out.

What two fish? There is not even one.

Fu Chaoyun asked, "Ayu, what did he catch? Is it big?"

"Well, it's big, but I don't know what kind of fish it is." Chen Ningyu covered his mouth to hold back his laughter.

Fu Chaoqing winked at her and said softly, "Good Ah Yu."

Chen Ningyu's face flushed slightly.

Fu Chaoyun was putting bait on the hook again and shouted, "It must be some lousy fish. What's so great about it? Watch me. A big fat fish will be caught soon!"

Fu Chaoqing laughed softly.

He is usually gentle and polite, but when he teases people, he becomes mischievous and very cute.

Chen Ningyu turned his head and concentrated on fishing.

As expected, Fu Chaoyun caught a big fish very quickly. He came over with a proud look on his face, wanting to compare whose fish was bigger with Fu Chaoqing. However, he discovered that there was not a single fish in the fish basket. He was so angry that he fell backwards.

Sometimes it is hard to accept that there is no opponent.

Fortunately, Chen Ningyu became his opponent and caught one fish after another. The two of them competed with each other and had a lot of fun.

But Fu Chaoqing didn't catch any fish in

the end.

Chen Ningyu specially picked out two big blackfish.

"Are we going to cook today?" Fu Chaoyun asked.

"I brought it back for my grandmother to eat."

Fu Chaoyun was surprised: "Are you leaving?"

"I've been here for a long time, but it feels like only a few days because you're busy."

Fu Chaoyun apologized, scratched his head and said, "Next time I know you're coming, I'll definitely make time. Ah Yu, when you get married, we'll have even less time to play together."

He really meant what he said.

After all, when they were young, the three of them were often together.

"It's still early, cousin. I just hope you can be careful. The Jinyiwei are also very dangerous." Chen Ningyu warned, "Don't make your uncle and aunt worry all the time."

"Got it, Ah Yu." Fu Chaoyun smiled, "I'll take you back."

"Don't bother me. You should spend more time with your sister-in-law when you have time."

Fu Chaoyun rarely saw her, and didn't want to go against her, so he agreed.

Chen Ningyu said goodbye to Fu Chaoqing, went to meet Fu Cheng and his wife, and prepared to return to the Chen family.

Fu Chaoyun asked Fu Chaoqing: "Why don't you try to keep her for a few days? If you had said so in the past, she would have stayed, and her mother would not want her to leave."

Fu Chaoqing said calmly: "You also said the same thing as usual. Ah Yu has grown up."

He turned and left.

Fu Chaoyun frowned, thought of Chen Ningyu's words, and went to see his wife.

Chen Ningyu returned to Chen's house in the evening.

The lady smiled and said, "You didn't stay a few more days? I just thought you were away for a long time this time, so you had to stay there for a month or so."

"I miss my grandma and can't sleep well every day." Chen Ningyu took the lady's arm. The lady poked her head and said, "Come on, you are always happy wherever you go. The princess loves you and gives you everything good. It's much more comfortable than our home, isn't it?"

"No, they say that no house is better than your own. No matter how good my aunt's place is, it's not my home. Besides, I always feel like something is missing when I can't see my grandmother."

The lady was pleased to hear this.

Chen Ningyu asked someone to take the mullet to the kitchen: "I caught it in the pond today, it's really big. My aunt said to cut the mullet into slices, grind it into big and flat, and then wrap some pearl fruit in it. It will be delicious."

The lady was overwhelmed with emotions.

At that time, the eldest princess had a very good relationship with her eldest daughter-in-law, Zhou, and often invited her over. Knowing that Zhou loved eating fish but didn't like to pick bones, she ordered the kitchen to prepare this dish carefully.

After tasting it, the lady liked it very much and ordered the cook to learn how to make it.

But after Zhou passed away, no one ate it again.

Because of this incident, the eldest princess never visited the Chen family again.

The lady did not speak for a long time.

Chen Ningyu didn't know the inside story. Seeing the lady like this, he wondered if he had said something wrong. Maybe his aunt had other intentions?

The lady said, "Well, this dish is delicious, let the kitchen prepare it tonight."

Only then did Chen Ningyu breathe a sigh of relief.

In her heart, she only hoped that the princess and the lady could get along, but unfortunately, it seemed too difficult. The past events of the past could not be forgotten just like that, although, to her, they were insignificant, after all, she did not exist in this world at that time.

In the evening, she had dinner with the lady-in-waiting and told her that she had taken over the property.

When the lady asked about Fu Chaoqing, she replied that he looked good, but the princess did not say anything specifically.

The lady sighed.

After returning to Furong Garden, Chen Ningyu saw a tall and handsome figure standing in the courtyard from afar, and immediately walked over quickly.

Chen Xiu turned around and said with a smile: "You have planted these flowers well, which shows that you don't grow them randomly."

"I planted it because I love it. My daughter doesn't want to ruin the flowers."

Chen Xiu rubbed her head: "Did you have dinner with your grandmother?"

"Well, has father just come back?" she asked.

Chen Xiu nodded, and was about to say something, but swallowed it back. After a moment, he said, "You must be tired from the journey, so rest early."

Her father was very handsome, but whenever he looked at her, there was always a kind of sadness hidden in his eyes, which made people feel distressed, but Chen Ningyu was happy about it.

Yes, the father must love her mother, his ex-wife, which is always a good thing.

That's why he has been so caring towards his daughter over the years.

Chen Ningyu grabbed Chen Xiu's sleeve and said, "Dad, my aunt gave me the land and house deeds."

Chen Xiu was startled, then he seemed to understand: "It's time to give it to you, Yu'er, but this is not a small amount of money, you have to keep it well, if you don't understand anything, ask your mother." He paused, "or ask the lady."

"Don't you know, father?" she laughed.

Chen Xiu pinched her nose: "Father only knows how to spend money, doesn't Yu'er know?"

Chen Ningyu laughed out loud.

Chen Xiu was indeed such a person. He never asked about money, just like the men in many families who took care of the outside affairs but not the inside.

After seeing Chen Xiu off, Chen Ningyu returned to her room and took out the account book that the princess had given her and flipped through it.

From now on, she could no longer wait for money to come to her door, she had to manage everything on her own.

Speaking of which, it's still very upsetting.

She looked at it carefully.

☆, Visitors

By June, the old man of the Wu family had recovered and invited them to his house for a gathering.

The intention of the two families this time is very clear, they are going to get married.

Madam Zhang was extremely happy, and all the gloom in her heart caused by the Li family was swept away. After all, Wu Jian was much better than Master Li. Even looking around the capital, how many people could surpass him?

She was very satisfied.

The lady was also very happy. They were old friends and now the relationship was strengthened. Naturally, the relationship between the two families became even closer. The Chen family was so happy, as if they were marrying above their station, but in fact, it was indeed the case.

The Yongchun Marquisate is just a name, which can be used to show off the prominence of ancestors, but that's all. Since the founding of this dynasty, civil officials have been valued, and if a military general does not have extraordinary merits, he is basically inferior to the civil officials.

As for meritorious service, now that Chen Xing has injured his leg, it would be difficult for him to make further meritorious service.

Therefore, they attach great importance to the Wu family.

In Hibiscus Garden, two maids were chatting. Bai Tao said mysteriously, "The Madam brought out a box of South China pearls and rubies yesterday. The South China pearls are big and round, and the rubies are beautiful in color. She said she wanted to make a headpiece for the second young lady."

This news was also told by her mother, Mrs. Liu.

"Last time the eldest daughter got married, didn't the lady give several pieces of beautiful jade? What's the big deal?" Bi Tao disagreed.

Bai Tao chuckled, "I'm just curious about what the lady will give our girl when she gets married."

Bi Tao rolled her eyes at her and said softly, "It's just between us, don't mention it to the girl."

Bai Tao sighed, "I know. I originally wanted to ask for favors, but my mother always asked me to go and ask for favors. In the end, the girl didn't take it seriously. I won't go either."

She was not stupid and she saw that Chen Ningyu would not buy it.

Bi Tao smiled and said, "Your mother is doing this for your own good, but it's unnecessary."

"Yes, yes. I told her to stop talking about it today, so as not to be in trouble with both sides. She left angrily." Bai Tao smiled, "But she came back and stuffed a few pieces of walnut cakes into my pocket. They were given by the Madam. Would you like to try them?"

Bitao brought it and the two of them sat on the steps to eat.

Chen Ningyu and Danqiu came out. They had just finished eating and were busy wiping their mouths.

"Miss, are you going out?" Bai Tao asked, "It's very hot today."

"If you have nothing to do, go sit in the pavilion and hold an umbrella for me." Chen Ningyu instructed Bi Tao, "Go to the kitchen and find some leftovers and steamed buns."

That means we are going to feed the fishes, Bitao responded.

The three of them went to the fish pond on the east side of the garden.

Unexpectedly, Chen Ningrou was there too. Seeing her, she greeted her, "Fourth sister is also interested today."

"It's just to kill time." Chen Ningyu stood in front of the vermilion railing, looking at the fish in the pond that had been attracted by the fish food, and his interest suddenly decreased by half.

"Actually, there's nothing interesting about them. They're just a bunch of stupid fish. I throw stones or food at them, but they just flock to me. They're really stupid." Chen Ningrou wiped her hands, pulled Chen Ningyu over, and said with a smile, "Why don't we talk?"

"What does Fifth Sister want to say?"

"What can a girl like me say? I'm just happy for my second sister, marrying into such a good family!"

Chen Ningyu nodded: "Second sister is blessed, but it is also what she deserves."

"That's right." Chen Ningrou rolled her eyes. "Isn't it the Fourth Sister's due? We are both girls from the Marquis' Mansion, so who can compare to who?"

"That's not what I meant." Chen Ningyu chuckled twice in his heart. Seeing Bitao coming, he stood up to get the food and threw it into the pond.

Chen Ningrou came over and stood shoulder to shoulder with her: "I heard that the pond in the Princess's Mansion is very big, and there are many beautiful fish, right?"

"It is very big, but as for the fish, my eldest cousin put a lot of mullet, crucian carp, bream, etc. in it, so there are not many left."

Chen Ningrou's eyes sparkled: "It's really interesting, why doesn't anyone in our family do this? After releasing it, we can catch fish and eat them, how fun!"

She has this romantic and innocent look about her, which is very endearing.

Chen Ningyu's eyes softened a little: "Only my cousin would let it go."

When mentioning Zhang Jiwan, Chen Ningrou curled her lips. She didn't like this person at all.

"I heard from my grandmother that the eldest son Fu got married. Now that I think about it, I only saw him when I was young. I don't know when the second son Fu will get married. Why don't they come to our house to play?"

Chen Yuning didn't know how to answer this question, for he was afraid that the princess might not agree.

"Maybe he is too busy. My eldest cousin is a member of the Imperial Guard. Even at home, I rarely see him." As for Fu Chaoqing, she did not mention him.

Chen Ningrou didn't say anything else. She just looked at the fish in the pond, her fingers circling the hem of her blouse.

After feeding the fish, Chen Ningyu was about to leave when she saw Bitao coming, followed by Chen Ningrou's maid Baozhu.

The two said together, "There are guests in the mansion, and the lady wants the young lady to come over."

"Which family?" Chen Ningrou asked first.

Baozhu shook her head: "I'm not sure, it seems to be some cousin, a woman, with two children."

"Strange, who is it?" Chen Ningrou frowned.

"You'll know when you get there." Chen Ningyu walked forward first.

When Chen Ningrou arrived at Ci Xin Garden, she realized that these were guests who had been there before. About seven years ago, they came to the Marquis' Mansion and brought a lot of local specialties. The lady had also treated them well.

The woman was the daughter of a cousin of the Dowager Lady. Her hometown was in Daming Prefecture and her family ran a small business. The cousin missed the Dowager Lady and asked them to come and visit her.

But things don't always go as planned. After they returned, the cousin died soon after. The woman's husband later fell ill and also died.

The lady cried when she thought of her cousin.

When she was young, her cousin came to live with her for a few years, but he went back because he failed to pass the imperial examination. The two of them had some feelings for each other and occasionally exchanged letters. When she heard that he had passed away, she was sad for a while.

She is the only one left of that generation, and none of them lived long.

"Come and meet your cousin." The lady wiped her eyes and asked a few girls to come and meet her.

The woman, Ms. Zhao, was very reserved. She stretched out her hand to tug at the hem of her clothes, not knowing where to put her hands. She called out to several girls first, making her sound like a servant.

Zhang frowned and Jiang curled her lips.

Zhao's daughter, Lü Yun, blushed and held her mother's hand.

Zhao's other son, Lu He, just stood straight with his lips slightly pursed.

The lady-in-waiting saw this and asked her granddaughters to sit down. She said to Zhang, "Please prepare a place for them later. They must have been very tired on the journey."

Zhang nodded: "There is an empty yard, it will be cleaned up soon."

Zhao said hurriedly: "We don't need a yard, we can live anywhere."

The lady waved her hands: "How can this be possible, Shuliang, we are relatives, so don't be so polite." She looked at Lu Yun again, as if she liked her very much, "The last time I saw Yun'er, she was only eight years old. Now she has grown into a big girl. She looks sensible."

"She studied with her grandfather for a few years and can read and write a little."

Hearing her praising her daughter, Zhao couldn't help but relax and smiled happily.

Lu Yun hurriedly said, "Compared to my cousins, they are nothing."

"That's pretty good, it shows your family loves you very much." The lady looked at Lu He again, "He'er is strong and healthy. Although he is a younger brother, he acts like an older brother."

"He does most of the housework, so he's naturally strong." Zhao felt distressed and sighed, "It's all because of the family that he hasn't been able to study in the past few years."

"Mom, why are you saying all this? I'm the only man in the family, can you just sit there and watch?" Although Lu He was young, he had his own ideas. He actually didn't want to come to the Yongchun Marquis'

Mansion, but he couldn't persuade his mother and sister, so he had to come.

The lady nodded slightly. A man who is responsible is a very good person.

I think they are really penniless and would not leave their hometown if they had a little livelihood.

It's really hard to say, in the end only the widow and the orphan were left.

Zhang quickly asked someone to tidy up the yard.

Chen Ningan smiled and said, "Sister Lu has been traveling a lot, and her skirt is dirty. Grandma, why don't you give the new ones I made to Sister Lu? They seem to be the same size."

Zhao clasped her hands and said, "Second Miss is really kind-hearted, but how can my Yun'er wear your clothes! We brought our own."

The lady gave him a look of praise: "Ning An is very thoughtful. A girl should dress beautifully. From now on, you will live here and become a family."

Zhao was so moved that tears welled up in her eyes.

Chen Ningrou snorted slightly. She couldn't stand Chen Ning'an being a good person.

Chen Ningyu did nothing but noticed that Lu Yun's face turned red again.

After Zhang had taken care of her affairs, she turned back and spoke to the Madam, "Mother, do you really want them to stay here permanently?"

They weren't too close, so she had her objections to this.

The lady looked at her and said slowly, "I am old now, and I always feel that I should be more lenient to others. Since they have come to seek refuge, there is no way to drive them away. My cousin still misses me until his death, so how can I not take care of his descendants? Our family can't tolerate these three people."

Zhang said hurriedly: "My daughter-in-law doesn't mean that either, but how should we arrange it?"

Especially Lu Yun, who is at the age to get married. Could it be that she is treated as a girl in the mansion?

"Just give her some monthly allowance." The lady realized that she had not thought it through carefully. She paused and said, "My cousin is still young and honest. It's fine to find her any job. As for He'er, let him go to the academy. The Lu family is also a family of scholars. We can't lose their education. As for Yun'er, the little girl has a lot of self-respect. Don't bother her too much. When it's time for her to get married, her mother will tell her. You can ask her about her requirements and find someone to marry her off to."

Zhang thought, it is easy to say, but there is always one more family, which makes her feel a little dissatisfied. The lady's kindness has caused a lot of trouble!

When she got home, she couldn't help but

complain to Chen Xing.

But Chen Xing was a grown man, so he didn't think so meticulously and spoke to the lady in the same way. Zhang was so angry that she had no choice but to ignore it for the time being.

Chen Ningyu had been looking at the account books these days and felt dizzy every time. He realized that he was not cut out to be an accountant. Later he thought about it and realized that he was being stupid. The princess managed it so well, could it be that she had done it herself?

She actually lacks someone to take charge.

Fortunately, there are still people I can trust.

She called Gu Qiu and said, "Gu Qiu, when I was learning arithmetic, you also learned some of it. From today on, you have to show me these account books and make every entry clear."

After hearing this, Gu Qiu was not unhappy about this tedious matter, but was ecstatic and nodded repeatedly: "I will definitely take good care of it, please rest assured, young lady!"

Ever since Chen Ningyu got the account book, she has also reviewed arithmetic seriously in private, and Chen Ningyu knows it.

Sometimes, you don't have to be afraid of being ambitious. In the eyes of the master, subordinates who do nothing are a headache.

Jiang soon found out about this and was very dissatisfied. When Chen Xiu came back, she said to him, "It turns out that Ning Yu has started to manage the household business. I don't blame her for not telling me, but how can a little girl like her handle such a big thing? What if something goes wrong?"

Chen Xiu said calmly: "She told me early in the morning."

Seeing that he had no intention of blaming Chen Ningyu, Jiang had no choice but to swallow her anger and continued to speak softly, "Are you really confident in letting her take care of herself, sir?"

"It's hers."

"Everyone knows this. After her grandmother passed away, she left all the property to her. I am worried about her. She has never had to worry about food or clothing since she was a child. How could she have learned these things?"

Chen Xiu turned to look at her: "Why, do you have any good ideas?"

"I am thinking about it for her. My husband, think about it. These properties were originally managed by the eldest princess. Most of the people in the farm and the shop were hers. Now they are given to Ning Yu. I heard that some people have been taken back. Isn't this a shortage of people? I think it would be better to send some capable people to Ning Yu. As a girl, she can't go out all the time, right?"

What he said was not without reason. Chen Ningyu was going to get married in the future. Could it be that she would continue to use the eldest princess's people? He nodded: "Then you go and talk to Ningyu. If she agrees, send a few people."

Jiang agreed with a smile.

When Chen Ningyu came to pay her respects one day, Jiang would bring it up.

"My husband said that it's too tiring for you to take care of all this. It would be better to find some experienced people to come."

Chen Ningyu could understand the meaning of this, but no matter how much gold and silver she had, they were all hers, and she would not allow others to interfere, especially when that person was from the Jiang family.

Although she did not have much resentment towards her stepmother, Jiang cared about her very much, and it was considered good that some of her was sincere. Chen Ningyu knew very well that since they were not biological children, they were different.

So she never expected any of this.

"That's what mother was thinking. I'm worried about this and want to borrow a few people from grandmother." She carried the lady out.

Jiang's face looked a little unhappy: "Madam, at your age, it is really better for you to worry less. Now that you are older, you should learn from me how to manage the household."

Chen Ningyu smiled gently.

In the past, she only knew how to teach Chen Ningrou. Now that she has inherited a large share of the family business, Jiang realized that she is the older sister. Should she teach her first?

But it's too late.

Chen Ningyu lowered her head and stroked the purse on her waist: "I have already told grandma that mother is busy on weekdays, so I won't bother you. Although grandma gets tired easily, she really likes to teach me. She is free anyway."

After hearing this, Jiang's mouth corners twitched slightly.

Most of the affairs of the Marquis's Mansion were handled by the First Madam Zhang. How busy could she be? She also said that the Madam Tai really liked it. The listener was thoughtful. Jiang was not a stupid person, so she was naturally very annoyed.

But she was afraid to act rashly. After she married Chen Xiu, even though Chen Ningyu always did things that displeased her, she did not dare to rebuke him and just wanted to let it go.

As a result, Chen Ningyu looked more and more like a lady from a noble family, and was better than Chen Ningrou in every way.

Now, he doesn't even take her as his mother seriously!

Jiang sneered: "You always have a lot of ideas. Well, since the lady is willing to teach, that's great."

"Thank you for your concern, mother." Chen Ningyu nodded.

After she left, Jiang couldn't help but smash a teacup.

☆, Chapter 10: Little Birthday

Chen Ningrou came over and saw her mother's gloomy face, so she asked, "But did Fourth Sister make Mother angry?"

Jiang didn't answer, she slowly exhaled and said, "Rou'er, you have to stand up for me and stop being like a child. I will rely on you and Li'er in the future."

"The headband for grandma is almost ready. I'll send it to her tomorrow." Chen Ningrou comforted her, "Mom, don't be like this. Daddy is still very good to you."

That depends on who he is comparing with. If he has to choose between Chen Ningyu and her, Chen Xiu would definitely choose the former. Originally, he married her just to find a mother for Chen Ningyu.

Jiang sighed and stroked her daughter's face: "Your father's birthday is in two days, do you have any plans?"

Chen Ningrou was stunned.

Apparently forgotten.

Jiang frowned angrily and scolded, "That's your father. Your fourth sister has even made the shoes, and you haven't thought of anything yet?"

This daughter needs her to tell her about everything!

Chen Ningrou took her arm and shook it: "Mom, Dad doesn't need anything. In my opinion, there is no point in giving him shoes."

"My husband is outside every day, and his shoes are the easiest to wear out. How can you be so bored?" Jiang frowned, "Your father loves and protects you every day, so why do you have no filial piety?"

"Mom, how could I be such a person?" Chen Ningrou's eyes turned, "Daddy likes to eat dumplings, why don't I make dumplings for him myself?"

Jiang's expression finally eased: "Your father will be happy if he eats it. Dumplings are often eaten during the Chinese New Year."

"My daughter doesn't understand why such delicious food can only be eaten during the Chinese New Year. I'm afraid daddy misses it a lot too, and this is a good opportunity for him to satisfy his craving." Chen Ningrou giggled.

Jiang shi thought for a while and said, "I'll ask someone to teach you later."

"Okay!" Chen Ningrou said with a smile, "I'm sure Daddy won't be able to stop eating."

On the day of Chen Xiu's birthday, the lady would also have dinner with her son in the evening to celebrate, so the six of them gathered together for dinner at noon.

When Chen Xiu saw the dumplings being served, he was very happy. He ate more than twenty of them and praised the filling for being delicious.

The dumplings are really good, with a thin and smooth skin, and a variety of fillings, more than ten kinds. The most delicious one is the fish dumpling, which is fresh, tender and fragrant. Even Chen Ningyu ate several of them.

"It's new and it's my first time eating it. Whoever made it, please give me some money." Chen Xiu was in high spirits and asked someone to bring some wine.

Jiang smiled and said, "What do you think, sir?"

Chen Xiu was puzzled: "How can I guess this?"

"It was made by my fifth sister." Chen Li couldn't wait to say, "I went to see it. My fifth sister had flour all over her face. It took her a lot of effort to make it."

"Oh, Rou'er can make dumplings now?" Chen Xiu laughed and joked, "Is it difficult for you?"

"I'm doing this for Daddy. No matter how difficult it is, I have to do it well."

Chen Xiu laughed: "Just now he said he would reward the cook. Since you cooked it, my dear daughter, what do you want your father to reward you with?"

"Daddy, will you give me everything?" Chen Ningrou looked at him expectantly.

"Of course, as long as Daddy has it."

Chen Ningrou twisted her fingers and sighed, "Forget it. My daughter is not as clever as my fourth sister. It's just food. How can it be as good as the shoes made by my sister? Dad will remember them wherever he wears them."

Chen Xiu was slightly stunned, then he quickly stretched out his hand and pinched Chen Ningrou's cheek, coaxing her: "Daddy will remember Rou'er after eating the dumplings. You and Yu'er are different, so why compare? You are both Daddy's good daughters!"

Chen Ningrou became happy and let Chen Xiu eat a few more dumplings.

Seeing her being entertained by her father, Chen Ningyu kept smiling and asked, "What kind of fish is this? It doesn't seem to be commonly eaten. It is indeed delicious."

Chen Ningrou didn't answer immediately, Jiang said, "It's Spanish mackerel. Rou'er said this fish has more meat and less bones, so she wanted to try cooking it. Who knew it turned out really good."

"My sister is really thoughtful." Chen Ningyu picked up the chopsticks and ate two more with a smile.

Chen Ninghua didn't say much, and only said a few words of congratulations. She was always very reserved in front of Chen Xiu, and outsiders might not think of them as father and daughter.

Chen Xiu just praised Chen Ningrou, and after dinner, he put on the shoes made by Chen Ningyu.

Chen Ningyu joked, "With the brocade socks

made by my third sister, my daughter will wear them out of filial piety, and dad will be warm in winter and cool in summer, and feel comfortable all over, right?"

Chen Xiu laughed: "You are good at talking, but I can wear them myself." He paused, and finally looked at Chen Ninghua, "Your socks are very finely made. You have made great progress as a female worker."

Chen Ninghua didn't know how many years it would take for Chen Xiu to praise her, and she almost cried with excitement.

Jiang curled her lips secretly.

Speaking of the two daughters, she likes Chen Ningyu a little more. Although she is disobedient, she has her own ideas. Chen Ninghua's submissive look always makes her feel more upset.

A concubine's daughter is always different from a legitimate daughter. Who are you showing pity to?

After coming out, Chen Ningyu and Chen Ninghua walked together.

"I made a few more pairs of socks. If you like them, you can wear them." Chen Ninghua asked the maid to bring two pairs. The socks were made of brocade and embroidered with lavender flowers.

Chen Ningyu smiled and said, "It's so beautiful, of course I like it, thank you, second sister."

"It's my duty." Chen Ninghua's face was gloomy.

As a concubine's daughter, her father and

mother dislike her. Whether in her childhood or now, she always feels more bitterness than sweetness. But who in this family can truly understand her?

Chen Ningyu sighed secretly and comforted her, "Don't be sad, Third Sister. Father will understand your kindness sooner or later."

Chen Ninghua looked at Chen Ningyu, who was still bright and beautiful under the moonlight, and smiled and said, "It's also true that I'm not as likable as my sister, but you're right."

The two walked forward side by side, and only separated and went back when they reached a cave entrance.

The Lu family has been living in the Marquis' Mansion for more than a month. Although Zhang is not happy, the lady is very happy.

Zhao had a hard life since her father and husband passed away and her family business failed. What had she not experienced? She had worked as a farmer, sold embroidery, set up stalls, and even washed dishes in restaurants. So she looked reserved and honest, but her words were interesting because she had seen so many things.

The lady dowager often chatted with her, and the relationship between the cousin and niece became better and better. Both Lu Yun and Lu He were children with strong self-esteem and did not cause any trouble to the mansion, so they lived in peace.

That day, Chen Ningyu went to the lady's house and saw Zhao there again, so she called her cousin aunt.

Zhao stood up quickly: "But I have something to say, I'm leaving now."

The lady smiled and said, "Don't bother. We are all family. What is there to avoid?"

Chen Ningyu also said: "I just came to ask grandma for a few people."

Zhao sat down again.

The lady asked Chen Ningyu to sit on a couch and said, "I have thought about this over the past few days and have just made a list. They are all capable people and are most suitable for you."

She asked Mother Hu to bring the list.

Chen Ningyu didn't even look at it: "Grandma's picks are always the best. I just saw that it's been a long time since there's anyone in charge, and the people down there are going to make a fuss, so I came to ask Grandma."

The lady smiled and said, "Forget it. You have always trusted me, so how can I not pick the best for you? But you have to spend some time on it. How many years can an old woman like me live? You will have to rely on yourself in the future."

The lady was optimistic and open-minded, and she never avoided talking about her own age.

Chen Ningyu's nose felt sore, and she said hurriedly, "Grandma can live to be a hundred years old!"

The lady laughed and squeezed her shoulders: "Silly child, everyone dies. But my children and grandchildren are filial and promising, so I have no regrets in this life."

Chen Ningyu buried her head in her arms and whispered, "Although grandma is not afraid of death, I am afraid when I hear it."

In this world, she loves three people the most: the lady dowager, her father, and the eldest princess.

She thought that she lived a carefree life, and that she was blessed by them. But people are not plants, so who can be heartless? In the past few years, she felt that she had a real blood relationship with them. She had become Chen Ningyu, although she was not the one before.

The lady reached out and stroked her hair, saying lovingly, "Okay, Ning Yu, I've been following the advice of the imperial physician Wang recently. I'm not eating too much meat, just to live longer. Silly child, how can your grandmother really bear to leave you?"

Only then did Chen Ningyu smile.

Zhao praised: "The fourth girl is really filial."

"You two children are also filial." The lady smiled, "He'er studies very hard. He hasn't touched it for many years. Compared with others, he is still much harder. I heard from Li'er that he always goes to ask the teacher for advice."

Zhao smiled happily: "He'er is lucky that he can continue to study."

The lady said, "Say some more polite words." She looked at Chen Ningyu, "You should recognize the people on this list. If you don't understand something, Mother Hu will tell you."

Chen Ningyu responded with a "OK".

As she was looking at the list, Zhao asked the lady curiously, "So the fourth young lady has a shop and good farmland?"

"It was left by her maternal grandparents."

Zhao had lived here for a while, so she understood the situation and sighed softly.

The lady also taught Chen Ningyu some of her experience as the housekeeper. In fact, to sum it up, it means knowing people and using them well, trusting people when you use them, and not using people if you are suspicious of them.

However, the lady had a lot of experience and was not just good at talking about general principles. She could give countless real examples, and Chen Ningyu benefited a lot from listening to them.

After Zhao went back, Lu Yun was practicing calligraphy.

"Oh, why don't you take a rest? It's still hot out here, why are you writing?" Zhao felt sorry for her daughter and quickly took out a fan to fan her. "Life is better now..."

Without even looking up, Lu Yun interrupted her and asked, "Mother, do you still expect to live here forever?"

Zhao was stunned: "Why can't I live here? Madam Tai is such a nice person."

Lu Yun smiled and said nothing.

Zhao was surprised. She looked around and asked, "Didn't the Madam send two maids to serve you? Where are they?"

"I dare not trouble them." Lu Yun said calmly, "I will do what I can do myself."

Although she had anticipated that living under someone else's roof would not be a comfortable thing, for the sake of her brother, this was the only hope for their Lu family. In fact, she had also proposed this to Zhao.

Zhao sighed, "They are a marquis' mansion after all. We should know our place when we live here."

Lu Yun didn't respond, but picked up the pen and wrote another word.

"I just found out today that the fourth young lady's dowry was so generous. There wasn't much people in her maternal family, so all the money was left to her. No wonder what she wears and what she uses are so good, no worse than the second young lady's." Zhao also grew up in a wealthy family when she was young, and this can be seen.

When Lu Yun heard this, she suddenly couldn't write anymore.

We talked about dowry, but I wonder what will happen to her when she gets married? Without these, I'm afraid she will be looked down upon when she goes to her husband's house.

She sighed slightly.

"I just hope my brother can have a promising future and pass the imperial examination to become a Jinshi."

She said something out of the blue. Although Zhao was surprised, she smiled and said, "He'er will definitely not let us down. He is now with the Second Young Master and no one looks down on him."

"Why does mom always talk about their family?" Lu Yun frowned.

"We live together, so how can we not talk about it? You also said that the Marquis' Mansion is good, and you also said that you remembered that the Madam and the others were very kind when you came last time. Why don't you allow me to mention it now?"

Lu Yun was a little annoyed and waved her hand: "Forget it, mother, you can say whatever you want. The three of us are just staying here temporarily."

Zhao smiled and said, "That will have to wait until He'er gets an official position in the future, then we can move out and live with him."

Lu Yun didn't know what else to say to Zhao, so she simply stopped talking.

Zhao said, "I'm going to go out and wash the clothes. You can take a rest after writing for a while."

Lu Yun responded reluctantly.

After Zhao left, she looked up at her back,

thinking of the past days, her heart was sour and bitter. She thought that they were originally a wealthy family, but unfortunately fate played a trick on them and they ended up like this!

Who says good people are rewarded? Her grandfather, father, and mother were all good people.

She lowered her head and slowly drew a line.

☆、Chapter 11 Ceremony

The Mid-Autumn Festival is coming. During this festival, every family will send mooncakes and fruits to show their affection. Therefore, Zhang is the busiest one and must not miss any family. The lady reminded her, "Send one to the eldest princess as well."

Although the eldest princess had severed ties with them over the years, the lady-in-waiting had never forgotten her and would send her gifts every year during every festival.

Zhang sighed and wanted to persuade the lady, but she didn't know where to start, so she could only agree.

But who would have thought that Fu Chaoqing would come today.

The lady couldn't believe her ears.

"Who? Chao Qing?"

Mother Hu smiled and said, "Yes, it was the eldest princess's second son. He came to deliver the mooncakes in person."

"Please come in." The lady was overjoyed.

Fu Chaoqing came in and performed the greetings as a junior.

Seeing that the boy who was a child in previous years has grown into a handsome boy now, the lady's eyes reddened slightly. How much she liked this boy back then, and how much she felt sorry for him!

"Chaoqing, come here, let me take a closer look." She waved.

Fu Chaoqing walked over as he was told.

The lady looked at him and said with emotion: "It has been a long time! But you," she paused, "was it your father who asked you to come here?"

Fu Chaoqing smiled and said, "My mother also agreed, and she even asked me to buy mooncakes with jujube paste filling."

"Okay, okay." The lady was overwhelmed with emotion and hurriedly asked him to sit down.

Fu Chaoqing said apologetically: "You look healthy. I have been rude and have not come to visit you in these years."

"You are also taking care of your health, why are you saying this?" The lady said in a gentle voice, "I see that you look good today. Your father and mother have spent a lot of effort and finally found a doctor who suits you."

Fu Chaoqing said quietly: "I am a burden to my father and mother."

"Don't say that. Who wouldn't like a good kid like you?" The lady felt sad when she talked about this, so she changed the subject and asked, "Chao Yun is very busy now that she has joined the Jinyiwei, right?"

"Yes, I'm not at home often."

The lady shook her head: "He is like a monkey spirit, he can't stay still, it suits him, but he has to be careful, this job is not easy."

"I will tell my brother. Madam is very concerned about him."

"After all, I watched you two grow up, just like my grandchildren." The old lady's face was full of love.

The two talked for a while, and then the lady asked, "It's rare for you to come here, maybe you can stay here for a meal?"

"I'm afraid I'll bother you."

"You often loved to eat here when you were young. Now you are so polite." The lady asked Madam Hu to go to the kitchen and tell them to prepare some good dishes. She also asked someone to call Chen Li and a few other girls.

Chen Ningyu was also surprised when he heard it.

Come to think of it, Fu Chaoqing hasn't been here for four or five years. No wonder the lady asked them to go.

Because she had just slept on the couch, she combed her hair before going there. On the way, she met Chen Ningrou and Chen Ninghua.

Chen Ningrou wore a turquoise jacket with a gold lotus pattern, and a plum-red skirt with scattered flowers. She had her hair in a bun, and wore a butterfly hairpin and a pearl and jade hairpin on her head. She also wore a string of small sapphires on each ear, making her look delicate and cute. Chen Ninghua, on the other hand, was always simple, wearing a moonlit white bamboo-patterned blouse and a green lotus-colored pleated skirt. She only had a white jade hairpin in her jet-black hair, and was extremely beautiful.

The two of them were dressed as if they were meeting a distinguished guest.

Chen Ningyu thought about it and it made sense. To them, Fu Chaoqing was just a strange guest, but to her, it was different.

When we arrived at Ci Xin Garden, Chen Ning'an and Chen Li were already there.

Although Chen Li is only nine years old, he already has his own courtyard. He and Chen Ning'an live relatively close to here, and they don't happen to go to the academy today.

But Fu Chaoqing was not there.

Chen Ningrou asked curiously, "Grandma, where is Mr. Fu?"

"What second young master? He is your cousin." The lady said with a smile, "He went to your great uncle's place."

Chen Li asked again: "Cousin? But I don't seem to remember him at all."

The lady sighed slightly: "It's been many years since we last met. When he came, you were still very young, how could you remember him?"

Chen Li nodded: "Then I have to get closer to my cousin later. However, I already have a cousin, grandma, so which cousin should I call this cousin?" He was a little confused. Zhang Jihe and Zhang Jiwan are his eldest cousin and second cousin respectively.

The lady laughed and said, "Then you should just call him Cousin Qing, so as to avoid confusion."

This is the result of having many relatives. Just counting one, two, three, or four can no longer solve the problem.

Chen Ningan asked: "He was not in good health. Now that he can come, is he better?"

The lady nodded: "That should be the case."

Chen Ningrou said happily: "It's really God's blessing!"

This expression was so sincere that Chen Ningyu couldn't help but look at her in surprise.

As he was speaking, Fu Chaoqing came over after visiting Chen Xing.

Today he was wearing a turquoise robe with bamboo patterns, his black hair was combed up, he wore a white jade crown, and a beautiful jade hung around his waist. When he walked in, he was like a fresh morning breeze, and whoever saw him felt comfortable, just like the handsome young man in the painting, pleasing to the eye.

Chen Ningrou's eyes widened a little.

In her memory, Fu Chaoqing was a handsome

boy. She was only eight years old at that time, and she couldn't take her eyes off him. Who would have thought that he would grow up so much now? She looked at him carefully again and sighed. It was a pity that he was a little thin and his skin was a little pale, but no matter what, he was still very handsome.

The lady smiled and said, "You haven't seen your cousins for a long time, so you don't recognize them, right?"

Fu Chaoqing said, "You have grown up now, so I must be a stranger to you." He looked at Chen Li and asked with a smile, "Li'er, I once held you in my arms. You liked to play with bamboo dragonflies at that time, so I carved one for you. Do you remember?"

"Bamboo dragonfly?" Chen Li's eyes lit up. "Is it the bamboo dragonfly that can fly? I remember, I remember, it was given to me by my cousin Qing!"

For children, things that can fly into the sky always leave a deep impression on them, but they can't remember the person who gave them the gifts.

At that time, the princess had stopped communicating with them. Fu Cheng had brought the two children here during those visits. It was not until four years ago when Fu Chaoqing caught a cold and his health suddenly worsened that he stopped coming here.

The lady said, "Your cousin Qing is good at calligraphy and painting, Li'er, you should ask him for advice."

Chen Li suddenly became close to Fu Chaoqing because of the bamboo dragonfly, and immediately pulled him to his study. As he was leaving, he whispered, "Cousin Qing, please make me another bamboo dragonfly. The previous one is broken."

Fu Chaoqing smiled and said, "Okay."

Chen Ningrou came up from behind and said, "Li'er, don't be rude. Cousin Qing is here as a guest, so don't act naughty."

"Fifth sister, I'm not rude." Chen Li felt aggrieved.

Fu Chaoqing also said: "Li'er is very well-behaved. I also want to go to his study to take a look."

His eyes were clear and moving. Chen Ningrou blushed and said softly, "Since cousin Qing is willing to go, that's great. Li'er's handwriting is not good enough, please give me some advice."

Fu Chaoqing nodded, looked behind him, and called softly, "Ayu."

His voice is very gentle.

Chen Ningyu walked over, with confusion in her eyes.

Fu Chaoqing knew what she was thinking and said softly, "I asked to come here on my own initiative, and my mother agreed."

Chen Ningyu smiled happily: "That's great!"

Fu Chaoqing also laughed.

These two people, one is extremely handsome, the other is beautiful, standing side by side, they are truly a perfect match. Chen

Ningrou felt sad and stood beside them, feeling a little at a loss as to what to do.

"Ayu, why don't you go to Li'er's study too?" Fu Chaoqing invited.

"Well, it's a rare visit from a distinguished guest like you, so I have to accompany you." Chen Ningyu blinked.

Seeing that his elder sister didn't say a word, Chen Li hurriedly said, "Fifth sister, go too."

"I'm not going." Chen Ningrou glanced at Fu Chaoqing, lowered her eyes and said, "Men and women shouldn't touch each other. Even though they are relatives, it's always inconvenient."

Chen Ningyu was stunned.

Having said that, she felt it was not appropriate to go.

Fu Chaoqing said indifferently: "Forget it, Ayu, you are coming to my house anyway."

He left with Chen Li.

Chen Ningrou felt a little regretful, but words spoken were like water spilled, and could not be taken back.

She bit her lip and turned away.

Chen Ning'an and Chen Ninghua arrived at this time. Chen Ning'an asked, "What happened to the fifth sister?"

"Maybe she's not feeling well." Chen Ningyu was actually thinking that there must be something wrong with her brain. It would have been fine if she was being stubborn and didn't want to go, but he dragged her into this. She and Fu Chaoqing grew up together, so going to Chen Li's study was nothing. It wasn't like they were a single man and a single woman being alone together. Besides, Chen Li asked her to go with him, so there was nothing wrong with just a few of them. In the past, when Zhang Jihe and Zhang Jiwan came, they often talked together, didn't they?

But it's better this way. She doesn't want Fu Chaoqing and Chen Ningrou to get close. That girl is really hard to like.

Chen Ninghua suggested: "Why don't we go for a walk in the garden? It's neither cold nor hot today, which is the most comfortable. There aren't many weather like this in a year. It won't be long before it starts to get cold again."

"Yeah, it snowed early, it's really annoying." Chen Ning'an said with a smile, "Just go sit in the garden and ask the maids to bring some fruit snacks."

Chen Ningyu thought it would be fine, so she naturally agreed.

The three of them drank tea and chatted. At noon, they went to have dinner with Mrs. Tai.

At this time, the Zhang family, Jiang family, Chen Min, Cao Xiangmei, even Zhao family, and Lu Yun were all here, but Chen Xiu was the only one missing. However, with his position, he rarely had time to come back for lunch. He was always working in the Yamen. Yes, sometimes even dinner has to be late, so I didn't see Fu Chaoqing.

Speaking of which, he was still quite regretful and asked Ms. Jiang how the child was doing.

"Of course he is one in a hundred." Although Jiang didn't like the eldest princess, it was hard for anyone to say bad things about someone like Fu Chaoqing. "It's a pity that his health is not good. He stopped drinking after a few sips of wine."

Chen Xiu sighed, and was thankful: "Finally it's all right, otherwise the princess might not let him go out."

"That's right." Jiang nodded. "It looks like he's fine. If he's really not well, it would be a pity for the child."

A few days later, the Zhang family came to deliver mooncakes.

When they deliver the gift, they don't just send someone once, but the whole family comes.

The lady was very happy. Although she thought Zhang Zhijing was too harsh as a father, she still liked him from the bottom of her heart. This son-in-law was capable, had good character, was good-looking, and knew how to be filial to his mother-in-law. Naturally, the more she looked at him, the more she liked him. She hurriedly asked the kitchen to prepare a banquet.

Chen Ningyu went back after meeting his uncle and aunt. Zhang Jiwan followed him and asked, "How is my water bottle? Is it useful?"

"Yes, it looks good, thank you."

"As long as you like it, cousin." He smiled and came up to me and whispered, "Cousin, I got some money a few days ago. Qiu's business is booming, and he gave me some money!"

"Congratulations." Chen Ningyu smiled and said, "I will definitely find a chance to try it someday."

"Next time you can just go with me. I don't have to pay for the meal."

Chen Ningyu smiled and said, "Okay, but if I go with you, what excuse can I find?"

Zhang Jiwan was stunned and scratched his head: "That's right, forget it, next time I will bring some dishes for you to try. Tell me, do you like fish or duck? Oh, do you like lion's head?"

"It's all fine, but it's too much trouble for my cousin." Chen Ningyu knew that Zhang Jiwan wanted to share the joy of making money with him. It was his little secret, and she didn't object.

Zhang Jiwan was very happy: "Just wait and eat. I think some of the dishes are better than those cooked by your chef."

The two of them unknowingly walked to Furong Garden.

"You've made me thirsty, cousin, do you have any tea?"

"Who doesn't have tea?" Chen Ningyu laughed and asked Danqiu to make a pot.

Just as Zhang Jiwan picked up the teacup, Zhang Jihe arrived. He was furious and scolded, "You disappeared again in the blink of an eye. My father ordered me to look for you. Why are you here again?"

Zhang Jiwan said nonchalantly, "I came to play with my fourth cousin. What's wrong? Can't I even drink tea?"

"Go away!" Zhang Jihe reached out and pulled him.

Zhang Jiwan was also a stubborn person. Zhang Jihe was only his brother, not his father, so he naturally didn't want to listen. He pulled his hand back, glared at Zhang Jihe and said, "What are you doing! I can walk by myself if I want to!"

Zhang Jihe was very annoyed and took out his anger on Chen Ningyu: "Ji Wan is not sensible, and you are not sensible either? He wants to come and drink tea, and you let him drink it?"

Chen Ningyu was puzzled: "Why shouldn't I let him drink? He is my cousin."

Zhang Jihe sneered: "You are good at deceiving people. Isn't it because of you that Ji Wan always comes here?"

Chen Ningyu also got angry. What does it mean to confuse people? She frowned and said, "Cousin, please speak clearly! Don't throw dirty water on me!"

"Need I say more? Isn't this obvious to you, Mr. Li? And what happened to you last time when Mr. Wu came? You know it very well in your heart, why do you need me to tell you?" Zhang Jihe showed no mercy and tried to pull Zhang Jiwan again, "Why do you keep talking to someone like her?"

This was the first time Chen Ningyu was spoken to like this in person, and she was so angry that she wanted to hit someone.

Zhang Jiwan was stunned at first after hearing those words, but after a while she came to her senses and shouted, "Brother, why do you say that about my fourth cousin? Mr. Li is not good enough, and Mr. Wu's talk is nonsense. It was clearly me who called my fourth cousin that time, and she came out!"

"You are so bewildered that you are speaking for her. Come with me!"

"I won't leave. If you want to leave, you leave first!" Zhang Jiwan was also angry.

"Are you going to leave or not?"

"No!"

In anger, Zhang Jihe tore Zhang Jiwan's clothes with force.

"You actually ruined my clothes?" Zhang Jiwan was a more irritable person, and he reached out to grab Zhang Jihe's collar.

The two men soon started to fight.

☆, Chapter 12 Fighting Incident

The two brothers started fighting, and Chen Ningyu was a little dumbfounded.

Forget about Zhang Jiwan, but it was also strange that Zhang Jihe, who was always well-mannered, actually fought with his own brother. However, thinking of his harsh words just now, Chen Ningyu was not surprised.

However, this happened in her house, which would definitely seem weird.

She raised her voice and asked, "Do you two want your uncle to use family rules?"

Zhang Zhijing's name has always had a deterrent effect, and the two men really stopped, one wiping his face and the other straightening his clothes.

But who would have known that at this moment, Zhang Zhijing and his wife appeared at the gate of the courtyard.

"You two rebellious sons, come out here!"

There was a sudden thunderclap.

When the two brothers heard their father's voice, they turned pale with fright.

"Who told them?" Chen Ningyu was also a little panicked. She originally wanted to suppress the matter, to make a big deal out of it and not let Zhang Zhijing and the old lady know about it. But now it was clear that someone had gone to inform them.

Gu Qiu and Dan Qiu were both in the room and shook their heads.

Bi Tao came in and whispered, "Just now when the young master was fighting, a maid happened to come over. She was from the laundry room and came to get the sheets and other things. She left without waiting for me to stop her."

What a confusing person!

Chen Ningyu cursed inwardly.

Zhang Jihe and Zhang Jiwan had already walked out, both with their heads down, waiting for the coming storm.

Chen Linzhi knew Zhang Zhijing's temper and quickly advised him, "Husband, the children are just fooling around with each other, it's nothing, and besides, it's not appropriate to say anything in Ning Yu's courtyard."

Zhang Zhijing thought about it and scolded him with a dark face, "You bastard."

A few people went to the lady's place.

On the way, Zhang Zhijing couldn't help scolding his two sons again, and the two brothers didn't dare to say a word.

The lady was also puzzled. These two were usually very good friends and never quarreled. Why did they suddenly fight? But when asked, neither of them mentioned the reason. Later, when they returned home, Zhang Zhijing beat them with a stick for more than ten times, and their facial features were distorted with pain.

But he still refused to tell the reason. Although Zhang Zhijing was strict with his sons, he would not really beat them to death, so he had to let it go.

Chen Linzhi was so distressed that her eyes turned red from crying. She called a doctor for them and applied medicine.

The two were helped back by the servants.

Zhang Jiwan walked for a while and stopped, looked around, stretched out his hand to hold on to a crooked tree, and said to Zhang Jihe, "This matter is not over yet, let's talk it out here!"

Zhang Jihe was not done yet, so the two men told the servants to move away.

Zhang Jiwan looked at Zhang Jihe and asked, "Are you happy this time?"

"You deserve it!" Zhang Jihe replied.

Zhang Jiwan sneered: "You're talking as if your butt doesn't hurt? I'm about to cry when I see you."

Zhang Jihe snorted.

When it comes to enduring pain, Zhang Jiwan is definitely the best, simply because he was beaten since he was a child.

Zhang Jiwan continued, "Forget it this time, but if you say that about Fourth Cousin again next time, I will fight with you."

Zhang Jihe was furious: "You still say you are not bewitched by her? I think she is a vixen, otherwise why would she repeatedly ruin my second cousin's marriage?"

"Young Master Wu doesn't have it." Zhang Jiwan frowned.

"Who knows? Anyway, she's not a good one."

"You are not allowed to say that about my fourth cousin." Zhang Jiwan waved his fist. "You are ruining her reputation. If this gets out, how will my fourth cousin live? Even her own relatives look at her like this. How can she bear it?"

Zhang Jihe lowered his voice a little: "I didn't say that outside." He stared at Zhang Jiwan, "Why on earth did you protect her?"

Zhang Jiwan sneered: "You don't know."

"How would I know if you don't tell me?"

Zhang Jihe was surprised.

Zhang Jiwan refused to say anything, and called the servant to help him walk away.

Zhang Jihe was so angry that his teeth were itching, but he still said that he was not bewitched!

He thought to himself, no, he must keep a close eye on his brother. He didn't want Chen Ningyu to be his future sister-in-law. Although it was unlikely based on the relationship between their two families, there were always exceptions.

Zhang Zhijing didn't figure out the matter. Everyone in Chen Ningyu's room was very loyal, and the old woman had never heard the two brothers talking, so no one else knew anything. But the lady found it strange, so she called Chen Ningyu to question him alone.

Chen Ningyu felt a little embarrassed. Such harsh words were spoken about herself, and she really didn't want to mention it.

The lady said, "Is there something else you are hiding?"

"Not really." Chen Ningyu sighed and finally said it.

The lady's eyes widened when she heard this, and she slammed the table and said, "What's wrong with Ji He? He actually said this about his own cousin!"

"Maybe my eldest cousin was just angry at the time. Didn't my cousin refuse to leave?"

"That's not right for you!" The old lady

was very annoyed. She had always liked Chen Ningyu. This granddaughter was not only good-looking, but also became more sensible as she grew older. She never caused anyone any worry. How could such a good girl be slandered like this, especially when that person was her own granddaughter!

"I must go and tell your aunt to take good care of it."

Upon hearing this, Chen Ningyu hurriedly said, "Grandma, please don't do that. My eldest cousin doesn't like me in the first place. If my aunt knew about it and scolded him, I don't know what he would think. It's better to forget it. My cousin is a boy after all, and he always thinks things too simply."

The lady rubbed her brows, looking quite distressed: "Ji He is a very intelligent child. He passed the imperial examination at the age of six. Now he is only seventeen, but he has already become a juren. At this age, he should have achieved a lot. Who would have thought that he would be such a jerk!"

This time, Zhang Jihe really refreshed the impression he left on her.

Without him, Chen Ningyu would not have known that there was someone among her relatives who hated her so much, and that person was not Zhang.

She originally thought that Zhang was the only one who hated her the most after the Li family incident.

On the contrary, Chen Ning'an was the most peaceful, so she always felt that Zhang's education level was quite high. Her two daughters both had the demeanor of ladies from wealthy families and were truly noble ladies.

The lady said again: "If I don't tell you, I will wrong you and let him scold you for no reason."

Chen Ningyu did not hide it: "I was really angry at the time, and I really wanted to hit him twice to vent my anger, but now I think that those who are innocent are innocent. Whatever my cousin says about me, it doesn't matter. Anyway, you, grandma, believe in me, and that's enough."

The lady patted her hands and said, "You are very broad-minded. Ji He will realize that he is wrong sooner or later, but I still need to inform your aunt."

Since she insisted on doing so, Chen Ningyu stopped trying to persuade her.

Chen Linzhi knew about it, and immediately went back to call Zhang Jihe into the room, and said with a stern face: "So it's about this matter, how can you say that about your fourth cousin?"

Zhang Jihe sneered: "She filed a complaint, didn't she?"

"What are you complaining about? She didn't say anything at first. She only told me when the Madam asked. She also asked the Madam not to tell me. You, how could your fourth cousin be such a person? You are so confused!" Chen Linzhi scolded her son, "Next time you have to apologize in person."

Zhang Jihe said disdainfully: "She is used to being a good person. If I don't tell her, how could my grandmother know that she is just taking revenge on me."

Chen Linzhi frowned and rebuked: "If she really wants to take revenge, won't she tell your father? If she tells your father, do you think you can get away with a dozen beatings? By then, I won't be able to protect you!"

Zhang Jihe had nothing to say.

Chen Linzhi said a few more words before he agreed to apologize.

Chen Linzhi had spent a lot of time and effort educating these two sons. Within two days, she urged Zhang Jihe again. Zhang Jihe had no choice but to find time to go to Yongchun Marquis' Mansion. When he saw the lady dowager, he could not avoid being scolded by her.

By the time he arrived at Furong Garden, he was already in a very bad mood.

When Chen Ningyu saw his face, she knew that this apology was just a pretense, but when she thought of what Zhang Jihe said that day, she would not let him off the hook.

Seeing this, several maids retreated.

It would be really embarrassing for the cousin to come and apologize if they were still here, but I'm afraid he wouldn't be able to say it.

Seeing that everyone had left, Zhang Jihe said with a straight face, "I was wrong last time. Please forgive me, fourth cousin."

"If you are not sincere, I cannot forgive you." Chen Ningyu said, "It is enough for us to understand each other. You can go now."

Zhang Jihe turned and left.

Chen Ningyu thought of something and called him again: "Second sister didn't blame me for the Ji family incident, and grandmother believed me. I don't understand why you are so angry, cousin?"

Zhang Jihe didn't say anything.

Seeing him like this, Chen Ningyu thought of Zhang Jiwan's behavior that day. One of the two brothers was good to her, while the other didn't like her. But this didn't mean that Zhang Jihe had no one to protect her. She seemed to have realized something and said calmly, "Even if you hate me in the future, you don't have to say it. Everyone has someone they hate in their heart, right? But, I hope you know why you hate me."

Zhang Jihe was stunned, frowned, and turned away.

The lady felt better knowing that he had apologized. She did not want her grandson to be someone who did not know right from wrong.

Mother Hu came in and said, "The Xu family just sent a festival gift."

"Oh? Why didn't Lin Ru come?"

In the past, during the Mid-Autumn Festival, both daughters would come in person.

"They said that a distant relative of the Xu family has come to stay for a few days and will not come this time." Mother Hu paused and was a little hesitant about the rest of her words, wondering how to tell the lady.

The lady looked at her expression and knew that it was not a good thing. She raised her eyebrows and asked, "Are you here to urge me again?"

Mother Hu sighed, "Yes, it is said that several months have passed and there has been no movement here. Madam Xu said that if there is no suitable one, she can only choose her niece."

The lady thought of the distant relatives that Mother Hu had just mentioned, and her expression changed: "Could it be that everyone is here?"

Mother Hu opened her eyes wide, "That's not going to happen, is it? If they really come, where will our mansion be? We agreed that the Madam will make the decision, Madam Xu won't really regret it, right?"

The lady's face was filled with anger: "This old woman has gone back on her word before. She has a good life because she gave birth to a good son!"

The lady is really regretting now. She shouldn't have been so hasty and only cared about Xu Ke's future. He is really not that good of a mother!

"Besides, Madam, Old Master Xu may not agree with Old Madam Xu." Mother Hu said.

The lady's expression eased a little. Compared with Old Madam Xu, Old Master Xu's status was obviously higher. As long as he didn't say anything, Old Madam Xu would not dare to act recklessly. After all, Old Master Xu was the first to express his intention and wanted to marry into their family.

"Why mention distant relatives? That's just a show of power." The old lady thought about it carefully and understood what Old Lady Xu meant. It was just to scare her so that she could find a suitable person as soon as possible to be Xu Ke's concubine and give birth to a son for the Xu family.

☆, Chapter 13 Madam Yang

The last time she came back, Chen Linru had already untied her knot and was chatting and laughing with Xu Ke. The old lady felt comforted seeing this. After all, the relationship between the young couple was still good. It was just that they had no choice but to deal with the issue of offspring.

Chen Linru also said that everything was left to the old lady. The old lady thought that her daughter trusted her, so she had to find a suitable concubine for Xu Ke.

If a concubine gives birth to a son in the

future, he will be the eldest son of a concubine. If the Xu family has never had a legitimate son, his position will be equivalent to that of the eldest son. If the concubine is not obedient, Chen Linru's life will be difficult. That's why she was so opposed to Xu Ke marrying Madam Xu's distant niece. Besides, it is not certain that Chen Linru will not be able to give birth to a son in the future.

Seeing that the lady was distressed, Mother Hu said, "Why not help Luzhu? She is a very honest person."

Lu Zhu was a maidservant brought by Chen Linru, and also a concubine. However, after serving as a concubine for many years, she was never promoted to a concubine, nor did she give birth to any children. Chen Linru still had some tricks up her sleeve.

The lady sneered: "It's because he looks honest that he's not stable."

Mother Hu was surprised: "Could it be that Luzhu also has this idea?"

"Who wouldn't have one? How many people wouldn't want to have children after becoming a concubine? Would being a concubine give them something to look forward to in the future?" The lady shook her head and turned the bodhi beads on her wrist. "I'm afraid she has already hated him. Others don't know that I carefully selected this green bead for Linru. But as time goes by, people will always change."

Mother Hu was shocked: "Madam Tai is still

very discerning."

The lady glanced at Mother Hu.

Mother Hu felt a little guilty. After all, when Luzhu's mother was still in the mansion, she had said many nice things and flattered her in front of her. After listening to her for a long time, she was inevitably biased. So she said the wrong thing.

Mother Hu forced a smile and said, "What is the Madam going to do? Choose a good girl, or another maid from the mansion?"

The daughters of ordinary officials would definitely not become concubines, as that would be a disgrace. The lady said, "I've been thinking about it these days, Qingtong."

Qingtong is also in the lady's courtyard. She has just been promoted to the first-class maid. She is pretty, but not as good-looking as Chen Linru. She is younger. What is strange to Mother Hu is that Qingtong has no father or mother. She is very lively and a bit naive. Compared with the other stable maids, she is really not suitable.

The lady took a few sips of tea and said calmly, "Prepare some nice clothes for her and send them over on a chosen day."

Seeing the coldness in the lady's eyes, Mother Hu suddenly understood that this was exactly what should be done!

She hurriedly gave orders.

After Qingtong heard the news, she couldn't sleep well all night. Qinghe, who was in the same ear room, congratulated her and said, "The Madam really thinks highly of you. Apart from anything else, the second uncle is handsome and elegant, and he doesn't like to flirt with other women. It's a blessing to serve him."

Qingtong blushed.

When Zhao heard about this, she said to Lu Yun, "The maids in the Marquis's mansion are really different. Look, she's just a maid, but she can actually become a concubine of such a family. If she gives birth to a son, she'll have a better life."

Lu Yun was somewhat interested in this: "Mother, are you saying that Qingtong is going to be the second uncle's concubine?"

"Yes, who else could it be?" Zhao said, "This second uncle is also young and promising, but..."

Lu Yun asked, "Second Auntie can't give birth to a son?"

Zhao said anxiously, "Speak more quietly."

"It's well-known, and it's not a secret." Lu Yun said calmly, "Qingtong is lucky, but it also seems that his luck is not very good."

Zhao was puzzled: "What does this mean?"

Lu Yun said nothing more and continued practicing calligraphy with her head down.

Recently her handwriting has been getting better and better. She also reads books regularly. When she encounters something she doesn't understand, she will ask Lu He. Thinking of the years she spent at home helping with farming and cooking, she was originally a girl from a poor family, but now, Zhao found that her daughter's words and deeds began to act like a lady from a wealthy family.

Zhao smiled so much that her eyes narrowed: "Yun'er, mother sees that you are beautiful. As they say, you are what you are made of. It's true."

Lu Yun was somewhat happy and looked up and asked, "Really?"

"Would mother lie to you?" Zhao looked at her. "Come to think of it, you will be sixteen next year, it's time to tell others."

Lu Yun was not shy and thought to herself that she had finally thought of this.

"But we are a stranger in this place, what should we do?" Zhao said to herself with a headache, "Not only do we have to live in someone else's house, but do we have to ask them to help find a son-in-law? I really can't say it."

Lu Yun sighed.

What Zhao said made sense. She was not the daughter of a famous family. She was just a guest in the Marquis' Mansion, and the people they interacted with in the Marquis' Mansion were all from wealthy and powerful families. Which family would be interested in someone like her?

She thought of the last time Yu Chaoqing came, and she felt frustrated again. Who wouldn't like a young man like this? But does he like you?

She was standing right in front of him, but he refused to even look at her!

But Zhao had no idea what she was thinking, so she said, "But their family knows a lot of people, so there must be someone suitable. Mother has to be thick-skinned and ask for help, but she can't delay you."

Lu Yun said nothing.

Zhao thought she was just shy and didn't mention it.

As the Mid-Autumn Festival approached, another guest came to the mansion, who was Madam Yang from the Wuding Marquis's Mansion, who often visited the Marquis's Mansion.

Although Madam Yang is older than the old lady, she likes to go out. She went to Jinling a few days ago and stayed there for about a month. She came back to celebrate the Mid-Autumn Festival and came in when she passed by.

The lady laughed and said, "You are unwilling to admit your age and are still running around. My body is not strong enough for this."

Madam Yang teased: "You stay at home playing mahjong for half a day, but I have a sore back and waist!"

The lady laughed out loud: "You are always so sharp-tongued. I can't argue with you!"

Although the two were not close friends when they were young, they became acquainted with each other because of each other's husbands, and found that they had similar interests. After they both became widows, they felt sympathy for each other, and their relationship became better than before.

Madam Yang said sourly, "I heard that your Ning An is getting married?"

The lady rolled her eyes at her: "It hasn't been decided yet."

"You're still hiding it from me. My daughter-in-law wrote to me and told me that she sent me a gift for the festival this year."

"Of course it will be delivered." The lady smiled and no longer denied it. The two families did have this intention. If nothing unexpected happens, it will be settled after the Mid-Autumn Festival. What's more, Lady Yang was only talking here. She was a sensible person and would never talk nonsense outside.

Madam Yang sighed: "What a pity for Ning An, I like her so much!"

The lady knew what she meant and joked, "I have several granddaughters."

Madam Yang laughed and said, "Hurry up and ask them to come out so I can have a look."

Mother Hu immediately told the maids to go and invite them.

Chen Ningyu was reading a book when she heard that Madam Yang had come. She was very happy. She commented on Madam Yang that she was worthy of being the Madam's best friend. Both of them had generous and open-minded personalities, which made them likable.

She changed her clothes and went.

When Madam Yang saw the girls coming in, her eyes narrowed into slits with a smile and she nodded repeatedly: "You are so beautiful, you should thank your grandmother. Back then, my sister was the most beautiful woman in Kyoto."

The lady almost spit out her tea.

The girls all laughed.

Mrs. Yang is a person who likes to joke.

The lady-in-waiting had no choice but to say, "You just came back from Jinling, so you must have brought some good things with you."

Madam Yang laughed and said, "You just want to share some with everyone you meet. I'm not afraid. Come, bring up all the brocades. Ladies, come and pick them out. Take what you like. I bought quite a lot this time. As for brocades, the ones from Jinling are still the best."

The girls all went up with a smile.

The lady said with a sigh: "Is there anything for me?"

"Needless to say, it has been prepared long ago." Madam Yang asked someone to bring it.

The lady was very happy, touched it and said, "This color is really beautiful. It happens to be cooler now, so I'll make a coat for you to wear."

Zhang and Jiang soon arrived.

Madam Yang also asked them to choose.

Zhang smiled and said, "Every time you come here, it costs a lot of money."

Madam Yang said, "Your mother-in-law loves to see me spend money. Just now she asked me what good things I had, so I had to bring Yunjin. Tell me, those who love playing leaf cards are different."

After hearing this, the lady laughed and hit Madam Yang.

After the girls had chosen their brocades, they came to express their gratitude.

Before leaving, Madam Yang said, "I am returning to Beijing now. I would like to invite you to visit me some other day."

The lady naturally agreed.

After Madam Yang left, Zhang laughed and said, "Madam Yang is just like a naughty child."

"That's right, that's why everyone likes to be with her." The lady said, "Her personality is very likable, and she married the most handsome man in Kyoto back then."

It is about the old Marquis Wuding Yang Shiren. The two of them also have a beautiful story. They were deeply in love with each other, but it was a pity that Yang Shiren passed away early. It was thanks to Mrs. Yang's sunny and optimistic personality that she was able to get out of the sadness. If it were someone else, I don't know what would have happened.

Jiang had been listening the whole time, and now she asked curiously, "Speaking of which, her grandson, Marquis Wu Ding, hasn't returned to the capital for several years, right?"

"Yes." The lady sighed, "Life is hard in the frontier. She is still worried about her grandson at her old age. Hey, who told their Yang family to guard the northwest for generations? The Northern Army was trained by their ancestors, and only the Yang family can command it."

Chen Ningrou listened, and leaned close to Chen Ningyu's ear and said, "Do you still remember that Young Master Yang?"

Chen Ningyu was confused.

Chen Ningrou laughed and said, "When he came to our house, I remember you fanned him in the face because he said you were beautiful and wanted to marry you."

The corner of Chen Ningyu's mouth twitched. She had no recollection of it, so it was definitely not her who did it.

Seeing that she didn't admit it, Chen Ningrou pulled Chen Ning'an over and said, "Second sister, do you remember? Later, Young Master Yang said it was a joke, and was severely scolded by Madam Yang. Young Master Yang also said that he was learning from Madam Yang. Madam Yang just likes to make fun of others."

Chen Ningan smiled and looked at Chen Ningyu: "Fourth sister was quite fierce at that time."

Chen Ningyu smiled awkwardly.

However, she felt that the original owner

did a good job, and that this young man who spoke nonsense as soon as he opened his mouth deserved a slap in the face.

☆, Chapter 14: Drunk Hibiscus

A few days later, it was the Mid-Autumn Festival. The lady had people set up a moonlight seat in the garden and offered fruits and moon cakes. When it got dark, she and everyone went to worship the moon, which was actually just burning incense and kowtowing.

After the ceremony, lanterns of various colors were lit all around, illuminating the mansion as if it were daytime. The servants set up tables and chairs and prepared a banquet.

Everyone was drinking, chatting and admiring the moon.

This night is very lively.

The old lady was also very happy. At her age, she felt that nothing could make her happier than enjoying family happiness.

She ate two crabs in a row.

Zhang said hurriedly, "This thing is very cold, mother should eat less."

The lady wiped her hands and smiled, "This year's crabs are really good. I ate so many that I don't know how many there are."

Chen Ningyu heard this and handed the peeled and broken crab to the lady, saying, "I have removed all the cold stuff. Grandma likes it. How about having half of it? It's rare."

She always felt that being able to eat was a blessing. The lady was already so old, she should eat a little more of the things she liked to make herself feel better.

The lady smiled happily: "Well, I haven't satisfied my craving."

She started eating again immediately.

Seeing this, Jiang reached out and pushed Chen Ningrou.

Chen Ningrou was busy eating mooncakes. When she looked up, she looked confused.

Jiang sighed.

Look at the right side, Chen Ninghua is asking Chen Xiu about calligraphy and painting. Naturally, they are talking about the moon painted by great talents.

Jiang wanted so much that she wanted to give Chen Ningrou a blow.

Chen Ningrou came back to her senses and smiled sweetly at the lady, "Grandma, Grandma, I'll make crab cakes for you tomorrow. They're not cold."

"Rou'er can also do this?" The lady laughed.

"Of course. Didn't grandma like the Spanish mackerel dumplings I gave her last time?"

The lady nodded: "It tastes good. Rou'er may not be good at other things, but the things she cooks are really delicious. I'll be waiting for your crab cakes."

Only then did Jiang laugh.

Zhang looked at it and curled her lips in disdain.

No matter how much Chen Ningrou tries to

please you, she is still a hopeless person!
After the dinner, Chen Ningyu returned to the house, feeling a little heavy-headed. He had just drunk a little wine, so his mind wasn't very clear.

Gu Qiu helped her to the inner room and whispered, "I just saw Aunt Su. She came to look for the Second Master, but before she could say a few words, she was scolded by the Second Master and left. She was crying miserably."

This concubine Su is quite evil. In Chen Ningyu's impression, it seems that Chen Xiu never liked her. I don't know why he married her in the first place?

That's also strange.

She yawned, and fell into a deep sleep as soon as she lay down.

A few days after the festival, the Wu family came to propose marriage.

The two families had already been in sync with each other, and the engagement process went smoothly, and the auspicious date was quickly set. The Wu family had only one son, Wu Jian, and the betrothal gifts had been prepared very early, so the date was set very soon, on October 26th.

Zhang finally breathed a sigh of relief. There were finally no more twists and turns this time. She started to get busy with the dowry. Because when Chen Ningrong got married, some good things were made in double portions, so it was easy to prepare.

At this time, the hibiscus in the Hibiscus

Garden had already grown buds. Chen Ningyu was sitting in the yard, with a teapot on her right hand, a plate of peanut biscuits on her left, and a plate of snow pears in the middle. She stared at the hibiscus again and again, shook her head and said, "Even after applying fertilizer, it still doesn't grow fast. Do we really need to dig a pond?"

Gu Qiu smiled and said, "What the flower farmers say always makes sense."

"But my yard is not very big. If I dig a pond, it will seem cramped." The flower farmer in the mansion had said this when she was planting hibiscus earlier, but she didn't take it seriously. Now she realized that the hibiscus would not grow well without water.

Danqiu pointed to the small rockery in the courtyard and said, "In my opinion, why not tear this down?"

There is a small rockery near the wall on the west side. It has been there for a long time. It doesn't look big, but it actually occupies a large area. The stones are also piled up in a disorderly manner, which does not quite conform to Chen Ningyu's aesthetic taste, so Danqiu's suggestion was exactly what she wanted.

When Chen Xiu comes back, she will go to see him.

When he heard that the rockery was going to be demolished, Chen Xiu asked curiously, "Or did you ask someone to build it because you liked it? Don't you remember it?"

Chen Ningyu naturally didn't remember it, and said vaguely: "I was still young at that time, and I just said it casually. Now I don't like it. I want to dig a small pond and plant hibiscus along the pond. It will surely look better."

Chen Xiu was not the kind of person who would fuss around, so he approved it without asking any further questions.

Chen Xiu would not object to any request made by Chen Ningyu. Jiang saw this and thought of the apricot tree in her yard. She took the opportunity to say, "It's the same if we move one or two. Husband, why don't we change the apricot tree too? They will look the same and won't look strange."

Unexpectedly, Chen Xiu's face immediately darkened.

Jiang's heart skipped a beat, and she said hurriedly, "I was just saying it casually. If you think it's unnecessary, you don't have to change it."

Chen Xiu said slowly: "Ning Yu is a little girl, she likes new things, I am used to it a long time ago."

Jiang didn't dare to mention it again.

Chen Ningyu's mouth corners curved.

Needless to say, this apricot tree must have been planted by her mother because she loved it. Now that time has passed, Jiang thought that Chen Xiu would no longer care about it, but in fact, this was not the case. This time, Jiang was afraid that she would be hit again.

Sure enough, Jiang secretly cried.

She had been married to Chen Xiu for more than ten years and had given birth to a son and a daughter for him, but in the end, she couldn't even change the tree!

But who can she complain to about this?

I heard that the lady also loved Chen Xiu's original wife very much.

Jiang cheered up again. After all, she was married to Chen Xiu and became the second wife of the Yongchun Marquisate. How many people envied her!

Besides, how can sugarcane be sweet at both ends?

Chen Ningyu went back and talked to the old lady about digging the pond. The old lady also agreed to everything she said and asked someone who knew about this to do it.

It took two days to dig the pond. The flower grower in the mansion transplanted the hibiscus flowers to the edge of the pond. The whole layout of the yard was changed, and it was quite beautiful, with flowers and water. Chen Ningyu thought that if she could raise some fish in there, she would not have to leave the yard to watch the fish in the future. How convenient.

When the servant who dug the pond heard this, he laughed and said, "Fourth Miss, you can't raise fish here yet. You have to improve the water first. Only when the water is good can you raise fish. Otherwise, they won't survive for a few days."

Since this matter concerns the life of the fish, Chen Ningyu took it to heart this time.

The old lady quickly ordered people to send Qingtong to the Xu family, and old lady Xu let Xu Ke marry Qingtong that day. As the principal wife, Chen Linru must have felt bad, but the matter had been discussed long ago, and if she was upset, she would seem ungenerous, so she had to swallow her anger. But she believed in the Madam, and Qingtong would not threaten her life.

By September, hibiscus flowers began to bloom.

The hibiscus she planted was a rare and precious variety called Drunken Hibiscus. It changed its color three times a day. The flowers that bloomed in the early morning and morning were as white as clouds, gradually turning into pink. From afternoon to evening, they turned into deep red, and now they were about to wither.

Such flowers are bright and lovely, and they are truly fleeting in beauty.

Chen Ningyu had already sent people to invite Chen Ningan, Chen Ninghua, Chen Ningrou, and Lu Yun.

Because Chen Ning'an is about to get married, she won't have much time left in the mansion. She wants to have a reunion with her family by looking at the flowers, which will also be a beautiful memory in the future.

Before this, she had invited the old lady,

but she said that she was old and her presence would only affect the girls' conversations. She smiled and ordered the kitchen to prepare a lot of delicious snacks: "Since you have this idea, grandma will give you some money and you can have a good time."

The lady sighed, she also thought of her blooming youth, but time passed so quickly, it seemed like in the blink of an eye, she was already gray-haired.

Chen Ningyu said, "Grandma, please come back and see it when you have time. These flowers are so beautiful."

The lady smiled and said yes.

In Furong Garden, there were already tables, brocade mats, tea, fruit wine, melons, fruits and snacks.

After a few girls came in, Chen Ning'an looked around and said with a smile: "I knew you dug a pond, but now you're doing it like this, it's really good." She looked into the pond, "But have you raised fish?"

"After raising them, the ones fished out from the fish pool are all the boss's koi." Chen Ningyu smiled.

Chen Ning'an was envious: "Looking at you, I want to redo the yard."

Chen Ningrou chuckled: "Second sister is going to marry into the Wu family soon. What have you done? That's a waste. If you want to get married, go to the Wu family. I think the yard of the second brother-in-law is quite big, compared to the second sister's. There are so many!"

Chen Ning'an blushed and spat: "What are you talking about? It's his yard. I can't control what he does with it."

There was intimacy in his tone.

Several other people were laughing.

The two met several times later and probably developed feelings for each other.

Chen Ningyu invited them to sit down: "This fruit wine is the same as the one we drank during the Mid-Autumn Festival. I didn't expect it to have such a strong aftertaste. You should drink less. I felt dizzy when I came back from that time."

"Yeah, I feel dizzy too, but it tastes good, sweet and fragrant." Chen Ninghua said with a smile.

Chen Ningrou sneered: "I thought Third Sister was talking to Dad about the moon, but it turns out that she drank a little that day."

Because of her two sisters, she was often criticized by Jiang, and she always felt a little uncomfortable.

But she only opposed Chen Ninghua.

Chen Ninghua felt a little embarrassed, but ignored him and just lowered his head to drink tea.

Chen Ningyu didn't want their good reunion to be ruined again, so she changed the subject and asked Lu Yun, "Sister Lu, I don't see you very often. You should go out for a walk when you have nothing to do. It's not good to be bored."

Lu Yun smiled and said, "I am practicing calligraphy. I used to love writing, but I just didn't have the time. Now I have a lot more free time."

"I didn't expect that Miss Lu also likes calligraphy." Chen Ning'an is proficient in music, chess, calligraphy and painting. "What kind of calligraphy do you usually copy?"

"It's an inscription."

The two had similar interests and talked a lot.

The color of the hibiscus flowers changed again and again. They admired and praised them, and the day passed like this.

Lv Yun truly experienced the life of the ladies from wealthy families. Who wouldn't like such a life? Unfortunately, life is not fair. She should have been like them, a daughter of a rich family. However, she was not.

And where will she marry in the future?

☆, Chapter 15 Wu Dinghou Mansion

The Wuding Marquis's Mansion soon sent an invitation, inviting their female relatives to visit their home.

The lady was very happy and said with a smile: "My elder sister invited me, so no matter how lazy I am, I have to go. Come to think of it, I haven't been there for more than a year."

Zhang said, "It's not that they didn't

invite you, but you don't want to go since Madam Yang is not here."

"It's boring when my elder sister isn't here. Her two daughters-in-law have nothing to say to me, so you should go." The old lady told Madam Hu, "Pick out something bright. We rarely go out, so we should dress up."

Mother Hu said with a smile, "Madam, even without dressing up, you are still an old beauty."

The lady snorted, "Look, you add the word 'old' in front of it, but you can't even say a nice word. I've kept you around for so many years in vain."

Everyone couldn't help laughing.

Mother Hu said hurriedly, "She is a beauty, a beauty, she doesn't look old at all."

The lady said, "It's getting late. Go get some clothes quickly."

Mother Hu left with a smile.

"You should go back and dress up too." The lady was quite interested. "The new clothes I made in the past won't go to waste. I haven't been going out much lately."

Everyone agreed.

In Furong Garden, Gu Qiu and Dan Qiu took out several sets, one said this one was good, and the other said that one was good. Chen Ningyu was dazzled.

She had a lot of clothes. In addition to the ones made by the mansion every season, the eldest princess also liked to send her some new styles of dresses. She herself had a considerable income every year from that business, so she would often buy some if she liked them. Now several of her cabinets were almost full.

"Let's go with this one." She chose a cross-collared jacket with deep rose red gold weaving and magnolia embroidered on the lapels, and a honey-colored corseted long skirt underneath.

Qiugu helped her put it on, combed her hair into a fairy bun, inserted a long red gold hairpin and a pair of small hairpins containing magnolia buds, and put a small dangling pearl earring on each ear.

Chen Ningyu put on some pink rouge, looked in the mirror and left.

When everyone gathered, their eyes were involuntarily focused on her.

It's just because everyone has dressed up once, but whoever stands next to Chen Ningyu will be outdone. A true beauty is like this, no one can hide her charm. If she dresses up a little more, she is gorgeous; if she dresses up a little less, she is elegant. Each has its own flavor.

Zhang frowned and thought to herself, who does she look like? She is so beautiful, but she surpasses her two daughters for no reason!

Not to mention Jiang. Ever since she gave birth to Chen Ningrou, the gap between the two girls has widened with every year. Now, her own daughter can never catch up.

Only the lady was very happy. She took Chen

Ningyu's hand and said, "Come with me in the car."

She took Chen Ningyu away.

Jiang said dissatisfiedly: "Look, he only loves Ning Yu."

But Zhang ignored her.

She didn't want to speak ill of the lady behind her back. Although she was a little unhappy in her heart, Chen Ning'an's marriage was settled and Chen Ningyu was also a legitimate daughter, so it would not be wrong for the lady to take care of her more.

But this third girl is in a miserable state. Zhang glanced at Chen Ninghua.

Chen Ninghua bit her lips, feeling very sad. It's her who's getting engaged now, not Chen Ningyu.

When Jiang saw this, she was moved and praised her eldest daughter: "Ninghua, you look really beautiful in this outfit today, but I think it's missing something." She took off a gold hairpin with kingfisher feathers on her head and put it on Chen Ninghua's head.

"That's better."

Chen Ninghua was flattered: "Mother, this is not allowed."

"Why not? I'm your mother. Giving you a hairpin is nothing."

Chen Ninghua had no choice but to thank him. Chen Ningrou saw this and angrily pulled her mother's sleeve: "Mom, why did you give Third Sister something? Why don't I have anything?"

Jiang said, "Isn't what I gave you enough? It's just a hairpin, and you're still jealous. When we get to the Yang family later, remember to not embarrass me. Your sisters are all very sensible."

"When did I ever cause any trouble for Nyonya?" Chen Ningrou frowned, "Mother still doesn't believe me!"

Outside, she would still control her temper and be likable.

Jiang smiled and rubbed her head.

The Mansion of Marquis Wuding is located on Yuhe Street. It is also an old house with a long history. It was once lived in by a prince. It is very spacious. Unlike the Mansion of Princess Huiying, which has the style of Jiangnan gardens, it is more like the style of the north. There are not so many small bridges and flowing water, only one garden. So if you say you go to the Mansion of Marquis Wuding to enjoy the flowers and have fun, that is just a casual remark. There are really not many flowers to enjoy, and there is no place to have fun. However, the Wuding Marquisate also has one strong point, which is listening to music.

Unlike other families who had to invite opera performers from other places, their mansion had its own. This was because the Marquis of Wuding had a grandfather who particularly loved opera. He was not the marquis, but the marquis's younger brother. He had an older brother to protect him and a mother who loved him, so he just loved opera.

Later, he found a lot of singing actors from somewhere, with all kinds of accents. This gentleman himself was well versed in opera, and he trained them carefully. These actors sang better and better, to the point that they were better than many famous actors. He became famous, and later those actors settled down in the marquis's mansion and became his people, singing for generations.

Until now, those actors still maintain their skills, and many wealthy families often come to borrow their talents, and they can get a lot of tips.

So when the lady left, she said to Lady Yang: "I have to listen to some music today."

Madam Yang smiled and said, "My daughters-in-law mentioned this just now. They said that every time they invited you, you didn't come. They just thought you didn't like to listen to music."

"That's not the case. I just have a lot of things going on at home lately."

Madam Yang raised her eyebrows and said, "You are just playing mahjong at home. Tell me, how much money did you win from your grandchildren?"

Everyone laughed.

The lady spat at her: "Don't expose me like this!"

Madam Yang smiled and said, "At our age,

it's better for us to walk around more. But today when you come to our house, there's nothing for you to see. Let's just listen to some music. Jin Ling and the others are ready."

Each of these actors has his own name. Jinling often plays the leading role, and there are also Yinling, Ziling, Hongling, etc., all of which are mainly named with the word "ling".

The lady said yes repeatedly.

Everyone followed.

Madam Yang had just met several girls, and now she said to Madam Tai: "Ning Yu is really a beauty. My two daughters-in-law praised her just now, saying that she is getting prettier every year."

The lady said, "Yes, she is my sweetheart too. I have to think about how to find her a good husband and pamper her every day."

Madam Yang said, "Who wouldn't love a girl like this? Why do you need to worry about her?"

"That's right, that's right." The lady smiled.

Speaking of Chen Ningyu, this is not her first time here. She comes several times a year. The two families are old friends. However, she often goes to the Princess's Mansion and has missed the opportunity several times.

There were two girls in the Yang family, one was named Yang Fu, the legitimate daughter of the second branch, and the other was named Yang Jing, the illegitimate daughter of the second branch. They also sat over and talked with the girls from the Chen family.

"What kind of play do you want to listen to later?" Yang Fu looked a lot like Madam Yang Er, with an oval face and almond-shaped eyes. She had an outstanding appearance and a rather fierce temper.

Chen Ningan said: "I like the singing of Yinling the most, just listen to Da Jinzhi."

"I like to listen to this, too." Yang Fu said with a smile, "Yinling's voice is very clear, unlike Jinling's. Her voice is lower, and both men and women can sing it."

"I love listening to Jin Ling." Chen Ningrou blinked her eyes and said, "She is so beautiful when she sings male roles. There is no gentleman in the world more beautiful than her!"

Yang Fu giggled and said, "See what you like. Give her more later. She must be very tired practicing this." She turned around and asked Chen Ninghua.

Chen Ninghua hesitated for a moment and said, "I like Zi Ling."

Several people were a little surprised.

Just because Zi Ling is the least outstanding among them.

Chen Ningyu tilted her head and said, "Although Zi Ling's singing skills are average, her posture, recitation, singing, and fighting all have a unique charm."

Everyone said yes.

After the maids served tea and snacks, the actors on the stage began to sing.

In his previous life, Chen Ningyu didn't like listening to these babbling sounds, but now, he feels it is a kind of enjoyment. Maybe people are like this, as long as the environment changes, many things that they don't like will gradually be cultivated, and they can even listen to the taste of them.

As she ate fruits, she felt that life was so comfortable and leisurely.

Before they knew it, they had listened to several plays, and when the performance was over, everyone gave tips.

The actors came to express their gratitude one after another.

The lady smiled and said, "You are getting better and better at singing. I will definitely invite you to my birthday party tomorrow."

"That's our blessing. Madam is as blessed as the East Sea." Jin Ling was very respectful.

Madam Yang asked them to leave, saying, "Why bother? I will send them over, but I remember it will take more than a year, right?"

"Yeah, I just thought of it. It's actually still far away."

Madam Yang said, "I am tired from listening to what you said just now. Go sit inside and have dinner soon."

The lady said hello.

Madam Yang said to the girls, "Would you like to sit down too?"

Yang Fu smiled and said, "Why are you sitting here, Grandma? Let's just walk around. We just sat for too long and it makes us feel uncomfortable."

"Okay." Madam Yang left with the other ladies.

"How about we go swinging on the swings? The weather is still warm recently. When it gets colder, we won't be able to go out to play." Yang Fu suggested.

It is September now. By October, the weather will start to get cold. By the end of October, it might even snow. By then, these ladies from wealthy families will generally have to stay indoors until next year before they can go out and play.

Girls are precious and cannot stand the cold.

All the girls said hello.

They went to the garden to swing.

☆, Chapter 16 A Glimpse

The garden of the Wuding Marquis Mansion is not small. There are not many flowers and plants, but the layout is grand. It is mostly made of stones, with many rockery piled up. Green trees are planted on the rockery, which are rolling and undulating. From a distance, it really looks like a group of mountains. It is surrounded by pools and is very imposing.

Chen Ningan smiled and said, "Every time I come back, I think this is Guilin."

Guilin's landscape is the best in the world. Yang Fu sighed, "I don't really like these, but my mother said that they were placed like that a long time ago, and my eldest brother likes them, so we can't take them down, so we have to give up."

Chen Ningyu thought it was a good idea. The scene of a military general's mansion was much more suitable than the gentle scenery of the south of the Yangtze River.

There are two swings on the west side of the garden, whose elegance is somewhat out of place here. Obviously, they were added later. However, there are always girls in the marquis's mansion, so it is inevitable that there will be a place for them to play. Several people took turns going up, and laughter could be heard from time to time.

Only Yang Jing didn't talk much, as if she was a little afraid of Yang Fu, and only said a few words when asked.

After playing for a while, they got tired and turned back.

Unexpectedly, I met two young masters on the road.

One of them Chen Ningyu naturally recognized, he was the third son of the Marquis' Mansion, Yang Yankang. But she did not know the other young man in brocade clothes and jade belt.

When Yang Fu and Yang Jing saw this man,

they hurriedly saluted and called him the Third Prince.

The girls from the Chen family were all stunned.

Chen Ningyu later thought that the aunt in their Wuding Marquis Mansion was a royal concubine, and they often went to the palace, so she would naturally know the prince. But why did the third prince appear in Wuding Marquis Mansion today?

The third prince Li Changluo smiled and said, "Sorry to bother you ladies, no need to be polite."

Although he said so, the girls still had to come and greet him.

Li Changluo looked over, and when he saw Chen Ningyu, his breathing stopped and he could not move his eyes away.

He had been born in the palace since he was a child. In fact, he had seen all kinds of beauties. But he had never seen someone like Chen Ningyu.

She was more gorgeous than the flowers in the garden, her narrow eyes were like sparkling gems, and a glance at her was full of indescribable charm, enough to make people's legs go weak. She also had a good figure, plump where she should be plump, thin where she should be thin, and she would lose this charm if she was a little more or less.

Yang Yankang saw Li Changluo's expression, smiled secretly, and asked, "Fourth Miss, it seems you didn't come last time?"

Chen Ningyu didn't want to talk, but when Yang Yankang asked, how could she not answer? She could only reply, "I went to my aunt's house."

Her voice was clear and pleasant, although it seemed a little suppressed at the moment, the low pitch had a different flavor.

Li Changluo paused for a moment before asking, "Aunt? Is it my aunt Huiying's family?"

"Yes." Chen Ningyu lowered his head even more.

Li Changluo laughed: "My aunt has never mentioned you. So, you are someone close to me."

How can you get close to someone you've never met? Chen Ningyu was silent.

Li Changluo no longer forced her to speak and turned away.

Yang Fu glanced at Chen Ningyu and frowned. She didn't know what was going on. As for the Third Prince, Yang Yankang had contacts with him, but this was the first time he brought him home. She was able to recognize Li Changluo because she met him in the palace.

No matter what, she had to tell her grandmother as soon as possible!

Each of them went to Madam Yang with different moods.

Madam Yang was originally joking with the lady-in-law, but when she suddenly heard the news, she was unable to react for a moment and hurriedly asked her eldest

daughter-in-law, Tang.
Tang didn't know, but was secretly annoyed. Yang Yankang was her son, and now he had brought the third prince here. As a mother, she knew nothing about it. It was really embarrassing. Madam Yang would naturally feel that she had not taught her son well.
When the old lady learned the news from her granddaughters, she was so shocked that she couldn't recover.
Two old ladies sat together.
The Madam was a little angry and asked, "Sister, you invited us here today, why is the Third Prince here?"
Not only that, he also said these words!
Madam Yang sighed, "I'm still investigating, sister, you have to believe me, I know nothing at all."
The two had known each other for many years, so when she heard Madam Yang say this, she was naturally willing to believe it. After all, hiding the truth would damage their relationship. However, she could not sit still at all, so she said goodbye and left with her female relatives.
Madam Yang immediately called Yang Yankang over and asked sternly, "Why is the Third Prince here today? Why didn't you tell him in advance?"
Yang Yankang felt very aggrieved: "My grandson didn't know. The Third Prince heard that our garden is great, but he always couldn't find time. Today he happened to be free so he came. Can I stop

him?"

Madam Yang stared at him: "Are you telling the truth?"

"Of course it's the truth. How dare I lie to my grandmother!" he vowed.

Mrs. Yang didn't get anything out of the question in the end.

In fact, based on Li Changluo's relationship with their mansion, it would not be a big deal for him to come here once. It was just that he happened to come today, which offended Madam Chen. After all, they didn't know and had no preparation. Most importantly, Li Changluo met the girls from their Yongchun Marquis Mansion directly.

Madam Yang called Tang over again and said, "I have already told Yankang not to get too close to the Third Prince. In our family, no matter which prince it is, we should do what we should do."

Tang nodded quickly: "My daughter-in-law knows."

But after the lady returned, she was very nervous.

Mother Hu knew that she was worried about the fourth girl.

With the Fourth Young Lady's looks, it would be easy for her to enter the royal family no matter which dynasty. The Lady Dowager does not want that. But today, Li Changluo only spoke to Chen Ningyu, and everyone would think so!

"Ning Yu has to get married." The lady rubbed her brows.

Mother Hu said, "It's not difficult for the fourth girl to marry into any family she wants, but she's just afraid that she won't find someone worthy of her."

The lady sighed.

Among her granddaughters, she loved Chen Ningyu the most, simply because she lost her mother when she was young. Although Jiang was not a satisfactory stepmother, she was not as good as a biological mother. So the lady was particularly concerned about Chen Ningyu, and their relationship naturally became better and better after getting along with each other for so many years.

Therefore, the selection of the grandson-in-law became a problem.

"We have to marry Ning Hua first."

The lady has a headache again.

The next day, she couldn't get up early.

Zhang hurriedly asked for a doctor.

The doctor said that she was worried too much, and prescribed some medicine, telling her not to think too much and to be more open-minded.

Zhang thought to herself, the Madam Dowager is really afraid that the Third Prince will fall in love with Chen Ningyu!

In fact, this is not bad, but it is not good either. Once the people in this family are connected with the royal family, they always have more ups and downs than ordinary official families. No wonder the lady is worried.

Jiang took her daughters to meet him.

Chen Ningyu saw that the lady was listless and sat on the edge of the bed with red eyes.

It's not that she is so narcissistic, but Li Changluo suddenly showed up yesterday and only spoke to her, which always made people think wrongly. She didn't expect that she would also implicate the lady, and she felt really sorry.

The lady said, "It's nothing. It will be fine tomorrow. If you all come here, I won't be able to rest."

Jiang said, "We are all worried about you, how could we not come to see you?"

"Just leave after you finish your review." The lady waved her hand and glanced at Chen Ningyu. "I'm fine. I just got up a few times at night. What's the big deal?"

Chen Ningyu wanted to say something, but didn't know what to say, so he just held the lady's hand.

The lady smiled and patted her hands.

Jiang quickly led them away.

Back at Xingfang Garden, Chen Ningrou whispered to Jiang: "The Third Prince looks very young."

Jiang was amused: "She is only seventeen years old, how old do you think she is?"

Chen Ningrou held Jiang's arm and said in a softer voice, "Actually, it's not bad for Third Sister to marry the Third Prince, isn't it? That's the Emperor's daughter-in-law, why doesn't Grandmother agree?"

Jiang said hurriedly, "Don't talk nonsense. Your grandmother didn't agree for a reason."

Chen Ningrou didn't understand.

Jiang warned, "Don't ever say this again. If the Madam and your father find out, I won't be able to protect you."

Chen Ningrou felt more and more puzzled.

The third prince is handsome and has a noble status, so why can't he do it?

In fact, Jiang secretly thought that this was a good thing. She heard that the third prince was very much loved by the emperor. After all, it was not a bad idea for their mansion to marry him. She just didn't dare to disobey the lady dowager and Chen Xiu.

Chen Ningyu had spent the past few days in anxiety. Fortunately, nothing happened in the end. She was relieved, and the lady was also relieved.

In October, Chen Ning'an got married.

Chen Ningyu gave her a jade plum blossom hairpin as a make-up gift. On that day, firecrackers rang throughout Kyoto, the bridal sedan circled the city several times, a lot of wedding money was scattered, and naturally, there were countless guests who came to congratulate her.

Everything was exactly the same as when Chen Ningrong got married.

When it's my turn, I'm afraid I'll be in the same situation, but only the person involved knows how I'll feel.

But Chen Ningding was happy.

She could see Chen Ning'an's admiration for Wu Jian.

Marrying the person you love is always a happy thing.

Three days later, Chen Ning'an returned home and confirmed her thoughts: she was living well.

Naturally, Zhang liked her son-in-law Wu Jian more and more.

In fact, the mother-in-law is rarely dissatisfied with her son-in-law. This is because in this era of parents' orders and matchmaker's words, the son-in-law is basically chosen by the mother-in-law. Sometimes, it is true that the daughter does not like the son-in-law.

After the young couple left, the lady called Chen Xiu over.

"Now that Ning An is married, it's time to find a suitable husband for Ning Hua. She is only a few months younger than Ning An, so we can't wait any longer."

Chen Xiu nodded, thinking of what happened to the Third Prince last time, and said, "Ning Hua should get married as soon as possible. Just talk to mother and madam about this."

The lady looked at him and sighed: "Ms. Ning Hua is also your daughter, right?"

"Mother said this, she is naturally my daughter."

"But I don't think you are like her father." The lady's face was a little serious. "Don't think I can't see it. Do you treat her the same way as you treat Ning Yu and Ning Rou? This child is also pitiful. She is also a filial girl!"

Chen Xiu lowered his eyes and said nothing.

The lady said, "No matter what, she has grown up and is not a bad person. You should stop blaming her for what happened back then."

The muscles on Chen Xiu's cheeks twitched twice, and he slowly said, "I don't blame Ning Hua, it's just..."

But for some reason, he just couldn't love his daughter.

That year, Zhou became pregnant, and a few days later, Aunt Su also became pregnant. Since then, Zhou's health has not been good. She gave birth to a baby boy, but the baby was dead. That was her first son, and the son she had been looking forward to for a long time!

Chen Xiu reached out and slowly wiped his face, and said in a low voice: "It would be better if Ning Hua got married. Mother, please find a good husband for her."

The lady didn't know how else to persuade him, so she could only sigh.

☆, Chapter 17: The Youth's Ideal

The weather was already cold at this time. The brocade that Madam Yang had given her was all used to make jackets. It would probably be finished in a while. Chen Ningyu had been too lazy to go out recently

as she was most afraid of the winter here.
Even with a charcoal basin, it was still freezing cold.
She wore thick cotton shoes, drank hot tea, and watched Gu Qiu flipping through the account book.
Now, the manor and the shop are staffed by people selected by the old lady, all of whom are very loyal and capable, so she doesn't need to worry too much and just needs to settle the accounts.
Gu Qiu was another good talent. He was very skilled in using the abacus and the sound of it clacking could be heard in the room.
Bai Tao suddenly said outside: "Miss, the second young master is here."
Just as he finished speaking, the door was pushed open and Zhang Jiwan walked in with a gust of cold wind.
Although he is his cousin, he is actually only half a year younger than Chen Ningyu.
It's just that boys mature late, so although he is still young, he is half a head taller than Chen Ningyu.
Chen Ningyu was blown by the wind and shouted, "Close the door quickly, close it!"
Zhang Jiwan laughed out loud: "No wonder you are called a rich lady, you can't stand the cold at all."
"I'm not as rough and coarse as you." Chen Ningyu snorted.
The last time Zhang Jiwan quarreled with Zhang Jihe to protect her, it made them

closer.

Zhang Jiwan didn't care. He sat down and put the food box on the table. "See, I can do what I say. This is Qiu's food. Try it."

The fragrance comes out even before the lid is opened.

Chen Ningyu sniffed it and said with a smile, "It's an eel!"

"It's eel. Don't you like fish? There's also lion's head. Come and eat it."

It was noon now, and Chen Ningyu was hungry: "It's better to obey than to be respectful. I'll eat."

Zhang Jiwan said, "Just eat. I brought this for you. Stop nagging me. Women are troublesome."

Chen Ningyu rolled his eyes at him, asked Gu Qiu to bring chopsticks, and asked again: "Do you want to eat?"

"I've eaten." Zhang Jiwan waved his hand. "I was so full that I can't even eat a piece of meat now."

Chen Ningyu started to eat by herself. After finishing, she praised repeatedly: "This Huaiyang cuisine is interesting. The eel is cooked like this. It's delicious. The lion's head is also good and very fresh. What's in it?"

"Put in the shrimp."

"No wonder."

Seeing that she liked it, Zhang Jiwan smiled and said, "I'll bring it to you next time when I have time?"

"Okay," Chen Ningyu asked, "but are you

here alone this time?"

Then she remembered that she hadn't heard that her uncle and aunt were coming.

Zhang Jiwan chuckled.

The corner of Chen Ningyu's mouth twitched.

"You've skipped school again!"

Zhang Jiwan hurriedly said, "Don't tell grandma, I came in secretly."

Chen Ningyu held his forehead with his hand. This kid really is tired of studying and doesn't like to read at all.

"What are you going to do?" She wiped her mouth. "Not to mention skipping school, your father will beat you for failing the exam to become a scholar, right?"

Zhang Jiwan was also having a headache, but he had an idea in mind. He came over and said, "Fourth cousin, why don't you talk to my second uncle and ask him to teach me martial arts. Can I take the martial arts exam in the future?"

"This is not something that father can decide. I won't hide it from you. Grandmother said so last time, but my aunt refused. I think she is afraid that you will suffer. You see, my father is very tired every day. He is not as comfortable as my uncle. He just sits in the government office to handle things."

Civil servants mostly use their brains, while military officers mostly use their bodies.

Zhang Jiwan shook his head: "I'm not afraid of being tired. My butt hurts when I sit down!"

Chen Ningyu chuckled, but soon said seriously: "Are you afraid of death? Military officers may also have to go to the battlefield one day, and that is not fun. Look at my uncle, his leg has not healed yet, not to mention those soldiers who lost their lives."

Zhang Jiwan was silent this time, and remained silent for quite a long time.

Chen Ningyu thought he was backing down, but the boy suddenly pulled her up and said, "Come on, I'll show you how to shoot an arrow."

"ah?"

Zhang Jiwan was very strong and soon pulled her out of the door. Gu Qiu was about to stop him, but Chen Ningyu thought for a moment and waved her hand: "Give me my fox fur cloak."

Gu Qiu was stunned for a moment and went to get it.

The ancestors of the Yongchun Marquisate were granted the title of marquis for their military merits, so how could there not be a martial arts training ground in their home?

At this moment, they were standing on a field to the north of the Marquis' Mansion, where all kinds of weapons were stored, including targets.

Although Chen Xing can't come now due to a leg injury, Chen Xiu still often comes to wield swords and knives. Chen Min and Chen

Li also come often. They are all children of the Chen family, and in addition to studying, they also need to show their skills.

Zhang Jiwan has already drawn his bow.

The posture looked good, but Chen Ningyu still didn't believe that Zhang Jiwan could shoot arrows, because he had never heard that he had any martial arts skills.

But when Zhang Jiwan shot an arrow, it actually hit the bull's eye!

Chen Ningyu's eyes widened, looking at Zhang Jiwan as if he were a ghost: "How did you do that? Are you lucky?"

Zhang Jiwan was so angry that he shot two more arrows. Although he didn't hit the center of the target this time, it was not far away. He said proudly: "Well, my archery skills are not bad, right? A talent like me, shouldn't I go to the battlefield? I am not afraid of life and death. A real man has ambitions. Even if I die on the battlefield one day, it is a worthy death!"

The young man stood in front of her, head held high in the cold wind, looking very high-spirited, and really had some heroic spirit!

Chen Ningyu was speechless for a moment.

It turned out that she had underestimated Zhang Jiwan and always treated him as a child, but he also had ideals.

But is this ideal just talk, or will it really make him move forward courageously? You know, she had many ideals when she was young, but as the years went by, they gradually faded away, and she even didn't want to mention some of them.

Childish, yes, childish, but also precious.

She smiled slightly and said, "Cousin, what you said is very good, but even if you are good at archery, it may not be useful."

Zhang Jiwan raised an eyebrow: "Why is it useless?"

"You want to learn martial arts and become a general, but you don't dare to tell your uncle yourself. You can only ask me for help and ask me to persuade father. Cousin, are you brave enough to go to the battlefield? Aren't the enemy's swords less powerful than your uncle's stick?"

Zhang Jiwan's face flushed, and he threw down the bow and arrow: "Fourth cousin, my brother said something bad about you last time, how could I protect you? Now I just want to ask you for one favor..."

"That's different, cousin. Don't you understand that this is a matter of your life? Who can take responsibility for it?" Chen Ningyu stretched out a finger and gently tapped his chest. "Cousin, only you can be responsible for yourself."

Zhang Jiwan was stunned.

He lowered his head and looked at her white fingers that looked like spring onions, and his heart began to beat violently.

She is right.

He was cowardly and he backed down. He didn't like studying in the first place, but he was afraid of his father and his mother's disappointment. He was afraid of so many things!

But he eventually grew up slowly.

"Fourth cousin!" He suddenly reached out and hugged Chen Ningyu tightly, "Fourth cousin, I know what to do!"

Gu Qiu and Dan Qiu were so shocked by his action that they almost screamed.

But Zhang Jiwan quickly let go: "I'm leaving."

Chen Ningyu nodded: "Okay."

He left happily.

Chen Ningyu squatted down and picked up the bow and arrow: "Put it back."

Danqiu took it and put it back in its original place.

Gu Qiu said softly, "My second cousin is really something. He scared us to death just now."

Chen Ningyu smiled.

Although Zhang Jiwan's hug just now scared her, she felt very warm.

At that moment, she finally understood why Zhang Jiwan liked talking to her, because she was someone who was willing to understand and tolerate him.

Although at first, she was unconscious.

She looked back at the martial arts training ground. Perhaps soon, Zhang Jiwan would appear here often.

But the fact is that Zhang Jiwan was beaten so badly that his skin was torn and he had to lie in bed for several days.

Chen Linzhi's eyes were red from crying, and she ran to the lady for help.

Although she didn't want Zhang Jiwan to become a military officer, she also didn't want to see Zhang Jiwan being beaten to death!

"It's useless for my father-in-law and mother-in-law to persuade me. My husband is determined not to agree. I don't know what medicine Ji Wan took. He refused to give in even after being beaten like this. Mom, my heart aches!"

The lady had a headache: "Why is my son-in-law so stubborn? What's wrong with being a military commander? Which of our ancestors was not a military commander?"

"That's right, I said the same thing." Chen Linzhi burst into tears, "Why don't you go and persuade him? My husband has always respected me, as well as my elder brother and second brother."

The lady was a little embarrassed: "This is the Zhang family's family affair, how can I interfere?"

"But if Ji Wan is beaten a few more times, he will be useless!"

The lady was so annoyed that she called Chen Xing over.

Chen Xing was delighted when he heard this: "Is there such a thing?"

"Brother, are you still laughing?" Chen Linzhi shouted, "Your nephew is about to be beaten to death."

"How is that possible? I'm a father too,

how could I not know? He was just trying to scare the child. Would he beat his own child to death?" Chen Xing frowned. "But my brother-in-law is indeed a little stubborn. Why bother? Ji Wan can't concentrate on studying anyway, so why not learn martial arts? He can also make achievements and establish a career."

"My husband said that Ji Wan is not the type to do this, and that he only knows how to be naughty and cause trouble."

As they were talking, Chen Ningyu arrived. She was also anxious when she heard the news. After all, she was largely responsible for Zhang Jiwan's beating. If she hadn't encouraged him, he probably wouldn't have gone to confront his father so quickly. But she estimated that it was only a matter of time.

"Grandma, uncle, aunt, this is all my fault. Last time, my cousin said he wanted to learn martial arts, and I told him to think it over before telling his uncle. I didn't expect him to be beaten so badly!"

The lady raised her eyebrows: "You said that?"

"Well, because my cousin doesn't want to study at all, he has things he likes to do, and he's very good at archery, so I think learning martial arts is also good."

Chen Linzhi didn't know what to say. She knew her child's temperament best. She also understood what her mother had advised before, that Zhang Jiwan was indeed not someone who could study. However, when she saw Chen Xing injured, she was afraid that her child would suffer the same thing. She was in a dilemma for a moment.

Chen Xingdao: "Then I'll go there."

The lady naturally agreed and said, "If you have anything to say, please talk about it nicely."

Chen Ningyu said: "I'll go too."

The lady did not object, and the three of them left together.

☆, Chapter 18 Persuasion

At this moment, Zhang Jiwan was still sleeping on the bed, lying on his stomach, and his butt could not touch anything, otherwise he would cry for help in pain.

Zhang Jihe was there to accompany him.

Zhang Jiwan was still restless after being beaten. He asked Zhang Jihe to bring him some water, read a military book, and eat some snacks. Zhang Jihe suddenly got angry and threw the book on the ground, saying, "You deserve it. How can you not be beaten for your character?"

Zhang Jiwan snorted, "I knew you were just pretending. You don't really care about me."

Zhang Jihe was so angry at him that he cursed, "Are you possessed by a demon? Do you have to learn martial arts?"

"I'd rather die than not learn martial arts!"

Zhang Jihe sighed: "I've never seen you like this before, so why bother this time? You might as well follow Dad's wishes. Even if you don't study well, Dad won't do anything to you. At least I'm at home, so you won't have to worry about the future..."

Now it was Zhang Jiwan's turn to get angry. He shouted, "You want me to rely on you for the rest of my life? You're dreaming!"

Zhang Jihe was startled.

Zhang Jiwan's face was dark, and it was obvious that he was really angry. He clenched his fists and wanted to jump out of the bed.

Zhang Jihe was stunned.

Chen Linzhi brought reinforcements.

Zhang Zhijing still gave face to Chen Xing and quickly asked him to sit down. When he saw Chen Ningyu again, he felt strange that there was a little girl following them.

"Hua Liang, you should know why I'm here." Chen Xing got straight to the point. "We are all fathers, who wouldn't want our children to have a bright future? But I watched Ji Wan grow up, and I think he is like his uncle, so why don't you help him achieve his goal?"

Zhang Zhijing was not someone who could be easily persuaded. He said calmly, "He is just a child, and he is just being willful."

"If he is just willful, why doesn't he surrender even after you beat him like this?" Chen Xing said with a smile, "Although Ji Wan is naughty, I think he is very determined this time. Hua Liang, you just want him to have someone to rely on in the future. Isn't learning martial arts a good option? Ji He is learning literature, so it's a good thing that both brothers are good at both literature and martial arts."

Zhang Zhijing remained silent and did not respond.

Chen Xing sighed: "I'm still talking about Ji Wan, aren't you also very willful?"

Zhang Zhijing raised his eyebrows: "I am his father. It is only natural for a son to listen to his father."

Seeing that the conversation had no good effect, Chen Linzhi said anxiously, "Husband, you can't continue to beat Ji Wan! He is only a few years old, he doesn't understand, we can teach him well, do you really want to beat him to death, husband?"

"You rebellious son, you deserve to be beaten to death!" Zhang Zhijing became furious when he thought of Zhang Jiwan's resistance.

At this time, Chen Xing suddenly looked at Chen Linzhi and Chen Ningyu. They knew that he wanted to talk to Zhang Zhijing alone, so they left immediately.

"Aunt, can I go see my cousin?" Chen Ningyu followed, also concerned about Zhang Jiwan.

Chen Linzhi hurriedly asked someone to take her there, while she herself stood at the door waiting for the result as usual.

Zhang Jiwan and Zhang Jihe were staring at each other, and when they saw Chen Ningyu coming, the two brothers turned away. Zhang Jihe and Chen Ningyu were also not on good terms, so he said, "Fourth cousin is here to see you, I'm leaving first."

Zhang Jiwan snorted.

It looked like the two had just had an argument. Chen Ningyu sat down beside Zhang Jiwan's bed and apologized, "If I had known this would happen, I wouldn't have advised you and caused you to be beaten like this."

"It's nothing, but I broke two boards." Zhang Jiwan chuckled, "Don't underestimate my father, he was still scolded by my grandparents for a long time. Anyway, it was worth it."

This kid is really optimistic. Chen Ningyu smiled and said, "Now that my great uncle is here, he should be able to persuade my uncle."

"Really?" Zhang Jiwan was so happy that he turned over suddenly and hit his buttocks. His whole face was distorted. Only because of Chen Ningyu's presence, he did not shout or scream. He almost got a stitch in the side because of holding his breath.

The servant hurriedly helped him up.

Chen Ningyu wanted to laugh but was too embarrassed to do so, so she held back and said, "Be careful, don't move around, or else it will be disastrous."

"It's not the first time I've been beaten. It's okay." He hesitated for a moment, "But

can my father really be persuaded?"
"That's right."
Chen Ningyu couldn't guarantee it. In fact, after watching Zhang Zhijing today, he felt that he had a very hard temper, while Chen Xing was always very gentle. Maybe it was possible to overcome hardness with gentleness? Speaking of which, both of them were fathers, but their attitudes towards their children were really very different.
The two talked for a while, and then Chen Linzhi came.
"Aunt, how is it?" Chen Ningyu asked hurriedly.
Chen Linzhi first glared at Zhang Jiwan fiercely: "What a troublesome thing!"
Zhang Jiwan felt wronged: "Mom, as long as Dad agrees, it's fine. I'm not going to do anything bad!"
"Well, luckily your uncle came, and my husband finally agreed to let you give it a try."
Zhang Jiwan was overjoyed: "Really, mother, really?"
"Can I still lie to you? Remember, you owe your uncle a favor. Your uncle usually doesn't want to do this kind of thing."
Chen Linzhi smiled again. Her elder brother was really powerful and could convince her husband.
"Of course. I'll go and thank my uncle right away!" He was about to get up again.
"Lie down. You can thank me later. Take good care of yourself. Your father said

that he will give you three years of training. If you don't pass the martial arts exam, you have to come back to study."

The Zhang family is not like a marquis's mansion. The children of a marquis's mansion are all protected, so it is not difficult for them to become a military officer. But the Zhang family is a scholarly family, so to become a military officer one has to rely on one's own abilities.

Zhang Jiwan said: "Three years is three years, I will definitely not let my father down!"

Chen Linzhi sighed. Although she didn't want Zhang Jiwan to go down this path, she had no choice but to go along with him now that things had come to this.

After returning from the Zhang family, the old lady learned that Chen Xing had persuaded Zhang Zhijing, and she finally breathed a sigh of relief: "Zhijing is too strict. The two children have suffered a lot since they were young."

"At least Ji He didn't let him down, otherwise I'm afraid he wouldn't have spared Ji Wan."

The lady nodded and said, "That's fine. Let Ji Wan come and live here from now on. Otherwise, Zhi Jing will not like him and often beat him with a stick."

"That's what I meant." Chen Xing said with a smile.

Not long after, Zhang Jiwan moved in even

though his buttocks injury had not yet healed.

In fact, he was afraid that Zhang Zhijing would go back on his word, and then his miserable days would come again, so he was not afraid of the pain. While his father was away, he asked the servant to move without telling Chen Linzhi. His grandparents were also very dissatisfied with their son. How could they treat their grandson so harshly? So they pretended not to see it.

Later, when Zhang Zhijing found out, he wanted to beat Zhang Jiwan, but was stopped by Chen Linzhi. He threatened that he would just pretend he didn't have this son.

But in fact, of course, it is impossible, it is just a temper tantrum.

Zhang Jiwan's happy years finally arrived.

The lady is not like Zhang Zhijing. He lives here, has good food and good things to do, and has plenty of money every month. He lives a happy and carefree life, but in just one month, he has gained a lot of weight.

At this time, it is almost the Chinese New Year.

During this period, there were several families that wanted to marry Chen Ninghua, but the lady did not think highly of her. Although Chen Ninghua was a concubine's daughter, her character and talent were unquestionable. However, those families looked down on her because of her status.

Their own sons were not very good, yet they still wanted to marry her.

It's better to just refuse like this.

Aunt Su was so anxious that she found Jiang and begged her, "Second Madam, please consider Ning Hua's filial piety..."

Jiang interrupted her: "Why, am I treating her badly, or is it the Madam who treats her badly?"

"No, no." Aunt Su said hurriedly, "It's just that Ning Hua is not young anymore. I think she is good enough. She doesn't need to be from a very good family."

Jiang sneered: "It's rare, who wouldn't want their daughter to marry someone of higher status?"

"I just hope Ning Hua can live a good life. It doesn't matter what family she lives with. It's not necessarily the case that people from good families have a hard life. Can my husband be considerate of everyone? If Ning Hua marries someone of a lower status, maybe things will be better."

Jiang's sore spot was touched, so she married into a wealthy family. Chen Xiu never opened his heart to her, but just did a good job on the surface so that others would think she was living a happy life.

She slapped Aunt Su and scolded: "Shut up! Who do you think you are? Can you advise Ning Hua on who to marry? You are just a slave. If my husband hadn't seen that you had given birth to a daughter, he would have been killed long ago." You've been kicked out, get out of here!"

Aunt Su covered her face and cried, then stumbled out.

On the road, I met Chen Ningyu, Chen Ningrou, and Chen Ninghua.

When Chen Ninghua saw her like this, she felt as if she had been slapped, and her face turned red.

Chen Ningrou mocked: "I wonder what Aunt Su is doing again. She really has no self-awareness."

Chen Ninghua almost bit his lip.

This situation is not uncommon. Chen Ningyu has seen it several times. She just doesn't know whether to envy or pity Chen Ninghua. After all, Aunt Su is Chen Ninghua's biological mother and she really loves her. In this world, it is always a good thing to have such a person who cares about you. However, Aunt Su always brings trouble to Chen Ninghua.

The three of them came in, and Jiang said, "Just now your aunt called a doctor, and Xiang Mei is pregnant. Come with me to take a look."

Chen Ningyu smiled and said, "That's really good news. Auntie has been looking forward to having a grandson for a long time."

"That's right." Jiang was not happy at all. As a younger sister-in-law, she still had to do her best.

The four of them went to the main room.

The lady-in-waiting was also there, and they all surrounded Cao Xiangmei and asked about her well-being.

The child in her belly is the first in her life. If it is a son, he will be the great-grandson.

"Congratulations, sister-in-law." They all went to congratulate.

Cao Xiangmei gently touched her belly with a happy look on her face.

"Don't move around too much in the future, and take care of the baby." The lady advised, "Just tell me what you want to eat. You're pregnant, so your taste will change. Don't be afraid to trouble the cook."

Cao Xiangmei has a gentle personality, so the lady said this.

Zhang also looked at her daughter-in-law with a smile: "I wonder how happy she will be when Min'er comes back soon!"

Her daughter-in-law has been married for more than a year. To be honest, she was also anxious, but fortunately, she lived up to everyone's expectations.

"I'll ask someone to send a letter to my mother-in-law right away." She turned around and gave the order.

The master of the Cao family was a doctor in the Ministry of Revenue and is now the Minister of Shandong and Liaodong grain reserves, but Mrs. Cao is in the capital. Cao Xiangmei also has an elder brother who was also in the capital but was transferred out last year.

The lady smiled and said, "I think the old lady will come over soon."

She guessed correctly. As expected, when Mrs. Cao heard that her daughter was pregnant, she came.

Because there was going to be a new baby in the family, the whole family was happy, and the excitement lasted for a long time.

☆、Chapter 19 Intention

Chen Ningyu went to the lady's house in the morning and talked about the New Year's gift arrangements.

The lady was surprised: "What are you worried about?"

"I just don't worry about it in the past, and I don't know what to buy. This time, my cousin aunt returned the family property to me. I think she has worked hard for many years. It's rare for me to take care of it myself. I want to thank my cousin aunt, but I don't have an excuse at other times. This New Year is different. She is always my elder."

The lady laughed: "You are not married yet, how can you send New Year gifts alone?"

"Isn't the situation different?" Chen Ningyu took the lady's arm and said, "Grandma, please give me some advice on what to buy."

Seeing her sincere intentions, the lady said, "Don't worry about it. Just give me the money. I'll ask them to prepare another gift when they prepare the New Year gift and send it to you early. What do you think?"

"Grandma is so straightforward!" Chen Ningyu said with a smile, "Thank you, Grandma."

"Little girl, remember to treat me like this in the future!" The lady acted jealous.

Chen Ningyu said: "Needless to say, when I get married, there will be no shortage of gifts from my grandmother, and they will definitely be the best."

The lady laughed out loud.

Zhang Jiwan's injury had almost healed by now. Due to Chen Xing's leg injury, he only learned martial arts with Chen Xiu. When Chen Ningyu asked him about archery, she found out that he had been practicing secretly for a long time. It looked like he had mastered it overnight, but in fact it took him two years, all the time he would practice in the woods after skipping school. He came to play with Chen Ningyu just after practicing sword that day.

Chen Ningyu was so cold that she stayed in bed every day and rarely got out of bed, like a lazy cat.

Zhang Jiwan joked: "You were born in the wrong body. You are most suitable for doing something else."

"What?"

"Be a bear! You hibernate when winter comes, don't you?"

Chen Ningyu was so angry that she threw the book in her hand at his head.

Unexpectedly, Zhang Jiwan took it and took

a look at the book and said, "Oh, it's a travel note. Where do you want to go?"

"I want to go everywhere." Chen Ningyu wrapped the quilt tightly.

Zhang Jiwan smiled and said, "Okay, when I have learned martial arts well, we will go out and play. I tell you, the places outside the Great Wall are better. There are large grasslands, herds of cattle and sheep, and we can even ride horses."

It sounds really good. Chen Ningyu fantasized about it and felt quite yearning for it.

But this is just a dream.

"Come on, uncle will allow you to go."

Zhang Jiwan said disdainfully: "When I grow up, how can my father control me? I can go wherever I want."

This child is really rebellious.

But I'm afraid he is just like Zhang Zhijing. Zhang Zhijing's personality is so stubborn that he doesn't even listen to his parents. Otherwise, Chen Xing wouldn't have had to go there to resolve the issue last time.

Chen Ningyu stretched out her hand: "Give me the book."

Zhang Jiwan gave her the book and strolled around the room.

Chen Ningyu raised an eyebrow: "Why aren't you leaving yet?"

Even if he is a cousin you know very well, it is not good for him to come here all the time.

Zhang Jiwan was looking at her dressing table. Seeing several rouge boxes on her table, all in different colors, she casually took out a brand new one and said, "Cousin, you have so many rouges, can you give me one?"

Chen Ningyu was stunned.

She widened her eyes and asked, "What are you doing here?"

She really didn't understand what Zhang Jiwan meant for a moment.

"It's for Sister Lu." Zhang Jiwan smiled. "I heard Brother Lu and Aunt Zhao say once that Sister Lu didn't even have a box of good rouge. Aunt Zhao couldn't do anything about it. She said that after all, she wasn't a rich lady and didn't need good things. I felt sorry for her."

Chen Ningyu frowned: "Is there such a thing?"

The lady was very kind to their family and gave them a lot for their daily expenses. How could they not even have a box of good rouge?

She thought for a moment and said, "This rouge originally belonged to me. It is not appropriate for you to give it to others. Besides, you are a man, how can you give this to a girl? Miss Lu is not your close relative, you have to understand."

Zhang Jiwan disagreed: "We live in the same family, so what?"

Chen Ningyu still insisted on her idea: "Well, I'll go and tell the Madam, don't worry about it, Miss Lu will always have rouge to use anyway."

Seeing that she kept persuading him, Zhang Jiwan gave in.

After Zhang Jiwan left, Danqiu came over and said hesitantly, "Just now when I heard my cousin talking about Miss Lu, I remembered something."

"What's up?"

"One day I met Jin Ju and talked to her for a few words. At that time, Miss Lu was sitting in the pavilion embroidering a purse. When I was leaving, I took a look and saw two white cranes embroidered on it. I didn't pay attention to it at the time, but today I saw that the purse hanging around my cousin's waist was exactly the same as the one embroidered by Miss Lu."

Jinju was the maid sent by the lady to serve Miss Lu.

Chen Ningyu was surprised.

Gu Qiu's expression also changed slightly.

However, Chen Ningyu didn't say anything else, picked up the book and continued reading.

However, after a few days, she went to Lu Yun's place.

Lu Yun was reading a book and Zhao was pasting New Year pictures.

They both looked surprised to see her coming.

Chen Ningyu smiled and said, "I haven't been out much these days, so I came out for a walk and happened to pass by here."

Lu Yun smiled and said, "Fourth cousin, please sit down. My room is a little messy and my mother is cleaning up."

"No problem." She sat down and asked, "What do you need for the New Year? Just tell grandma if you need anything."

"A lot, a lot. The madam gave me a lot of things, more than I can use up." Zhao was very grateful, "How can I feel embarrassed?" While looking at Chen Ningyu, she felt that the whole room was brighter because of her.

She hurriedly made tea for Chen Ningyu: "It's cold outside, Fourth Miss, drink some to warm yourself up."

"Thank you for your help, cousin." Chen Ningyu picked up the tea, took a sip, and winked at Gu Qiu.

Gu Qiu took out the rouge and powder she had brought with her.

"I got some good things. Sister Lu, take them and try them out. It's New Year's Day, and we sisters should dress up beautifully, right?" She looked at Lu Yun with a smile.

Lu Yun declined: "How can this be good? Besides, I don't usually use it, so it would be a waste if I gave it to you."

The last time the women from the Marquis' Mansion went to the Marquis of Wuding's Mansion together, the lady-in-waiting did not invite her. After she moved in here, she really never left the house. What's the point of dressing up?

Chen Ningyu got the hint and smiled, "I

don't go out much either, but I'm in the mood, so I'll dress up a bit and look happy. Sister Lu, just accept it."

Lu Yun couldn't refuse again, so she said, "Thank you, fourth cousin. How about I make a purse for you? I have nothing to do, so I made a lot of them. I gave one to my cousin last time."

The one I am talking about is Zhang Jiwan.

Chen Ningyu didn't expect that she would bring it up herself, and was inevitably surprised, because she originally came to test Lu Yun, but Lu Yun behaved very frankly.

"Then I won't be polite. Sister Lu's embroidery skills must be good. Unlike me, my embroidery skills are not that good."

Lu Yun said, "My fourth cousin is a very kind-hearted girl. If I really want to learn something, there is nothing I can't do."

Chen Ningyu smiled: "My cousin thinks highly of me."

After talking for a while, Chen Ningyu finally went back.

On the way, Gu Qiu whispered, "Miss Yi, what is Miss Lu thinking about?"

Chen Ningyu shook his head.

It's hard to say, but Lu Yun is not young anymore, I wonder how she will plan her life-long affairs?

Now the lady is busy with Chen Ninghua.

A day later, good news came again that Chen Ningrong was pregnant. Zhang was naturally happy, but she was also worried that Chen Ningrong would not be able to take good care of the baby since she was away with her son-in-law. Chen Xing didn't think so. After all, his eldest son-in-law was a county magistrate. What could happen? He just asked someone to send some things to her.

Before the New Year, the marquis's mansion was very lively, with relatives from all over coming to give New Year gifts, and people coming in and out of the mansion constantly, and this continued until New Year's Eve, when the family gathered together to celebrate the Spring Festival amid the sound of firecrackers.

The second day of the first lunar month is the day for daughters-in-law to return home. If her parents' home is in Kyoto, she usually goes back at this time. Of course, some may delay until the sixteenth day of the first lunar month.

Zhang and Jiang usually took their children back to visit their grandparents.

The lady was very kind and never stopped them from doing this. She even asked them to stay for two more days. After all, a daughter-in-law would not come back unless there was something special after marrying into the Chen family. She was also a daughter and understood how difficult it was.

Seeing that they all went back to pack their things, the lady beckoned Chen Ningyu over and asked, "Do you want to visit your mother's family?"

Chen Ningyu shook his head as usual.

The lady didn't force it and smiled again: "It's the same if you have the eldest princess."

But this time, for the first time ever, Jiang actually called Chen Ninghua to go.

You know, before, Chen Ninghua, like Chen Ningyu, refused to go back to her parents' home with Jiang. The strange thing is that Chen Ninghua was willing to do so.

Chen Ningyu didn't understand why she did that.

They were not Jiang's biological children. Jiang's family treated Jiang and her two children like treasures, but they would never treat them as treasures because they were not Jiang's biological children. She had met one of Jiang's nieces, and she rolled her eyes when she saw her.

So she never went.

At this moment, in Qingyin Garden, Chen Ninghua's residence, Xia Lian was packing up her daily necessities, and said worriedly: "Miss, you usually don't go, why do you have to go this time?"

Chen Ninghua was helpless: "My mother said it, how can I refuse?"

"But the fourth young lady won't go, and the lady is fine. Besides, the lady-in-waiting is still here."

Chen Ninghua said, "Fourth sister is the same as me? Don't say anything."

Xia Lian had no choice but to stop talking. My daughter is indeed different from the fourth daughter. To be honest, she is much more pitiful, but the lady still loves her. Why should she go to the Jiang family to suffer? But she is just a maid, how can she make the decision? She can only sigh.

☆、Chapter 20 Lantern Festival

Before the Lantern Festival, the princess sent someone to pick up Chen Ningyu.

In fact, Chen Ningyu had spent the Lantern Festival in recent years at home and had never gone to the eldest princess's place. She had not expected that the eldest princess would call her over so early this year.

The lady seemed to understand something and said with a smile, "She sees that you are older now, so you should stay a little longer this time."

Chen Ningyu nodded: "Then I can't celebrate the festival with my grandmother this year."

"Silly child, why does grandma still care about so many things? Go quickly, so that Ezi won't have to wait for you again." The last time the princess agreed to let Fu Chaoqing come, the lady was already satisfied. She felt that the stone that had been pressing on her heart for many years was much lighter.

Chen Ningyu went to the Princess's Mansion.

It was still very cold at the moment, so she wore a thick coat and a fox fur cloak, wrapping herself tightly up. She didn't take off the cloak until she entered the house and saw charcoal basins everywhere.

The princess said, "Come and sit down. You must be cold on the way."

"It's okay. Just thinking of my aunt makes me feel warm inside."

The princess chuckled and said, "You are really good at making fun of me. Why did you give me such a valuable gift before the New Year?"

"Thank you for your hard work over the years, Aunt. It's all my duty." Chen Ningyu held the eldest princess' hand, "I will have to send gifts every year in the future. Aunt, please don't refuse to accept them, otherwise I won't come here."

"You dare to scare me? But that's all. You are so filial, and I love you well." The princess smiled and looked at her coat. Her eyes lit up and she said, "Oh, this is brocade from Jinling. The last time I sent people to Jinling, I couldn't buy such a good one."

Chen Ningyu smiled and said, "It was given by Madam Yang. She came back from Jinling last year and gave it to the mansion."

The princess nodded and said, "No wonder, their Wudinghou Mansion has always had a good relationship with your Mansion."

"Yes, he invited us to his house last year and we listened to some music."

"The actors in their family are really good. The Queen even invited them to sing several times. Others want to learn, but they can't." The Princess touched Chen Ningyu's face affectionately. "But you didn't like listening to music when you were young. I don't know when you started to like it."

Chen Ningyu smiled and said, "When I was young, I didn't like eating fish because I thought the bones were too troublesome. Don't you like it now?"

"They say girls change a lot when they grow up. I think it's true. Yun'er and Qing'er are still the same as when they were little. They haven't changed much."

"Of course he hasn't changed. I still remember that my eldest cousin was very naughty when he was little. He often scared me with toads. He was very happy to see that I was scared. Don't mention how hateful he was! Isn't he handsome now?"

The eldest princess laughed: "When Yun'er was young, he was very disliked. I even disliked him."

"What are you talking about?"

There was a loud shout outside the door, and Fu Chaoyun walked in with an angry face, shouting, "Mom, how old am I now? Why are you still talking about that time?" He looked at Chen Ningyu again and smiled sinisterly, "Ayu, someone said yesterday that they saw a snake in the pond."

Chen Ningyu hurriedly said, "Cousin, didn't you hear me say that you are handsome and elegant? I was really praising you."

Fu Chaoyun snorted and turned his head away. Fu Chaoqing also came in and smiled slightly, "How brave was he at that time? I told him a ghost story and he couldn't sleep well for half the night."

"Xiao Lan, you..." Fu Chaoyun's face turned dark.

Everyone else laughed, including Yu.

"Well, she's still like a child. I just thought of the past when I saw Ning Yu." The princess smiled for a while and said to Yu, "Tell someone to add two more charcoal basins to Ning Yu's room. She is very afraid of the cold."

Yu smiled and said, "Mother, I have already given the order. I know you love Ning Yu very much."

The eldest princess was quite satisfied.

Fu Chaoyun asked: "Ayu, how long will you stay this time? I'm not very busy recently."

"My grandmother asked me to stay a few more days."

The princess heard this and nodded: "Okay, I'll stay until the 17th and then leave."

Fu Chaoyun was delighted: "Let's go to the lantern festival in a few days."

The Lantern Festival in this dynasty starts on the eighth day of the first lunar month and ends on the seventeenth day. For the entire ten nights, every household hangs colorful lanterns, and there are performances such as lantern riddles,

dragon lantern shows, and lion dances.
Therefore, the nights in Kyoto have been extremely lively these days. No matter whether they are princes or common people, most of them will come out to watch the lanterns. Chen Ningyu has longed for this for a long time, but unfortunately the rules of the Marquis' Mansion are strict and the Madam will not let them go out. Now that she hears what Fu Chaoyun said, Chen Ningyu is naturally happy.

The princess said, "Ning Yu is a girl, how can she go?"

"Why not? With the child protecting her, what will happen to Ah Yu?" Fu Chaoyun said, "It's rare for Ah Yu to come here, so please allow me, mother."

The princess hesitated for a moment, then turned to look at Chen Ningyu: "Do you want to go?"

Chen Ningyu said aggrievedly: "Aunt, I have never been there once."

Seeing her like that, the princess smiled and said, "Okay, okay, let's go once. It doesn't have to be on the 15th, just the 9th. There won't be many people there. But it's only this once. You can't make any mistakes while you're here with me."

Fu Chaoyun made another promise.

Yu saw this and couldn't help feeling sad. She had never seen Fu Chaoyun like this since she married him. Last year during the Lantern Festival, she said she wanted to go, but Fu Chaoyun didn't show any reaction. He was not as attentive as he was today!

But who made Chen Ningyu so beautiful? Compared with her, she was just a supporting role.

Then why didn't Fu Chaoyun marry Chen Ningyu back then?

Their two families are not close cousins, so it's okay.

Yu didn't understand.

After everyone finished their meal, they left the main room and went back.

Chen Ningyu also walked with Fu Chaoyun and others.

Seeing them talking and laughing, Yu felt even more sad. Although she was the daughter-in-law of the Fu family, compared to Chen Ningyu, she seemed like an outsider and was completely out of place. She didn't know what to say.

Chen Ningyu was a girl after all, so she was more careful. Seeing that Yu was lagging behind, she turned back to wait for her and asked, "Did you go to the Lantern Festival, sister-in-law?"

Yu forced a smile and said, "No, my parents wouldn't allow me to do that at home."

"That's great, we can go together."

Yu hummed.

By the ninth day, every household had hung up lanterns. Since this day was neither the first nor the fifteenth, there were not many people around, so the princess allowed her to come and see on that day.

Chen Ningyu wore a not-too-conspicuous

jacket and skirt, and didn't do any dressing up as she went to watch the lanterns with Fu Chaoyun, Fu Chaoqing, and Yu, along with a few maids.

But since she was going out, she still wore a veiled hat. After she had only taken a few steps, Fu Chaoyun threw away her veiled hat: "Come to see the lanterns, can you still see them with this on?"

Chen Ningyu was speechless.

Fu Chaoqing frowned and said, "Why do you care so much? Ah Yu is still a girl."

Fu Chaoyun said, "It's thrown away anyway, so what? I'm here, so what are you afraid of?"

Fu Chaoqing didn't want to ruin his mood, so he turned his head and ignored him.

Fu Chaoyun enthusiastically told Chen Ningyu about the times they came to turn off the lights in the past.

It was Chen Ningyu's first time here, and she was very excited. She would linger for a while at every lantern she saw, and would guess the riddles. However, she was not very good at it and was always slow to react. Fu Chaoqing, on the other hand, guessed for her many times, and in a short while, she had won many prizes.

There was everything, baskets, candied haws, snacks, they were all stuffed into the basket and asked Fu Chaoyun to carry it.

Although Yu was in a bad mood these days because of Chen Ningyu, she was very happy at this moment. She was held by Fu Chaoyun and was full of happiness.

After all, she is his wife, so how can she be like Chen Ningyu?

As the four of them walked, it became completely dark and more and more people gathered.

Chen Ningyu suddenly realized that someone was holding her hand. She turned her head and saw that it was Fu Chaoqing.

He didn't look at her, but whispered, "Be careful not to get separated."

It seemed like a very casual move.

But his palm was solid, slightly warm, and wrapped around her hand.

She never thought that Fu Chaoqing's hands were not small. She only remembered that his fingers were long and graceful, not inferior to hers at all.

Her face turned a little red.

I wanted to break free, but for some reason, I still let him hold my hand.

When she was young, she often played around in the Princess's Mansion, and he often led her.

Although he is in poor health, he is very caring.

At that moment, she seemed to remember a lot of things.

"Let's go eat something," Fu Chaoyun had been walking in front. He turned around and pointed to a restaurant in front. "Let's sit by the window. The lion dancers will come over soon. How about we watch them from upstairs?"

"Okay." Fu Chaoqing agreed.

Fu Chaoyun didn't notice the hands of the two and walked forward again. However, Yu was a little surprised.

Chen Ningyu shrank suddenly.

Fu Chaoqing held it tightly and didn't let her move, but when they entered the restaurant, he let go and asked Chen Ningyu as usual: "Ayu, what do you want to eat?"

Without waiting for Chen Ningyu to answer, Fu Chaoyun said, "Let's eat fish dumplings. They are delicious!"

Yu was surprised: "Have you eaten it, sir?"

"Yes, otherwise why would I ask you to come?" Fu Chaoyun said with a smile, "Sometimes I don't go home, so I eat out with my colleagues. I think this one is good."

They naturally obeyed and ordered fish dumplings, a plate of fried bamboo shoots, a plate of shredded chicken with sweet potatoes, a plate of jade fish fillets, and a small jar of wine.

The four of them sat down and started eating.

Sure enough, not long after, there came a lion dancer downstairs. The lion's huge head was playing with a colorful ball in a very exciting way.

Chen Ningyu stood up and looked at it, and said with a smile: "What a big lion, so powerful!"

"Yes, great skills." Yu also praised.

Fu Chaoyun only drank with one foot on the

stool, looking quite rude and chivalrous.

Fu Chaoqing didn't drink. He stood behind Chen Ningyu and watched the lion dance. He smiled occasionally, looking gentle and handsome.

After watching, they were full and satisfied. Fu Chaoyun patted his stomach and said, "I'm almost dying of fullness. Let's go for a walk!"

Chen Ningyu found it funny.

Yu hurriedly put clothes on him: "Don't catch a cold, sir."

The four of them went downstairs and went to the street again. This time, after walking for a while, they saw three people coming towards them.

Although it was night, the surroundings were as bright as day. Chen Ningyu saw the person in charge at a glance, and his heart sank as if it was tied with stones.

Fu Chaoyun was the son of Princess Huiying and a frequent visitor to the palace. Naturally, he knew this person. He bowed and greeted him in a familiar manner, "Is the Third Prince also here to see the Lantern Festival?"

Li Changluo nodded, but his eyes fell on Chen Ningyu's face.

He saw her the moment she came out of the restaurant just now. Unlike that day at the Marquis Wuding's Mansion, he could see her unrestrained side from afar. Her every frown and smile was truly captivating, and he almost went crazy looking at her.

No wonder I can never forget her. Who in this world could be more beautiful than her? He stepped forward without hesitation.

☆、Chapter 21 Visit

"I came here to see the lights, and we just happened to meet. Why don't we go together?"

After all, he is the eldest princess's nephew, and of course he is a relative of the Fu Chaoyun brothers.

Fu Chaoyun did not refuse: "We are going to the east to have a look, so we can't go there."

Fu Chaoqing got a headache when he heard this. He did not ignore Li Changluo's staring eyes!

"Ayu is tired and wants to go back." He said calmly, "Brother, let's come back next time."

Fu Chaoyun was stunned and asked Chen Ningyu: "Ayu, are you tired? You were fine just now, saying that you wanted to take another look. Actually, it's just that side. Go back after you finish looking. You can't come next time."

Fu Chaoqing wanted to kick Fu Chaoyun.

Chen Ningyu certainly didn't want to have anything to do with Li Changluo, so she said, "I can't walk anymore. We've seen enough anyway, so let's go back."

Seeing that she was determined to do so, Fu Chaoyun did not force her and said to Li

Changluo, "Then we will leave first. Goodbye."

Li Changluo is not a stupid man, so he can tell the strangeness of the words just now.

He felt a little annoyed because Chen Ningyu was avoiding her.

"I'm tired of it, Zixia. Why don't I go with you? Come to think of it, I haven't visited Aunt Huiying for a long time."

Chen Ningyu pursed her lips. She was very anxious, but she didn't know how to refuse.

Fu Chaoqing immediately said, "It's getting late now, and I'm afraid mother needs to rest. Please come back another day, Third Prince."

Li Changluo's face darkened slightly.

Fu Chaoqing's expression remained unchanged.

No matter how slow Fu Chaoyun was, he still felt something was strange.

After Li Changluo left, he asked Fu Chaoqing: "What happened just now? You seemed to hate the Third Prince?"

"Do you like him?" Fu Chaoqing asked unhappily.

Fu Chaoyun frowned: "How could I like him? But he is a prince after all, so it's okay for him to come to our house and sit down, right?"

"Just don't like it." Fu Chaoqing refused to explain.

Yu did figure out something.

After returning to the princess's mansion, Chen Ningyu went back to her room to rest as it was indeed late.

But, just like last time, she couldn't sleep well.

Li Changluo's eyes flashed through her mind from time to time, those eyes were hot and a little scary.

In fact, the most terrifying thing is his identity.

If it were an ordinary prince, he would have been crowned a king and left the capital at the age of seventeen. However, Li Changluo never became a king and stayed in Kyoto, or even in the imperial city. Anyone with a little common sense should know what this means.

However, even if he understood, he could not guess what would happen in the future.

Chen Ningyu turned over in bed again.

The two girls, Gu Qiu and Dan Qiu, were also worried.

"I must tell the Madam when I get back." Gu Qiu sighed.

Danqiu didn't know what to say, so she thought for a while and said, "It should be fine. The eldest princess has the emperor's trust."

"But the Third Prince is the Emperor's son."

Now Danqiu was speechless again.

The next day, Chen Ningyu got up and still felt a little sleepy because he had a lot of dreams at night, but they were not good dreams and he was not in a good mood.

She went to pay her respects to the eldest princess.

The eldest princess smiled and said, "Did you have a good time yesterday? I went to bed early."

"It's pretty good. The lanterns are beautiful and there are lion dances to watch."

"As long as you like it," the princess said, "Do you still want to go today?"

Chen Ningyu hurriedly shook her head: "No." She answered quickly. The princess was just teasing her, but she didn't expect her to refuse outright. She found it strange.

As the two were talking, a servant came to report that the third prince had arrived.

The eldest princess was surprised.

Chen Ningyu clenched her hands tightly.

"Ask him in." The princess said to Chen Ningyu, "You go back first."

Even if the princess didn't say anything, Chen Ningyu had to leave in a hurry and went out without stopping for a moment.

Li Changluo came in and brought a lot of gifts.

The princess smiled slightly and said, "Why did you come here so suddenly? You didn't even tell me in advance. Does the emperor know?"

Li Changluo smiled and said, "I have already told my father, aunt, that my nephew was young and ignorant in the past and rarely came to visit. I hope you will not blame me. Today I am here to apologize."

The eldest princess was surprised again.

The current emperor now has five sons. Except for the eldest second prince and the third prince, one of them has already been made a king, and the other two are still young, one is eleven years old and the other is eight years old. To be honest, she is not very familiar with the third prince Li Changluo, but she did not originally want to get close to the other princes.

The eldest princess has always had a good sister-brother relationship with the emperor over the years, which has a lot to do with her ability to understand the times. She didn't want to get involved in the fight for the throne.

But today, Li Changluo came to the mansion. In fact, he had only come here a few times when he was young, and never came here after he grew up. How could the eldest princess not be surprised? She had no intention of cultivating feelings with any of the princes!

Li Changluo added: "Aunt, I met my cousins yesterday. I remembered that they had come to play here before. As your nephew, I have been a little immature over the years. Please don't take it to heart."

So there is such a thing, the eldest princess thought, Chen Ningyu didn't even mention it just now!

Thinking of her expression, the princess knew what was going on.

She smiled faintly and said, "Since you are here, how can I not welcome you?" Then she ordered the servants to call the two brothers.

When Fu Chaoqing heard that Li Changluo had arrived, he dropped the book in his hand onto the desk.

He put on his cloak and came out.

On the way, I met Fu Chaoyun, who said, "Come to think of it, the Third Prince hasn't been here for several years, right? I remember he was the same age as you, and he seemed to have come here once when you were eight years old, but I really don't remember anything else."

Fu Chaoqing said: "Yes, that was the last time he came."

"He is a stranger to us. I didn't expect to meet him yesterday. He actually came to our house." Fu Chaoyun said carelessly, without thinking about the reason at all.

He looked at Fu Chaoqing again and said strangely: "You really hate him!"

Fu Chaoqing walked away with a gloomy face.

The two of them came to the eldest princess, and Fu Cheng was there too. Li Changluo was talking to Fu Cheng, and when he saw them coming, he actually called them cousins.

The corners of the two brothers' mouths were crooked.

After talking for a while, Li Changluo said he wanted to go out and take a look at what changes had taken place in the Princess's Mansion.

Fu Cheng ordered his two brothers to lead the way.

Li Changluo was not interested in the wine, and he quickly mentioned yesterday's incident and asked Fu Chaoyun: "Is the girl I saw yesterday still in the mansion? She is my aunt's cousin's niece, if I remember correctly, the fourth daughter of the Chen family?"

Fu Chaoyun was surprised: "How do you know? Have you seen her?"

Li Changluo smiled and said, "I met him once at the Marquis Wuding's mansion."

Fu Chaoyun said: "I see."

"Is she still at home?" Li Changluo asked again.

"Yes, Ah Yu will stay until the 16th."

Li Changluo was very happy: "Why not call her out as well? After all, she is also my cousin."

Before Fu Chaoyun could speak, Fu Chaoqing said, "I'm afraid it's not very convenient. Ah Yu is very shy. Besides, we are a few men. What are we going to do with her?"

Fu Chaoyun glanced at Fu Chaoqing, wondering when did Ah Yu become shy? But he couldn't expose his brother, so he said, "Yes, yes, Ah Yu is also afraid of the cold, so forget it."

Li Changluo's wish was not fulfilled, so he spoke less.

However, he did not show any sign of anger. After all, the eldest princess's family were not ordinary people.

Not to mention the eldest princess, even these two brothers were very valued by his father. If Fu Chaoqing had not been in poor health, he would have been chosen to be the prince's tutor. Fu Chaoyun was also personally appointed by his father to be a Jinyiwei to serve his father.

Li Changluo thought to himself that if this could be accomplished, it would be killing two birds with one stone. It would be better not to be anxious and take a long-term view.

He never mentioned Chen Ningyu again. He walked around the mansion and then said goodbye to the eldest princess and left.

The eldest princess asked her two sons, "Did you meet the third prince yesterday?"

The two sons answered yes.

The princess's eyes narrowed slightly: "What did he say to you just now?"

Fu Chaoyun scratched his head and said, "Nothing."

Fu Chaoqing said, "He wanted to ask Ah Yu to come out and meet him, and he also said that he had met Ah Yu once at the Marquis of Wuding's mansion."

The eldest princess's face suddenly turned very ugly.

It seems that Li Changluo's unusual behavior this time is mostly because of Chen Ningyu, otherwise why would he come here in person? At his age, he should get married. The last time he went to the palace, he heard the Queen Mother mention that she wanted to find a wife for Li Changluo.

Seeing that his mother and brother were very serious, Fu Chaoyun belatedly asked, "Could it be, could it be that the Third Prince has taken a fancy to Ah Yu?"

Fu Chaoqing gave him a look of contempt.

The eldest princess sighed.

Fu Chaoyun cried out, "That won't do. Although the Third Prince hasn't married yet, I heard he has many concubines! Rumor has it that he's a bit lustful. We can't marry Ah Yu to him!"

"Of course I know." The eldest princess treats Chen Ningyu as her own daughter, so how could she not think about her?

She grew up in the palace and had seen a lot of dirty things, so she didn't want Chen Ningyu to marry into the royal family. Not to mention, the identity of the third prince was the most bizarre. She didn't know what the emperor was thinking!

"Ask someone to prepare the carriage to send Ning Yu back." The princess ordered the servants.

Fu Chaoyun said: "Ah? Ah Yu has only been here for a few days."

"It is no longer suitable for her to live here. The Third Prince has no connection with the Yongchun Marquis' Mansion. I believe he will not go to the Marquis' Mansion, rather than our home." Fu Chaoqing explained, worry in his eyes.

Fu Chaoyun thought about it and agreed. Although he was reluctant, he had no choice but to do so.

The princess called Chen Ningyu over and said softly, "Don't worry, I'll take care of everything."

Chen Ningyu trusted the eldest princess, and the tension in her heart eased.

She quickly took the bus back.

There had been a green cloth oil cart parked in front of the Princess's Mansion. When it saw Chen Ningyu's carriage coming out of the mansion, it hurriedly followed it. When it arrived at the Yongchun Marquis' Mansion, it turned around and left.

☆, Chapter 22 Princess Meets Princess

The lady was also surprised to see Chen Ningyu come back so early, and asked her why she didn't stay a few more days.

Chen Ningyu was afraid that the old lady would worry, so she didn't tell anyone about this matter. She just said that it wouldn't be good to leave it for too long. In fact, she wanted to see how the eldest princess would solve it first. If everything went well, there was really no need to make the old lady worry anymore. The last time, she only met her once and the old lady didn't sleep well.

The lady didn't ask.

During the days that Chen Ningyu was away, Madam Yang came once, and the relationship between the two old ladies became a little subtle.

It was because Madam Yang's eldest grandson

Yang Yanling was coming back. He had not wasted the past few years on the border. He defeated the Mongolian soldiers years ago and drove them hundreds of miles away. The Mongolian Khan decided to submit to the dynasty and pay tribute every year. The emperor was very happy and summoned Yang Yanling back to Beijing.

This was great news for the Wuding Marquis' Mansion. When Madam Yang talked about it, her face was full of smiles. She was happy for her, but while she was happy, she realized that Madam Yang might want to marry them.

Speaking of which, that's also a bit of a high-end.

Not only does the Wuding Marquis's Mansion have a favored imperial concubine, but also their descendants have all made military achievements for generations, and the Northern Army is well-known. So when Yang Yanling returns, it will be difficult for him to marry a girl from any of these families?

But the lady was not willing to marry Chen Ningyu to Yang Yanling.

Just because this girl was the apple of her eye, she wanted to marry Chen Ningyu into a simple scholarly family, so her candidate was Chen Ninghua. However, Madam Yang would definitely not agree.

After all, Chen Ninghua was a concubine's daughter, and Yang Yanling was both a legitimate son and the Marquis of Wuding, so they were indeed not a good match.

The lady was very conflicted.

Chen Ningyu naturally didn't know about this matter. He said a few words to the lady and then went back.

After a few days, the eldest princess went to the palace.

When Empress Jia saw her, she smiled and asked, "Why are you here at this time? What a coincidence! Lingzi is here too."

Princess Huaying Li Lingzi is the emperor's sister. If the princesses are of noble status, this one is even more so. Even the queen would be a little wary of her. However, the princess did not give her any face and said indifferently: "If I had known she was coming, I would not have come, so as to avoid disturbing the queen."

Li Lingzi sneered: "Same here, I still don't want to see you!"

Jia has a headache.

One of these two is the emperor's half-sister, and the other is his biological sister. It would be fine if the emperor had a different attitude towards them, but he treats them the same way. The two are incompatible, or even have a deep hatred for each other. Even if the emperor tries to be a peacemaker, it won't work.

"We are sisters after all, why are you so angry?" Jia said with a smile, "Since you are here, it's just right for you to have a meal with me."

The princess was busy, so she stopped

fighting with Li Lingzi and sat down, smiling, "I couldn't ask for more."

Li Lingzi snorted, but finally she had to give Jia face and stopped speaking rudely.

Jia pulled her fur shawl closer and chatted with them.

Li Lingzi actually had something else to do today. After a while, she asked, "I heard from the queen earlier that she wanted to find a wife for Chang Luo. Have you found a suitable girl now?"

The eldest princess' eyelids twitched.

Jia sat up straight and said, "Not yet. The emperor attaches great importance to it, so I am also confused no matter how I look at it."

Li Lingzi rolled her eyes.

The eldest princess held her breath, she was curious about what Li Lingzi would say.

Seeing this, Jia asked, "Do you have any good candidates?"

Li Lingzi laughed and said, "I also see that Chang Luo is not young anymore. I am still his aunt, so I just want to do my best to help him."

"Tell me who the girl is?"

"It's not a wealthy family. The girl is the second child in the family. Her surname is Ge. Her father works in the Ministry of Rites. I once met her at another family. She was really dignified and polite."

Jia asked, "Is it the second daughter of Ge Xiandao, the master?"

"Yes, so the queen also knew it."

"I have considered this before." Jia's eyes fell on Li Lingzi's face and she smiled meaningfully, "It's okay, but I'd better talk to the emperor about it. It's not that easy to decide."

"Of course." Li Lingzi said with a smile, "I just mentioned it casually."

The eldest princess curled her lips.

She was really casual enough to make a special trip just because I mentioned it casually.

Jia turned her head and looked at the eldest princess: "Ezi, what do you think? Have you seen Miss Ge Er?"

Li Lingzi also stared at her.

The princess smiled slightly and said, "I haven't seen it before. Your Majesty knows that I don't interact with other families very much. But since my sister mentioned it, it should be good."

She sincerely hoped that the Third Prince could marry Miss Ge Er, so that she wouldn't have to worry about this.

Li Lingzi was a little surprised. It sounded like Li Ezi was actually somewhat on her side.

Of course, that was only her opinion, but it was different in Jia's eyes, because the two princesses were definitely not the same kind of people, so she felt that the eldest princess was just speaking casually and had no thoughts at all.

Unexpectedly, the princess asked again: "Does Chang Luo plan to get married this year?"

Jia replied: "That's not necessarily true. For a man, it's okay to wait for a year or two. The emperor just hopes that he will get married as soon as possible, saying that he will be more stable after getting married." She felt very bitter when she said this.

It's a pity that her son, the original crown prince, died, otherwise she could have seen this day. Now, her son is gone, what fun is there in her life? It's just watching a show.

The princess' heart skipped a beat when she heard this. One or two years? There are so many variables involved!

After the three of them had their meal, the two princesses said goodbye.

On the way, Li Lingzi looked at the princess several times, and finally couldn't help asking: "Don't you have someone you like who wants to marry Chang Luo?"

"No." The eldest princess raised her eyebrows, "I'm not like you."

Li Lingzi sneered: "Then why did you come? I don't usually see you coming so often."

The princess looked at her, her mind moved, and she said calmly: "Actually, Chang Luo came to my house once, and I thought it was strange, so I came to the palace."

"Oh? He came to your house?" Li Lingzi frowned. Li Changluo was usually not very close to others. Between the two of them,

Li Changluo was closer to her. Why didn't he come to her house, but went to Li Ezi's place instead?

The eldest princess said, "I think he is a little impatient. Just as the emperor said, it's time for him to get married so that he can calm down."

Li Lingzi snorted: "When did you start caring about him?"

"He is our nephew after all, and we have watched him grow up," the eldest princess said slowly, "maybe I should find him a suitable wife? If he gets married, he will still remember me as his aunt, right?"

Li Lingzi's face darkened and she walked away with a flick of her sleeves.

The eldest princess sincerely wished in her heart that Li Lingzi could help the third prince get married as soon as possible!

However, it seems that Li Changluo has not mentioned the matter of Chen Ningyu to the emperor and the queen, and it seems that he is not sure either.

In Li Changluo's current position, he should not have chosen his own wife. He is not stupid. Of course, as one of the princes, Li Changluo is liked by the emperor and is not a stupid person.

The eldest princess guessed half right. In fact, Li Changluo went to find Concubine Shu.

Shufei was the eldest aunt of the Marquis of Wuding's Mansion. Li Changluo was originally the son of a concubine of low rank, who died soon after giving birth to him. The emperor gave him to Shufei to raise, but Shufei had no son, only a daughter.

These two have some mother-son relationship. Concubine Shu was eating snacks. After listening to Li Changluo's words, she wiped her mouth and asked curiously, "Is it the fourth young lady from the Yongchun Marquis's Mansion? I heard from my mother that she is really as beautiful as a fairy?"

Li Changluo blushed a little: "Yes, mother, I would like you to make the decision."

Concubine Shu nodded: "It's not difficult, but you should marry a virtuous woman. Why do you have to marry someone from the Yongchun Marquis's Mansion?"

In her opinion, there was absolutely no need for Li Changluo to do this.

Li Changluo said hurriedly: "The Yongchun Marquis's Mansion is not an ordinary family. The eldest aunt married into the Zhang family, and the second aunt married into the Xu family. The maiden family of their eldest wife, Zhang, is also a scholarly family for generations. Old Master Zhang is a scholar of the Hanlin Academy."

Concubine Shu nodded again, and after a moment's silence, she said, "You are right."

"Does mother agree?" Li Changluo was overjoyed.

Although he couldn't tell his father, the

emperor, and his mother, it was different with Concubine Shu. In this palace, Concubine Shu was the only one who treated him sincerely. At least that was what Li Changluo thought. He didn't believe that the queen could find a wife he was satisfied with.

In that case, you might as well just marry the one you like!

Concubine Shu glanced at Li Changluo and said, "You really care about this. In this case, I will think of a way for you."

Li Changluo was naturally overjoyed when he saw that she agreed.

Yuanniang, a middle-aged maid behind Concubine Shu, who was also her confidant, asked softly, "Should we invite the Madam Dowager to come over?"

The lady in chief was Lady Yang, the mother of Concubine Shu.

Concubine Shu said, "It's the Lantern Festival. I should come as usual. My mother just came back from Jinling. I haven't seen her yet."

Shufei is different from other concubines. It is not difficult for her to see her family.

Yuanniang smiled and said, "Marquis Wu Ding has returned to the capital with great achievements this time, and the lady will be very happy too."

Speaking of this nephew, Concubine Shu was in a very happy mood and said with a smile: "That's right. It will take another month for him to arrive in Beijing, otherwise he would have been asked to come along. Please give orders and ask the Madam to come the day after tomorrow."

Yuanniang responded and left.

☆, Chapter 23 Concubine Shu

Madam Yang was very happy to hear the news. After all, she was going to see her daughter. She hadn't seen Concubine Shu for more than two years.

When Concubine Shu entered the palace, Madam Yang cried secretly until her heart ached. But when she went outside, she had to cheer herself up. She couldn't let anyone know that she was unwilling to give her daughter to the emperor as a concubine.

However, Madam Yang still felt uncomfortable every time she thought of this.

If Concubine Shu had not been so beautiful, she would not have been favored by the emperor when he was on a secret tour.

She packed up and went to the palace.

Concubine Shu stood up to greet him and threw herself into Madam Yang's arms.

The mother and daughter have a good relationship. Madam Yang's eyes were red: "I have been playing everywhere and I haven't seen you."

Concubine Shu said, "As long as mother likes it."

Madam Yang looked up at her daughter and

saw that she looked radiant and did not look like a woman in her thirties. She felt relieved that the emperor was kind to her and that she did not have a hard life in the palace.

Concubine Shu pulled Madam Yang to sit down and said with a smile, "Mother is in good spirits, and I am finally relieved."

"Your brother and sister-in-law are here, don't worry about them."

Concubine Shu hummed.

Madam Yang thought of Yang Yanling and asked, "The emperor has called Yanling back this time, but he is not going to let him go to the border again?"

"Yes, I have talked to the emperor several times. Fortunately, Mongolia has surrendered this time. Yanling will live in the capital permanently."

Madam Yang clasped her hands together and said, "Amitabha."

Concubine Shu smiled and said, "Next time, mother and sister-in-law will worry about Yanling's marriage again."

"I do have a choice for this one." Madam Yang sighed, "But it's still a bit of a pity. The girl I originally liked got married because Yanling never returned to the capital. This one is also okay, but her biological mother died early."

"Oh? Whose girl is she?" Concubine Shu was curious.

"She is the fourth young lady from the Marquis of Wuding's mansion."

"What?" Concubine Shu was startled. She didn't expect that Madam Yang also fell in love with that girl. She couldn't help but become curious. "I haven't seen her. After all, she was not born before she entered the palace."

Their two families have always had contacts. When she was young, she often met the two aunts of the Chen family. But after entering the palace, she never summoned them. After so many years, they became even more estranged.

However, this time, the fourth young lady of their Marquis' Mansion was involved.

Madam Yang said, "She is as pretty as you were back then."

The reason why Concubine Shu has been able to remain prosperous in the palace for a long time, besides her abilities, is that her face is also one of her important weapons. Not to mention the batch of girls who entered the palace back then, even now, there is no girl who can compare to her, and the Queen is far inferior to her.

After hearing what Madam Yang said, Concubine Shu knew what was going on. She was indeed a beauty. No wonder Li Changluo was obsessed with her.

"To be honest with you, mother, Chang Luo has also mentioned this girl." said Concubine Shu.

Madam Yang raised her eyebrows. She thought of the time when she invited Madam Chen and others to the mansion and met the Third

Prince.

"Yankang brought the Third Prince here, and he met Fourth Miss Chen." Madam Yang looked at Concubine Shu seriously, "You said so, could it be that the Third Prince also likes her?"

Concubine Shu did not tell the truth, and smiled and said, "I just mentioned it. After all, she is a beauty."

Madam Yang thought for a moment and said, "My daughter, let me advise you not to interfere in the Third Prince's affairs. There is always the Emperor and the Empress. We have no right to control who he marries."

Concubine Shu sighed: "I raised him."

"But he is not your biological son!" Mrs. Yang's tone also became stern.

Concubine Shu pursed her lips. She didn't want to conflict with her mother, so she just asked, "What do you think, mother? Should we go to the Yongchun Marquis's Mansion to propose marriage?"

"Not so soon. Yanling hasn't returned to the capital yet. Besides, how can we be careless about this important matter? Yanling may not like it, so we have to ask his opinion."

Yang Yanling is the Marquis of Wuding, not a child anymore. Madam Yang will still respect his ideas. This time it is his marriage and the woman he is going to marry, so she cannot take full charge of everything.

Concubine Shu didn't know what to say, so she was silent for a while and said, "I just want to see mother today, let's not talk about anything else."

In fact, she originally wanted to tell Madam Yang about Chen Ningyu. After all, their two families were on good terms. But it was not easy to say it now, otherwise Madam Yang would be angry. She would just wait and see what the situation was first.

But she really wanted to meet Miss Chen Si.

"Why don't you bring Miss Chen Si to the palace next time? Mother said she is no less capable than me." Concubine Shu smiled.

Madam Yang said, "This is not very convenient."

It's okay for her to be a concubine.

The two talked for a while before Mrs. Yang went back.

After the fifteenth, the weather gradually became less cold, the snow stopped falling, and tender green buds appeared on the branches.

The lady called both Chen Xing and Chen Xiu over that day.

The two of them just thought it was nothing, but the lady started talking about the two girls.

The cause was naturally that Yang Yanling returned to Beijing and brought the Mongolian Khan to Beijing to pay homage. The emperor rewarded him with a thousand taels of gold and promoted him greatly to the position of Left Commander-in-Chief of the Five Military Commanderies. He was in great glory.

The lady asked, "What should we do?

Chen Xing was surprised: "Isn't this a good thing? Naturally, we can just marry Ning Yu to him."

Chen Xiu is Chen Ningyu's father, and he has always cared for her the most. Hearing this, he said, "The Wuding Marquis Mansion is not a simple family either."

Although the Wuding Marquis Mansion and the Yongchun Marquis Mansion were conferred the title of marquis at the same time, the Wuding Marquis Mansion has always been more prominent than the Yongchun Marquis Mansion. Its ancestors had produced the Minister of War, the General, and several other high-ranking officials. However, the saying that wealth and honor are sought in danger has always been true.

Now, the Wuding Marquis's Mansion has a royal concubine who raised the third prince personally. The old Wuding Marquis and his wife died early, and Wuding Marquis's mother is a second wife. To put it simply, it is a complicated family, so the Yongchun Marquis's Mansion has never taken the initiative to propose a marriage.

Madam Yang seemed to know this as well, so she did not mention other grandchildren and only found a wife for Marquis Wuding.

She felt that with the status of Wu Dinghou, the Yongchun Houfu would not refuse. Of course, in the Hou family, no one would do anything only based on the depth of feelings. Mrs. Yang also liked the foundation and foundation of the Yongchun Houfu. connections.

The Yongchun Marquis Mansion itself seems to be ordinary, but all the relatives have great powers. In recent years, it was only because of the vision of the old Marquis and his wife that such a situation could exist.

When Chen Xing heard what Chen Xiu said, he pondered for a moment and said, "But we have to get married."

The wife said: "I never wanted to refuse. After all, our two families have been friends for so many years. Not to mention what happened to your grandfather and grandpa, their Wuding Marquis Mansion helped a lot, otherwise the title would be gone."

Chen Xiu hummed: "What mother said is true, we are not ungrateful people."

The three of them discussed for a while, and Chen Xing said, "If the Marquis of Wuding is not bad, then that's fine. If Ning Yu marries him, can they still treat her harshly? Besides, Madam Yang is also a person who knows her limits. She also gave an explanation for the matter of the Third Prince last time."

The old lady also admitted that she could trust her elder sister. After thinking for a long time, she said, "Perhaps it's too early to say it. After all, she didn't say much. It all depends on Marquis Wu Ding. I watched that child grow up. He was a little naughty when he was young, but I didn't expect that he could become a general."

Chen Xing sighed: "Mother, how can a person who has been through battles not change?"

"That's true." The old lady looked at her eldest son and was glad that he was by her side. To be honest, she was also very worried at home during those years when he went to the battlefield, but everyone's path is destined and there is nothing they can do about it.

But now that Chen Ningyu has to marry such a man, she feels really distressed.

"How about this, we can test Madam Yang's opinion later. It would be best if Ning Hua married him. She is a little older anyway, and it is not Ning Yu's turn yet." Chen Xing said, "If Madam Yang really doesn't agree, then we can talk about it later."

The lady-in-waiting shook her head: "How can this be possible? Marquis Wu Ding is both the legitimate son and the marquis, while Ning Hua is a concubine's daughter. Although this child is also good in every way, if I tell her, won't my elder sister be angry?"

She thought about it and decided that it was definitely inappropriate.

Chen Xing frowned, "Then it can only be Ning Yu, what else is there to say?"

Looking at the old lady again, Chen Xiu said, "Mother, brother, don't be reluctant to let Ning Yu go. She is a girl, so why not get married? After all, the Yang family knows her background well."

The lady sighed.

"Anyway, when we meet Marquis Wuding next time, they clearly have that intention, so we don't have to hesitate. Since they have already decided to get married, we might as well do it. Marquis Wuding was able to pacify the northwest, so he is not an ordinary person. The future of their mansion will surely be good!" Chen Xing made the final decision.

The other two had nothing to say.

Back at Xingfang Garden, Jiang asked Chen Xiu tentatively, "Is there something important that needs to be done, mother?"

"Nothing serious." Chen Xiu's face was indifferent.

Jiang smiled and said, "My husband, you don't have to hide it from me. Mother must have found a good marriage for Ning Hua!"

Chen Xiu glanced at her and said, "You seem to care a lot about Ning Hua."

"She's my daughter after all, how can I not care about her? Ning Hua is a really good child, filial and polite. Last time I said your socks were wearing out quickly, she sent you several pairs, all of which were sewn stitch by stitch."

Chen Xiu had complicated feelings towards Chen Ninghua. He lowered his eyes and said, "Ninghua is a good daughter. You can make her a few more sets of clothes someday."

Jiang nodded: "Ning Hua is going to get married, so it's time for her to dress up more. I wonder which young man mother has taken a fancy to?"

Chen Xiu was annoyed by her questions and said, "It's not Ning Hua."

"What?" Jiang was stunned.

She was about to ask again, but Chen Xiu took his clothes and went inside to change them.

Jiang sat on the edge of the bed, thinking and thinking, and suddenly it dawned on her that the last time Madam Yang came, she talked to her for a long time, and her grandson, Marquis Wuding, returned to the capital again. Could it be that he was going to marry Chen Ningyu?

It must be like this!

Otherwise, he would not have surpassed Chen Ninghua. Marquis Wu Ding is not young at all. He must be in his twenties, right?

She frowned slightly.

☆, Chapter 24 Gift

By February, it already looked like spring. The girls in the mansion took off their heavy coats and put on padded jackets. This time, Chen Ninghua got two extra pieces. When she heard Jiang say that it was Chen Xiu's special order, she touched her new dresses and felt very happy.

This move was indeed the right one. Although Jiang was not nice to her, she was the mistress of the second house after all. When she reached out to her, there was no reason for her not to accept it. As long as Jiang said more good things to Chen Xiu, she would always get some favor from Chen Xiu.

Seeing that his daughter was in a good mood, Qiu Bai said with a smile: "I saw a magpie when I woke up this morning. There must be good things happening this year."

Chen Ninghua said with a smile: "There are always magpies every year. There are so many trees in our yard. You always come to coax me."

Qiu Bai said hurriedly: "Not really, it's really rare in the past."

Chen Ninghua didn't take it to heart. Although she had been neglected by her father and mother for all these years, she was able to leave a good impression in front of the lady. Her reputation as a talented woman was also well-known in Kyoto. It was not just luck.

What can it decide whether it is a magpie or not?

She stood up: "Let's go."

Several people went to the place of Madam Ci Xinyuan.

I met Chen Ningyu on the way. She was wearing a moon-white cross-collared blouse embroidered with orange-red peach blossoms, and a royal blue long skirt. Her hair was loosely tied into a bun on the left, with her long hair hanging down. She looked indescribably lazy and beautiful.

Chen Ninghua pursed her lips before she smiled and said, "What a coincidence, I meet the fourth sister again."

They didn't live in the same courtyard, so Chen Ninghua usually arrived earlier. Chen Ningyu smiled and said, "It's not cold now, so I'll get up earlier too."

Her eyes flickered over Chen Ninghua. The last time she was making spring clothes, Jiang specifically mentioned Chen Xiu's words, which actually surprised Chen Ningyu. Jiang was praising Chen Ninghua in every word, which was very rare.

Are they going to stand on a united front? Chen Ningyu thought to himself, who is this targeting?

She didn't think that Jiang would suddenly have a change of heart and be nice to Chen Ninghua. If she wasn't targeting anyone, she must have other intentions.

The lady was having breakfast at the moment. Seeing them coming one after another, she smiled and said, "That's great, that's great. Come eat with me for a while. Having you eat together will help my appetite."

The girls sat down.

The ladies are always like this, so they never feel too full when they eat by themselves.

Anyway, the breakfast here is rich, with porridge, steamed buns, sweet and salty cakes, biscuits, and various pickles, which can fill an entire table. The lady is a person who likes to enjoy life.

Zhang smiled and said, "They think we are too old, so they don't allow us to accompany them. They insist on them coming before they ask them to eat."

The lady laughed: "You are old, and you don't know how to tidy up. Look, you are wearing even plainer clothes than me. These clothes are just made. Look at the embroidery. You should learn from her!"

Xiuwen is Jiang.

Jiang was not like Zhang. She liked to dress up. She always dressed up well, eyebrow pencil and rouge. She never used them even for a day. When she heard the lady's praise, she laughed and said, "Sister-in-law is naturally beautiful. How can she be like me?"

Zhang said calmly, "My husband and I are an old couple, so we are often lazy and not as good as my younger sister."

Jiang's face froze immediately.

Women dress up for their friends, isn't she the same? She just wanted to please Chen Xiu.

Zhang's eyes were full of contempt.

Jiang was so angry that her teeth were itching.

There is a reason why Zhang is superior to Jiang. Not only does she come from a noble family, but Chen Xing is also good to her and she doesn't have any concubines around her. But Jiang is different. How can the two of them be truly harmonious?

The lady was used to it and pretended not to know.

After leaving the Madam's place, Chen Ningyu took only a few steps when she saw a maid coming over with a small wooden box and calling out, "Fourth Miss, Fourth Miss, the Princess's Mansion has sent something."

Chen Ninghua and Chen Ningrou both stopped.

Gu Qiu took it, opened the box and said with a smile, "It's perfume powder."

Chen Ningrou curiously leaned over and saw more than a dozen small jade bottles lined up in the box. The jade bottles were transparent and the scented powders inside were colorful and there were many kinds. Some of them she had never heard of, so she enviously said, "They all look like top-quality scented powders."

Chen Ninghua stood not far away and did not come to see.

Chen Ningyu was not a stingy person, so he said, "Pick out a few that you like. I can't use them all anyway."

Chen Ningrou was very happy. She took Chen Ninghua and Chen Ningyu to Furong Garden.

Gu Qiu took out all the small jade bottles.

Chen Ningrou said: "Then I won't be polite, Fourth Sister!"

"Take it, it's nothing." Chen Ningyu had so many good things that she didn't care at all. Although Chen Ningrou and Chen Ninghua were not very close to her and their friendship was usually as pure as water, and she even disliked Chen Ningrou a little bit, but they were sisters after all and saw each other every day.

Chen Ningrou took three and asked the maid to put them away.

Seeing that Chen Ninghua didn't move, Chen Ningyu chose two for her, both of which were light and more suitable for her.

Chen Ninghua thanked him and accepted it.

"This perfumed powder smells special. I wonder where the princess bought it from."

Chen Ningrou was loved by Jiang and had always used the good ones since she was a child.

"I don't know. My aunt loves these things. She must have asked someone to buy them somewhere else."

Chen Ningrou sighed: "It's great to have a cousin like this!"

Chen Ningyu smiled.

Gu Qiu was about to put the wooden box away, but she found that the jade bottle had been taken away, and there was a small compartment underneath. She smiled and said, "Miss, what else is there?"

She took the thing out and looked at it.

Everyone gathered around and saw that it was a praying mantis carved out of green jade. If this praying mantis was real, the girls would be scared when looking at it, but this jade carving looked simple, cute and full of childlike fun.

Gu Qiu said: "There is a note underneath."

Chen Ningyu took it out and looked at it. It turned out to be a gift from Fu Chaoqing.

He saw it on the road on his way back and thought it was interesting, so he bought it. Coincidentally, the eldest princess gave her perfume powder, so she also brought it together.

Chen Ningrou was curious: "What did you write?"

"My second cousin bought it." Chen Ningyu answered casually.

Chen Ningrou took the jade mantis and looked at it carefully, wishing she could stick her eyes on it.

Gu Qiu looked at it and frowned.

They talked for a while, played for a while, and then Chen Ningrou and Chen Ninghua said goodbye and left.

As a result, somehow, the jade mantis on the table was knocked to the ground with a bang and broke into three pieces.

The room was very quiet for a moment.

Chen Ningrou's face changed drastically, and she asked in panic, "What's going on?"

But no one saw it. When they finished talking about the perfume powder, Chen Ningrou pulled Chen Ningyu to the study to play. When they came out, they said goodbye. The perfume powder and the jade mantis were on the table, and I don't know how they fell down.

Chen Ningyu was filled with anger.

She squatted down and picked up the jade mantis pieces one by one.

Gu Qiu hurriedly said, "Miss, be careful not to cut your hands!"

When the jade is broken, it has edges and corners.
Chen Ningyu seemed not to hear it and picked it up anyway.
Chen Ninghua saw that her face was a little red.
She rarely saw Chen Ningyu angry, like today. Even if she was angry, it would be very difficult for others to notice. But this time, Chen Ningyu was obviously very angry, so angry that she didn't even try to hide it.
"It's all our fault. If we hadn't followed them, we wouldn't be in such a rush and mess and knock things over." Chen Ningrou pulled Chen Ninghua into the water.
Chen Ningyu took a breath and said, "It's okay. It's just a small thing. It's an accident. Who can stop it?"
Although her tone was light, it made people's hearts skip a beat.
"I need them to clean up here." She ordered them to leave.
Chen Ninghua also apologized, said goodbye to Chen Ningrou and left.
Chen Ningyu gathered the broken pieces of the Jade Mantis together, put them in a wooden box, and said to Gu Qiu, "Put them away."
"Young lady..." Danqiu interrupted, "I think it must have been dropped by the Fifth Young Lady. She picked it up to play with it at first, and then she went to the study with the young lady. No one noticed

it at the time. It seems that it was placed on the edge of the table, and it fell when it was touched."

After listening to this, Chen Ningyu nodded and said nothing.

Seeing her like this, Gu Qiu and Dan Qiu didn't dare to say anything more.

Chen Ninghua and Chen Ningrou were walking on the road.

Chen Ningrou looked at Chen Ninghua and said, "Third sister, can you see how the jade mantis fell?"

Chen Ninghua shook his head.

"What a pity, such a beautiful jade carving." Chen Ningrou sighed, "I liked it when I saw it, and even wanted to ask someone to buy one according to the same pattern, but it ended up breaking into pieces, and Fourth Sister was very unhappy when she saw it."

She invited them to play and gave them perfume and powder, but the jade carving that Fu Chaoqing gave her was broken. How could Chen Ningyu be happy?

Chen Ninghua said calmly: "Fourth sister has a lot of fun things to do, so she probably doesn't care too much."

"That's good. I was afraid that Fourth Sister would be mad at us."

Chen Ninghua lowered his eyes and said nothing more.

Seeing that the New Year had passed and it was a new year, her daughter was one year older. Zhao was very anxious. Although Lu

Yun did not react, she could not bear it anymore and talked about Lu Yun's lifelong affairs with the lady that day.

The lady apologized: "I was so busy that I really forgot. Don't worry, I will find a good son-in-law for Yun'er. Tell me, what kind of son-in-law do you want to find?"

Zhao had naturally thought about it, and said a little embarrassedly: "My daughter is at least literate. Although our family is not, our ancestors are also a family of scholars."

Zhang frowned as she listened.

With this tone, I'm afraid her demands are quite high, and then the lady will be annoyed with her!

The lady nodded: "That's right, please continue."

Zhao smiled and said, "He must be a scholar, right?"

"Of course."

Zhao said again: "It would be best if he could be a juren."

The lady nodded again: "It's not difficult to become a juren."

When Zhao heard this, she was so delighted that she wanted to kneel down in front of the lady.

The lady smiled and said, "I like Yun'er, too. She looks like a lady from a wealthy family. We can't let her down. I'll take care of this matter."

Zhao thanked him repeatedly.

After she left, the lady looked at Zhang.

☆, Chapter 25 Matching

Zhang's eyelids began to twitch. She pressed them down with her hand and forced a smile.

The lady said, "You heard it just now, didn't you?"

"My daughter-in-law heard it. Mother is going to find a marriage for Miss Lu, and it has to be a juren." No matter how much Zhang wanted to hide her dissatisfaction, she couldn't hide it. She really felt it was too absurd.

The lady nodded and said, "I know you are in trouble."

Zhang sighed, "Mother, it's good that you know. It's not that my daughter-in-law doesn't want to, but I'm afraid no one in the capital knows about the Lu family now. How can there be a good marriage? And it must be a juren?"

The lady smiled, took a sip of tea and said, "You, the Juren got a better score."

These words woke Zhang up from her dream, and she understood immediately, thinking that the lady was really powerful!

There are several levels of Juren. One type is those who can pass the Juren exam and also the Jinshi exam. One type is those who pass the Juren exam but may not pass the Jinshi exam. And another type is those who pass the Jinshi exam after going through a lot of hardships and can never pass any other exams.

The lady looked at Zhang and said, "Parents are like mothers in the world. My niece is always a mother, so it is natural for her to want to find a good son-in-law. However, I also know their situation. No matter how much I want to do good for them, I am unable to do it. You should find a suitable one, and look among our distant relatives."

Let alone the Zhao family, what about their Yongchun Marquis Mansion? Her most beloved granddaughter might not be able to find a grandson-in-law that suits her heart!

Zhang responded.

Zhao happily ran to tell Lu Yun and Lu He the good news.

"She said she was going to find you a husband who is a juren scholar!" Zhao was overjoyed. "I was a little hesitant to bring it up, but luckily the lady agreed. If you are a juren scholar, your life will not be hard at all."

Juren already had social status and were no longer ordinary people.

Zhao's thoughts were actually very simple. Just as the lady had said, as long as he could be a juren, that would be enough.

Lu He was surprised: "Really? That's great, my sister is married, and I feel more at ease."

Only Lu Yun didn't quite believe it. She was more thoughtful and asked, "Can you tell me which family it is?"

"How can it be so fast!" Zhao laughed, "It

will definitely take some time. Your cousin's grandmother is also busy, and the third daughter is also going to get married. It's not settled yet. I had no choice but to tell her. I didn't want to cause trouble for the lady."

Lu Yun said calmly, "Then let's talk about it after we find it."

Zhao called Lu He, "Help me open this box."

When they came, they brought four large boxes. This was one of them, and also the most valuable one. It was made of mahogany, with copper edges around it and carved with patterns of intertwined flowers. It was very exquisite.

This is the last bit of property left to the Lu family.

Lu He opened the box.

There were several pieces of clothing, a wedding dress, a box of jewelry, and dozens of books inside.

"So there are these things!" Lu He was surprised.

Zhao reached out her hands and touched them one by one and said, "Of course, these are all handed down from our ancestors, so no matter how hard or tired I was, I didn't pawn them. I just wanted to use them as betrothal gifts and dowry for you, so that you won't be looked down upon."

Lü He felt sad when he heard this, and he comforted Zhao, saying, "Wait until I pass the imperial examination and become a Jinshi, and our lives will get better and better."

Zhao nodded and said, "You will have a bright future. Mother believes in you." She opened the jewelry box and called Lu Yun to come and see.

Lu Yun said: "I have seen it, mother, don't you remember it?"

Lü Yun had grown up very early, and Zhao always consulted with her. Now she remembered and said with a smile, "Look at my memory, Yun'er, when you get married in the future, I will bring these jewelry with me. There are also some fabrics, so you can make some new clothes."

No matter how good the material is, it has become old and faded after so many years. Lu Yun sighed, "It's not as good as what I have now. Don't worry, mother. If she really dislikes our poor dowry, she will never marry me."

When Lu He heard this, he said, "Yes, the one who is going to marry my sister in the future will naturally know our situation."

Zhao smiled and said, "I know, but it's always good for us to have some." She took out a long hairpin with a golden butterfly and colorful jade and inserted it on Lu Yun's head, nodding with satisfaction, "How beautiful it is, this is what your grandmother used to wear."

There were only two or three good items, and the rest had been sold. Lu Yun was a little impatient, but to cooperate with Zhao, she forced a smile.

At the end of February, Madam Yang and Yang Yanling, Marquis of Wuding, came to visit.

No matter how much Yang Yanling was a marquis, he was still a junior in front of the lady dowager. He used to come here often when he was young. He had been busy since he returned to the capital this time and only had time now. It was only out of courtesy for him to come and pay his respects.

As it was a holiday, Chen Xing, Chen Xiu and Chen Min were all present. However, Yang Yanling had returned to the capital, and they had already met and talked in the court, so they came mainly to see the lady.

Only a few girls were not seen, as the lady did not ask them to go.

Chen Ningrou was very curious and asked Baozhu to find out the situation.

Baozhu came back and said timidly, "Everyone has left, and I didn't see them."

"It's useless!" Chen Ningrou cursed, "You're leaving so soon?"

"I heard that just after I had a few words with the Madam, someone came to report that it seemed that all the soldiers in the guards were causing trouble, and the Second Master was also there."

Chen Ningrou curled her lips: "You really know how to pick a day, what a coincidence!"

In fact, she just wanted to know what Yang Yanling looked like. She thought he was a handsome boy back then. In her memory, no one could surpass him except Fu Chaoqing. He was just a little naughty, and Madam Yang often called him a naughty boy.

Who would have thought that a few years later, he would become a great general. Could such a man win a war?

He is so different from my great uncle.

Chen Ningrou didn't quite believe it.

The old lady also felt a little regretful. Before she could take a closer look, the man had already left. When Chen Xiu came back, the old lady hurriedly asked, "What's the big deal? Is this the guard post you are in charge of?"

Chen Xiu said: "No."

The lady breathed a sigh of relief.

Chen Xing was also very concerned and asked about the whole story.

"It was about the delay of military pay. Someone took the lead and went to the Ministry of Revenue to make trouble, and a fight broke out. Fortunately, no one died, but some were slightly injured." Chen Xiu shook his head. "To be honest, it was also the Ministry of Revenue that did not handle it properly. How could they not be angry just because they delayed the soldiers?"

The lady nodded and asked again: "Is the treasury so empty that it can't even pay the soldiers?"

"There have been severe disasters in recent years. Many places have no harvest. We have given out a lot of money, but we can't get it back. So we are a bit tight."

Chen Xing frowned, "No matter what, we can't lose the soldiers! We shed blood for our country, and firstly, we have no other income, and secondly, our salary is low to begin with. This is really unjust! How will Wu Dinghou deal with it?"

Chen Xiu said solemnly: "They arrested him immediately, saying he violated military discipline and ordered him to be beaten with a stick."

"Isn't it that he has offended people just after arriving? They are all his subordinates. If they become alienated, can he still control them?"

Chen Xiu smiled again: "After the fight, the Ministry of Revenue also had a hard time. He took the Ministry of Revenue's Left Vice Minister to see the emperor."

The lady took a deep breath and patted her chest, saying, "I heard that the Minister Wang also has a bad temper, but there was no fight?"

"What are you hitting? It's like catching a chicken!" He was sweating coldly as he watched.

But Yang Yanling just took Lord Wang away, and no one dared to stop him.

As for what would happen if he went to the palace, no one knows.

However, after a few days, the military pay was paid, not a single copper coin less.

Speaking of Zhang, she has been very worried these days. The task assigned by the lady was not easy to do. She tried her best and finally found two people. At the request of the lady, both of them were juren, but their future was not very good. One of them was surnamed Zhu and opened a private school to teach. The other was a distant relative of their Chen family. He had taken the imperial examination three times but failed. Now he helped to manage the accounts of the mansion and earned some monthly salary. He planned to try again.

She reported it to the Madam, who said, "They are both not young anymore, right?"

"One is twenty-five, and the other is twenty-two."

The lady said, "Is there no better one?"

Zhang felt wronged: "I have tried my best to find a daughter-in-law, but when others heard about the current situation of the Lu family, who would be willing to marry her? Young scholars are either full of confidence and waiting for the exam, and are not in a hurry to get married, or they have already found someone they like!"

The lady had no choice but to give up and called Zhao over to tell her what had happened.

Zhao was very satisfied. She felt that Chen Mingshan, a distant relative of the Chen family, was not bad. He was not too old and there was a possibility that he could pass the exam. Even if he failed, he could still be an accountant in the Marquis' Mansion and would have no problem supporting the family.

She immediately expressed her satisfaction: "But we just have to look at the person."

The lady smiled and said, "He is also a handsome boy. Actually, he is the son of my husband's cousin."

Zhao was even happier.

She went back and told Lu Yun about it, and said with a smile: "You can meet her next time. If you think she's good, then it's settled. I'll feel relieved that you're married. Your father loved you very much when he was alive."

Lu Yun held the brush tightly in one hand and asked, "Is Chen Mingshan also seeking refuge in the Marquis' Mansion?"

"Yeah, it's just like us, isn't it perfect?"

Seeing Zhao's silly smile, Lu Yun put down the brush with a snap.

Seeing the anger on her pretty face, Zhao was startled: "Why, you don't like it?"

"What's there to like or dislike? People like us can only match this." Her eyes were slightly red. "Just think that mother has found something good, so happy. If father were alive, would he also be happy to see me marrying such a person?"

Zhao was stunned.

Lu Yun turned around and ran out.

☆, Chapter 26: Unexpected

Zhang Jiwan had just finished practicing martial arts and came out of the martial arts training ground. He was wearing only a short suit and was covered in sweat. He was holding a sword in his hand and walking briskly. He was recalling the sword skills he had just used in his mind and thinking about how to make the dance more powerful.

As a result, when he reached a cave entrance, he heard a faint crying sound coming from inside. He was curious and walked over to take a look.

Lu Yun was crying there. She stopped crying when she heard footsteps. She turned around and saw that it was Zhang Jiwan.

Seeing her face full of tears, Zhang Jiwan asked in surprise: "Sister Lu, what's wrong with you? Did someone bully you?"

Lu Yun wiped her eyes and shook her head: "Nothing."

"How can it be nothing? You're crying." Zhang Jiwan walked closer. "You're the same as me, staying in someone else's house, but I'm better. Tell me, is it because the servants did something?"

"No, really not." Lu Yun wiped away her tears and said softly, "I'm just sad."

Zhang Jiwan was cheerful by nature and liked to make friends. Lu He also lived in the mansion, so he gradually became familiar with Lu He and treated him as a friend. He also treated Lu Yun as a sister and showed some concern for her.

Seeing that she was unwilling to speak, Zhang Jiwan did not force her and said, "Then I will take you back."

Lu Yun nodded, and seeing the sword in his hand, she asked if he was going there to practice martial arts.

Zhang Jiwan smiled and said yes.

He is fourteen years old this year. Unlike Zhang Jihe, who is thin, he is very tall. Even a tall girl like Chen Ningyu is half a head taller than her. Because he looks like Zhang Zhijing, his facial features are also handsome.

He walked with her on the road, chatting and laughing from time to time. When Lu Yun saw his profile, her face suddenly turned red and she quickly lowered her head.

Zhang Jiwan accompanied her all the way to the gate of the courtyard before saying goodbye and leaving.

When Zhao saw her coming back, she rushed over and said, "I was so worried. I just figured it out. Yun'er, you are my sweetheart. I shouldn't have married you off so hastily. If you don't want to, that's fine. I'll go and ask the Madam to help me. Please don't be angry. It's my fault!"

Lu Yun sighed: "I'm afraid the Madam will be unhappy."

"Madam Tai is kind-hearted, why would she bother with me?"

Lu Yun said, "Then you can just go back."

Zhao looked outside and asked, "Was that the second young master just now?"

"Yes, he saw me and sent me back."

Zhao smiled and said, "My second cousin is

a good person. He doesn't put on airs at all."

Lu Yun didn't say anything, thinking that Zhang Jiwan was naturally a good person, not like other young masters. Lu He also often said that he was good, and it was true. Although Chen Min and Chen Li in the mansion were also young masters, they didn't pay much attention to her when they saw her.

It can be seen that Zhang Jiwan never despised her identity.

"Why don't we make food next time and send a portion to our second cousin?"

Zhao was surprised: "My second cousin, how can he be so good at eating?"

Because Zhao felt that it was too much of a disturbance to the Marquis's residence, and they were not from the capital and had their own taste preferences, and the two children also liked what Zhao cooked, so a small kitchen was built in the yard, and Zhao cooked by herself every day.

Lü Yun took Zhao's arm and said with a smile, "Mother's roast chicken is extraordinary. No other chef in this mansion can cook as well as you!"

This is Zhao's specialty. Zhao said proudly, "That's right. I'll make it for my second cousin some other day."

Lu Yun happily went back to practicing calligraphy, as if what had just happened had never happened.

In March, the Wuding Marquis' Mansion sent

an invitation, inviting them to visit.

This time, many families were invited, because Marquis Wu Ding returned to the capital and was promoted. Many families sent gifts, but they did not have the time to invite them one by one, so they invited them all at once to make things lively.

On the way there, the lady smiled and said, "That's good too. I haven't seen many of the old ladies for a long time, so let's get together at their house."

Chen Ningyu disliked such grand parties the most, but there was nothing she could do. As the daughter of a marquis, she had to face it. Besides, she would probably not be able to escape getting married in the future. When she thought of getting married, a shadow fell on her face.

I don't know if the eldest princess has resolved the issue of the third prince. There has been no news yet.

Or is no news good news?

When they arrived at the Wuding Marquis's mansion, they saw a line of carriages waiting to enter. Zhang said with a sigh, "It's really lively here."

The lady said in a calm tone: "It was usually deserted, but now that people are back, it's different after all."

At that time, Yang Yanling was only a teenager when he served as a deputy general with his second uncle Yang Dongping to lead troops to fight against Mongolia. As a result, Yang Dongping was injured and returned to Beijing, but he stayed. Many people questioned that this young man who originally went to gain experience took on such an important task, but the emperor decided to trust him this time.

Who would have thought that he would be gone for six years, with countless wins and losses, and no one knew whether he could succeed, but today, no one doubts it anymore.

The lady sighed: "My elder sister finally made it through."

She knew the position of Yang Yanling in Madam Yang's heart. After he left the capital, the two of them only communicated through letters. Madam Yang was worried about him to the core. Finally, she could not sit still at home and often went out to see the mountains and rivers to distract herself.

When they reached the second gate, all the women came down.

There were quite a few people in the huge yard, dressed in jewels and jade, with elegant clothes and beautiful hair, which made people's eyes dazzled.

Madam Yang came over to greet them in person. After exchanging a few words with the Madam, she took Chen Ninghua's hand and praised her for looking dignified and generous today, but she did not praise Chen Ningyu at all.

Chen Ningyu didn't notice anything, but the lady was surprised, but she didn't show it.

Seeing this, Jiang followed Madam Yang in praising Chen Ninghua and saying all kinds of good things, which made Chen Ninghua blush and feel embarrassed.

After that, Jiang gave Chen Ningyu a meaningful look.

Chen Ningyu was puzzled.

To be honest, she really doesn't like others praising her like this!

After everyone greeted each other, Madam Yang invited them to listen to some music.

These gatherings all follow the same routine: meet, say polite words, admire flowers or listen to music, have a meal, and then talk again. Although wealthy families have money and power, they can't do much to play. Of course, men may have more, such as hunting.

Chen Ningyu found a seat to sit. The girls all sat in the second row at the back. The first row was for the old lady and the other ladies in the mansion.

When the actors began to sing, everyone became quiet.

Sitting next to Chen Ningyu was the second daughter of Mr. Qi, a doctor in the Ministry of War. Mr. Qi was Zhang Zhijing's cousin and often visited their house. The second daughter, Qi Shuqin, was on good terms with Chen Ningyu, so Chen Ningyu sat next to her.

"Where did you buy the perfume and powder you are wearing today? It smells so good and has a bit of sweetness." Qi Shuqin likes Chen Ningyu's exquisiteness the most. What she wears and uses are rarely seen in Beijing.

Chen Ningyu said: "It was given by my cousin."

Qi Shuqin envied: "Every time I ask you, I always hear you say this. The eldest princess is different!"

"Of course, who is my cousin?" Chen Ningyu smiled, "If you like it, I'll give you some next time you come to our house. I don't use it often, and I only bring it with me when I go out."

Qi Shuqin nodded repeatedly: "Okay."

Chen Ningrou poked her head out from the side: "I have one too. It was given to me by my fourth sister. I brought it with me this time. How about I give it to you?" She took out a sachet.

Qi Shuqin took it without hesitation and thanked Chen Ningrou.

Chen Ningyu frowned, and she thought of the jade mantis again.

Well, I'm still taking the things she gave me as a favor!

Chen Ningrou smiled and said, "Fourth sister, don't be angry. I always give it to Sister Qi. We are family."

Chen Ningyu said calmly: "I finally understand what it means to offer flowers to Buddha through borrowing flowers. Next time, I will offer them myself."

Next time, Chen Ningrou will never get her things again, and Chen Ningyu has hated this person even more since then.

Seeing that she was angry, Chen Ningrou didn't dare to say anything more.

After listening to the song, Madam Yang talked to the old lady. The two had known each other for so many years. In fact, Madam Yang had noticed earlier that the old lady was reluctant. What's more, after this incident, she could only give up the idea.

Madam Yang smiled and said, "Yanling is old enough to get married, and I have been thinking about it. Today, I have to ask my sister to help me."

The lady then realized that Madam Yang had changed her mind and did not want to marry into their family. Although she was a little surprised, she also felt that it was just what she wanted. She joked, "I was afraid that you would be overwhelmed by the choices today, so no wonder you called me here. I must be here to help you."

At this moment, Chen Ningyu was chatting with a few girls.

Bai Tao came over mysteriously and said a few words to Gu Qiu. Gu Qiu felt that this news was still of some value, and her expression changed a little, but she didn't want to go over and report to Chen Ningyu directly.

The master and servant have been together for several years, and Chen Ningyu could see it, so he found an excuse to leave the crowd.

"I need to go to the bathroom too, let's

talk while we go."

The two asked for directions and set off.

After exiting a cave, there was a small bamboo forest with lush green leaves. Gu Qiu said softly, "Mrs. Bai Tao only found out about this today. She was afraid that the young lady didn't know, so she asked Xing Hong to tell Bai Tao that Madam Yang originally wanted to marry into our mansion."

Chen Ningyu was stunned: "Is there such a thing?"

The two families have known each other for many years, but although Madam Yang has a legitimate grandson and two other grandchildren, she has never heard of such an intention. Why is it that Wu Dinghou wants to get married as soon as he returns? Is he waiting for him?

She thought of Madam Yang's praise of Chen Ninghua today, and Jiang's look, and finally found the reason!

Could it be that Madam Yang wanted Chen Ninghua to be her daughter-in-law? But considering Chen Ninghua's status, it was unlikely. Just a few compliments might not mean anything.

Gu Qiu sighed: "It turns out that the third girl is quite lucky."

She also saw that scene today, but she felt that her master was the legitimate daughter, and logically, Chen Ningyu should be the one to marry him. How powerful the Marquis of Wuding is now, both the marquis and the

left commander-in-chief!
She felt sorry for Chen Ningyu.
Chen Ningyu smiled and said, "Who said that Wu Dinghou is good?"
Gu Qiu was surprised: "Marquis Wu Ding is not good enough, what kind of man do you think is good enough?"
Chen Ningyu's eyes turned: "I think obedient ones are the best."
Without waiting for Gu Qiu to react.
Then there was a "puff" sound in the bamboo forest, and the bamboo leaves began to shake.
Gu Qiu was shocked.
Chen Ningyu was also shocked.
I saw a tall figure slowly walking out of the bamboo forest, holding a small wine jug in his hand and wearing a navy blue robe.
He looked lazy but also had a huge sense of oppression that made people feel breathless.
Gu Qiu took several steps back.
Chen Ningyu also took a step back.
The man's eyes fell on her face. Because of the sunlight, he squinted slightly and said in a low voice: "Chen Ningyu?"

☆, Chapter 27 Do You Still Remember Me
Chen Ningyu's heart started beating fast.
She didn't know him, but he called out her name right away!
who is he?
A name popped into her mind, and she opened her eyes wide: "Marquis Wu Ding?"

"Yes." He smiled, and his stern face seemed to soften a little. "Do you still remember me?"

Chen Ningyu stopped talking.

She didn't remember him, but logically, she should remember him.

Yang Yanling picked up the wine pot and put it to his lips. He raised his head and took a sip. He looked down at her and said lightly, "You are still as beautiful as before. It's just that it's not easy to find an obedient husband."

Chen Ningyu's face turned red.

An obedient husband is definitely the best, but he doesn't want to be the kind of submissive husband. In Chen Ningyu's ideal, she really wants to find a gentle and considerate man who can think of her in everything.

But she also knew it was hard to find.

Chen Ningyu bowed to him and said, "My Lord, please make yourself at your leisure. I have something else to do. Bye."

Yang Yanling smiled and said, "Goodbye."

Sure enough, not long after she walked back, Yang Yanling came.

The looks of the women were very enthusiastic.

But Chen Ningyu no longer had that curiosity.

So this is what Marquis Wuding is like.

Chen Ningrou leaned close to her ear and said, "Fourth sister, do you still recognize him? Do you think he looks the same as before?"

Chen Ningyu naturally didn't know him, that was the first time she met him.

As for whether they looked alike, she had no idea, but it was undeniable that Marquis Wu Ding was a very handsome man, handsome enough to make young girls' eyes even hotter.

But what's the use of being so enthusiastic? There is only one man and there are so many girls. I'm afraid Madam Yang has already selected several of them. Marquis Wu Ding's coming at this time must have been arranged by Madam Yang, who wanted him to leave an impression.

In fact, this is true.

Yang Yanling received instructions from Madam Yang early in the morning to wait until the time was almost right and then come over under the pretext of paying his respects to the old ladies.

A few days ago, Madam Yang had brought up this matter to him, and he had agreed reluctantly. He was used to the desolate and empty northwest, and today's hustle and bustle made him a little bored. He perfunctorily left the crowd and took time to drink in the bamboo forest. Unexpectedly, he happened to hear the conversation between the master and servant.

In fact, it was not just them. There were others passing by before. He had excellent hearing and did not miss a word. But it was Chen Ningyu who said something obedient,

which made him spit out a mouthful of wine.
Is he, Marquis Wuding, not as good as a man who listens to a woman?
Yang Yanling felt angry and amused.
When he walked into the house and greeted the old ladies, there were several girls in the room. He glanced at them and his task was completed.
The party is almost coming to an end at this point.
After a while, each family said goodbye.
Madam Yang asked Yang Yanling, "What do you think of these girls? If you like any of them, you can propose marriage. There are two girls among them whom you have seen since you were young."
"So urgent?" Yang Yanling was stunned.
Madam Yang frowned, wishing she could punch her grandson: "Impatient? Don't you see how old you are? Other young masters already have children, and you still don't want to get married? Even if you don't want to, Yanshou will have to get married too."
Yang Yanling smiled and said, "Then let my second brother get married first."
Madam Yang was almost angry to death.
Yang's eldest wife, Tang, hurriedly advised, "Mother, Yanling has only been back for a short time, there is really no need to rush. This is a big deal!"
"Yes, mother, there is no rush for this matter. Besides, didn't you say earlier that you would marry into the Yongchun Marquis's Mansion?" Second Madam Fan

objected, "I think the fourth Miss Chen is pretty good, why didn't mother let Yanling take a look at her?"

Yang Yanling had already had doubts in his mind. He lifted his white robe, sat down and asked calmly, "Grandmother, why not the fourth girl?"

Madam Yang's face changed slightly, and she asked hurriedly, "Why, are you interested in Miss Chen Si?"

Seeing that she was facing a formidable enemy, Yang Yanling became even more suspicious. In fact, based on the relationship between the two families and what Madam Yang had revealed earlier, if he were to marry, it would definitely be Chen Ningyu. But Madam Yang suddenly changed her mind, so how could he not be suspicious.

Yang Yanling said, "Let's not talk about whether you like it or not, grandma, you also need to give me an explanation, right?"

Mrs. Yang looked a little embarrassed.

Just because of this reason, she couldn't say it!

"What's wrong with those girls? They are all well-educated and well-mannered, and their status is also suitable. I think they are good."

Seeing that Madam Yang was avoiding the question, Yang Yanling raised his eyebrows and said, "Since Grandmother is unwilling to talk, then let's wait a while. I have just returned to the capital, and I have not yet adapted to the climate here, let alone marrying a wife. Today, I have shown my face and met people in accordance with Grandmother's wishes. Let's leave it at that for now."

Madam Yang was anxious: "How can this be possible? We can't drag other girls along."

"Why are you holding off?" Yang Yanling laughed. "Those girls want to get married, and we won't stop them. Or, grandma, have you already made an appointment with a lady behind my back?"

"That's not the case, but today is different."

Yang Yanling poured himself a cup of tea, picked up the teacup and shook it, saying, "When I came in earlier, there were several people in the room. Do you think you're going to marry all of them? I just took a look and I have to take this responsibility. I'm really too busy to handle it."

Seeing Yang Yanling bringing this up, Madam Yang's mouth twitched. Although this grandson had been away for many years and his temperament had changed a lot, his words and actions were still very unruly, which made her helpless. She was afraid that his willingness to show up today was already a big concession.

Seeing that Madam Yang was helpless, Tang scolded Yang Yanling again: "Yanling, your mother is doing this for your own good. Although you should be cautious about your lifelong affairs, you should still pay attention."

"What do you mean by 'care'? Just bring me some girls and I'll marry them." Yang Yanling drank the tea in one gulp. "That's all. I have things to do."

He stood up and left.

Tang's face turned red and white. Although she was a stepmother, she was also a mother, but Yang Yanling never took her seriously.

Seeing this, Fan smiled and said, "Mother, don't be angry, sister-in-law. Yanling has always been like this. Forcing him to come will only backfire. It's better to give him some time. He is so old now, I don't believe he really doesn't want to get married."

A gentleman desires a beautiful lady; this is human nature.

Madam Yang was so angry at Yang Yanling that she had a headache. She sighed and said, "Yanling came back this time with a lot of things from there. Send some to the Chen family tomorrow." Madam Yang ordered, "There are also a few sable skins. Give one to each of the three girls."

Mother Sun went to do it.

But Chen Ninghua returned to Qingyin Garden and had just taken off his coat to rest for a while when Aunt Su came.

Chen Ninghua hurriedly called her in, and whispered, "Why are you here, Auntie? Is there anything wrong?"

Aunt Su's face was full of joy: "I heard that Madam Yang likes you very much and came to see you specially."

Chen Ninghua frowned slightly. No one else would say this. It must have been a maid in the room who told Aunt Su. She was her biological mother and cared about her very much. The maids around her also knew it.

Seeing that she was a little dissatisfied, Aunt Su hurriedly said, "Don't blame them. I forced them to ask." She held Chen Ninghua's hand and asked again, "Is it true?"

Although she had never thought of Chen Ninghua marrying into a very wealthy family and just wanted her to live in peace, the Wuding Marquis's Mansion was after all extraordinary, and it would be a good thing for her to marry any of the young masters in the mansion.

Chen Ninghua said calmly: "He just praised me a few words."

Aunt Su said, "Didn't you praise the fourth young lady?"

Chen Ninghua pursed her lips and said, "Why are you talking about Fourth Sister again?" Does everyone have to praise Chen Ningyu?

Aunt Su laughed and patted her hands, "That's great. In fact, what's so special about the fourth young lady? She's just prettier. How can she be as virtuous as you, who is proficient in music, chess, calligraphy and painting? Madam Yang is very discerning."

Chen Ninghua's face changed: "Aunt, please stop talking nonsense. We are sisters, there is nothing good or bad about us. Besides, what does it have to do with Madam Yang?"

She was happy at first, but when Yang Yanling appeared, she realized that she was just overestimating herself. Although Madam Yang praised her, she had no other intention.

Aunt Su came here secretly at this time. She was afraid of being discovered, so she quickly took out a purse from her sleeve and said, "I don't have anything valuable. This is what I saved over the years. You can take it. It can be used to manage people or something."

Chen Ninghua frowned: "How can this be possible? Your life will not be easy either."

As for the mother and daughter, Chen Ninghua is okay, at least she has the lady dowager around, so she is not in financial difficulty. But it is different for Aunt Su, the lady dowager cannot take care of them so much, and apart from daily expenses, she has nothing else.

Aunt Su stuffed it into Chen Ninghua's hand and said, "Take it and don't say anything more. I'm counting on you, okay?"

She said this and went out.

Chen Ninghua held the purse, feeling sad and uncomfortable.

She hated that she was the daughter of Aunt Su. If she were not a concubine's daughter, the situation today might be different.

Given the relationship between their two families, if she were a legitimate daughter, it would not be difficult for her to marry Marquis Wu Ding.
She sighed and put away her purse.

☆, Chapter 28 Offending
On the second day, Mother Sun from the Marquis of Wuding's mansion came in person.
The lady was surprised.
Mother Sun smiled and said, "The Marquis brought it back from the north. The Madam said she had forgotten about it."
The lady exclaimed, "You are so polite!"
Mother Sun said, "Madam Tai knew you were going to say that. She told me to put my things down and then go back."
The lady laughed and said, "Forget it, forget it. I will shamelessly accept it."
Mother Sun asked people to bring some things, including Cordyceps sinensis, deer antlers, wild ginseng, etc., all of which were precious things, but fortunately there were not many of them, otherwise the Madam would not have accepted them. Mother Sun also took out three pieces of sable skin: "This skin is beautiful, the Madam said it is the best for the three girls to wear."
The lady is a person of such high rank that she naturally understands what this means.
She quickly called Zhang over.
"Find some good things tomorrow, and find a reason to send them to the Marquis Wuding's

Mansion." She couldn't take advantage of others for no reason. Although she had a good relationship with Madam Yang, one thing was another.

Zhang nodded, leaned forward and asked, "Did Madam Yang not mention the matter of Ning Yu?"

"I didn't mention it, but it doesn't matter. Ning Yu can marry anyone else."

Zhang was secretly surprised.

She learned from Chen Xing that Madam Yang had long intended to get married, and everyone thought it would be settled. But who would have expected that yesterday's behavior would lead to that. Why did Madam Yang suddenly dislike Chen Ningyu again?

The lady remembered something at this moment and said to Zhang: "On the Queen Mother's birthday in July, you must remember to prepare the backup ceremony. Although we are not royal relatives, we still have to follow the etiquette."

At that time, all civil and military officials will celebrate his birthday.

Zhang understood and left.

Chen Ningyu got the sable fur. He was very happy because of its smooth fur and beautiful color, so he asked someone to make a light fur coat for him.

Gu Qiu said: "I heard that the third and fifth girls also got the same."

Chen Ningyu thought that this might be sent by Madam Yang as an apology. After all, she had said that she had this intention before, but changed her mind later, so she must feel guilty.

As time went by, Li Changluo became more and more impatient. One day, he went to Concubine Shu again and asked about Chen Ningyu.

Concubine Shu said calmly, "I didn't know that mother still liked that girl."

"What?" Li Changluo was anxious, "Do you want her to marry Wu Dinghou?"

Concubine Shu glanced at him and sighed, "She's just a girl."

Li Changluo smiled awkwardly: "Mother, I only like her. After all these years, can't you see that I have never been like this before? Please help me fulfill my wish!"

"You have to know that I can't make the decision on this matter." Concubine Shu lazily forked a piece of fruit and put it into her mouth. The taste was sweet and sour. She narrowed her eyes slightly. "If your father knew about this, he would definitely be unhappy."

"I know I'm forcing you, but you still have a say in front of your father." Li Changluo complimented her, "Who in the palace doesn't know this? Mother, I will never forget this kindness!"

Seeing how anxious he was, I wanted to swear.

Concubine Shu smiled and said, "I'll think about it. Anyway, your mother hasn't found a suitable one yet." She raised her eyebrows and said, "I heard that Princess

Huaying wants to introduce Ge Xiandao's daughter to you."

Li Changluo's face suddenly changed: "It would be better for me to die!"

Ge Xiandao's daughters are all talented, but their looks are a bit disappointing to others.

Concubine Shu smiled and said, "Okay, go out now."

After Li Changluo left the palace, he was still distracted by the thought of Chen Ningyu. Unfortunately, he was born into a royal family, unlike other young masters. Otherwise, with similar family backgrounds, it would not be difficult for him to marry her. But here, it became particularly complicated.

"She still hasn't gone to Princess Huiying's mansion?" He turned around and asked Zheng Xie, a personal guard.

Zheng Xie replied: "No, I have only been to Wuding Marquis's Mansion once."

"I know that." Li Changluo waved his hands impatiently. Thinking of what Concubine Shu had just said, he felt particularly upset.

If this matter is delayed any longer, Chen Ningyu might really marry Yang Yanling!

The emperor values Yang Yanling very much. What should he do then? If he wants to steal his wife, it will be too difficult.

He thought about it.

Seeing this, Zheng Xie said, "Why don't you go to Yongchun Marquis's Mansion?"

Li Changluo frowned: "Not very

appropriate."

Zheng Xie gave another suggestion: "Ms. Chen Si will have to go out eventually."

Li Changluo was annoyed: "Forget it, just ask them to keep an eye on it."

He walked away.

Seeing that the old lady was a little free, Zhao shamelessly rejected the distant relative of the Chen family that Zhang had mentioned last time. The old lady was a little surprised, but seeing that Zhao was very satisfied, she just thought it was a success. Who knew that they still looked down on him.

But the lady did not get angry, she just said: "There is nothing better for now, can you wait a little longer?"

When Zhao heard about this, she became a little anxious, but she didn't dare to make her daughter angry again. She thought for a while and said, "Cousin, you also know that our family was not originally a farming family. Our ancestors were a family of scholars after all. They always say that daughters should marry high. I feel sorry for Yun'er."

The lady frowned slightly, but it was understandable.

Zhao said again: "I know I have caused trouble to you, Madam. We are eating and living for free, yet you are asking for these things. I am too embarrassed to see you."

The lady sighed and said, "Forget it. I'll

let my eldest daughter-in-law take another look."

When Zhang heard this, she was so angry that her face turned black.

What is this? You say others don't deserve it? You don't even know your own weight!

Only the lady is kind-hearted and tolerant.

Zhang said, "I'm still looking for one. I'll just leave it alone. If you ask, I'll tell you there's no good one and they don't think he's worthy of their daughter."

Madam Cai comforted her, "They are just people who don't know the rules of etiquette, madam, don't take it to heart."

Zhang sneered, "If you are worried, just let them wait and send the two maids away. If the Madam asks about it, just say you are busy and will come back to help for the time being. Anyway, they are very capable and don't need them to help."

She is not like Jiang who is sometimes straightforward, but she is aggressive in doing things. Otherwise, the lady would not have entrusted her with so many internal affairs of the Marquis' Mansion, and Chen Xing would not have been without a concubine. Now that Zhao has offended her, her life will definitely be a little difficult.

Mother Cai hurried to give instructions.

Chen Ning'an had not been back since he came back on the second day of the New Year. On this day, he took a day off and came to the Yongchun Marquis Mansion with Wu Jian and Wu Dairong.

It is because of the relationship between the two families that she can come here so often.

Three girls from the mansion came to see her.

Seeing that Chen Ningrong was still holding the needle and thread, Chen Ningrou's eyes widened: "What kind of important thing is this? Why would you bring it with you when you go back to your parents' home?"

Wu Dairong smiled and said, "I made it for my eldest brother. I asked my eldest sister-in-law not to bring it, but she refused. She said that my eldest brother's clothes are too thick and it will be uncomfortable to wear when it gets hot. Hers is the lightest and most comfortable to wear."

When they looked, they found that it was indeed an undergarment, and she was embroidering flowers on the corners of the garment.

Chen Ningyu joked, "It's true that things are different after getting married. In the past, when I saw my second sister, she would either drink tea or appreciate paintings."

"Yes, you have become an embroiderer. You bring her home with you." Chen Ningrou said, "Second sister, stop embroidering and go out with us."

But no matter what anyone said, Chen Ning'an would not stop.

It can be seen that her second sister is completely devoted to Wu Jian. Chen Ningyu thought, I don't know whether it is a good thing or a bad thing. Women are always more sentimental than men and are more easily hurt. If it were her, she would not be like this.

However, if two people have feelings for each other and neither of them lets the other down, it cannot be said to be a bad thing.

She looked at Chen Ning'an, and somehow she suddenly thought of Fu Chaoqing.

Thinking of that night when he held her hand.

Think of the jade mantis.

But she quickly shook her head and continued chatting and laughing with them.

☆, Chapter 29 Sending Off

In early April, the crabapple trees in front of the mansion bloomed again. Zhang Jiwan picked several crabapple flowers in one hand and walked in slowly with a basket in the other.

When Bai Tao saw him like this, she burst out laughing.

"My dear cousin, are you selling flowers?"

"Yes, one copper coin per plant, do you want it?" Zhang Jiwan has never been arrogant and he always responds to anyone who talks to him.

Bai Tao giggled and said, "Okay, I want

one."

She actually paid for it.

Gu Qiu came over and said, "What are you doing? Are you taking it seriously?" Then he said to Zhang Jiwan, "The girl just got up..."

"Oh, I'll just wait." Zhang Jiwan sat down with a big sword and golden horse, and handed her the crabapple flower. "Look at the fancy things in your vase. They are not as beautiful as this one. Put it in."

Gu Qiu felt that his cousin was no longer useful in his old age and originally wanted to persuade Zhang Jiwan to leave, but it seemed that this was not going to work, so he had to accept the flowers.

Chen Ningyu walked out without combing her hair, looking sleepy.

But her facial features looked like they were painted. Zhang Jiwan glanced at her and said with a smile, "Fourth cousin, no wonder everyone says you are pretty. Isn't it true? My mother can't go out unless she smears it all over her face!"

Chen Ningyu was sweating: "Don't talk nonsense, that's your mother."

Zhang Jiwan smiled.

Danqiu was busy combing Chen Ningyu's hair.

Chen Ningyu was not afraid of gossip, but it seemed that it was not easy for her to reject someone like Zhang Jiwan. Maybe the longer they were together, the less she rejected him. The two of them felt very relaxed together, just like her own brother.

She was indeed getting along well with him.

Chen Ningyu now acknowledged their relationship and became concerned about Zhang Jiwan, asking him how he was doing in learning martial arts.

Zhang Jiwan immediately went to the yard to dance with the sword for him to see.

This is a good posture. Chen Ningyu encouraged him, "You look almost as good as your father. You should work hard."

"It's not convenient to bring a spear. Next time you come with me to the martial arts training ground, I'll show you how to use it." He was very happy and wanted to show her other kung fu.

Chen Ningyu said hello.

Zhang Jiwan came into the room and waved to her: "I brought you some food, try it."

He opened the lid of the basket and found a roast chicken inside, emitting a rich aroma. However, Chen Ningyu's eyes fell on the basket, and she wondered why it wasn't brought in a lunch box. The last time he brought vegetables out from Qiu Ji, she remembered that it was put in a very exquisite lunch box.

"Isn't this from Qiu Ji?" she asked.

Zhang Jiwan's eyes widened. He originally wanted to fool her, but Chen Ningyu saw through it at a glance. He didn't know what went wrong.

"Are you a god or someone else?" he was surprised.

Chen Ningyu was amused and blinked: "You

guessed it all. I am a god in heaven."
Zhang Jiwan twitched his lips.
"If it's not from Qiu Ji, then where did you buy it?" She thought it smelled good.
Zhang Jiwan asked her to taste it, and Chen Ningyu tasted it.
"It's quite crispy and fragrant, but it doesn't seem to be made by our chef. Have you found a good restaurant again?"
Zhang Jiwan chuckled twice: "You guessed wrong, this was done by our cousin."
"Cousin?" Chen Ningyu didn't react for a moment. After thinking for a while, she asked in surprise, "Are you talking about Cousin Lu's mother, Cousin Zhao?"
"That's her. How is it? Is her cooking delicious?" Zhang Jiwan said with a smile, "She often sends it to me. I'll bring it to you to try."
Chen Ningyu put down her chopsticks, folded her hands and asked, "Does she really send you food often?"
"yes."
"Then why doesn't she ever give me any to eat?" she asked, "Why do you think that is?"
Zhang Jiwan was very proud: "Of course, it's because I'm likable!"
Chen Ningyu wanted to give him a slap on the face. The silly boy was just slow. She smiled and asked tentatively, "So, are you liked by cousin Lu? Does she come to see you often?"
"I don't come here often, but occasionally

he comes to ask me about my calligraphy practice." Zhang Jiwan smiled and scratched his head, "My handwriting is still pretty good."

Chen Ningyu felt angry and amused when she saw his silly look, but at the same time, she felt that the situation was a little serious. Last time it was the purse, but this time it was Zhao who stepped in, using delicious food, and there was also the excuse of practicing calligraphy.

Could it be that their family really has some intention?

"I'm full too. You should go back and practice martial arts well." She wiped her mouth.

Zhang Jiwan didn't think too much about it and said, "I'll leave this roast chicken here for you. I ate a lot anyway. You can have some more when you're hungry."

Chen Ningyu nodded, and after he left, she went to the lady's place.

The lady was very happy to see her and said with a smile, "It's time for dinner, why are you here? But it's good that you can accompany me."

Lunch has just been placed on the table.

Chen Ningyu didn't want to disturb the lady's mood for dinner, so he used a little as well.

She didn't speak until she finished eating.

The lady frowned and asked, "Did Ji Wan say this herself?"

"I wanted to test the purse issue, but

Cousin Lu said it was my cousin who suggested sending food. The roast chicken is still in my room. My cousin said they often send it. Cousin Lu also asked him about practicing calligraphy."

The lady slammed her hand on the table so hard that the teacup jumped.

"Grandma, maybe I'm just imagining things, but I'm worried about my cousin. He lives in our house, and nothing can go wrong."

She knew very well that if Zhang Jiwan really wanted to have something with Lu Yun, Zhang Zhijing would beat him to death, and Chen Linzhi would be so angry that she would die.

To be honest, for a family like theirs, even if Zhang Jiwan and Lu Yun loved each other, those two would not allow Zhang Jiwan to marry Lu Yun.

The lady patted Chen Ningyu's hand and said, "Thank goodness you told me. I really didn't know anything!"

Chen Ningyu felt a little ashamed: "My cousin is familiar with me and tells me everything. Logically, I shouldn't speculate like this, but I think this is a big deal about my cousin, so I still have to tell grandma."

"You haven't done anything wrong to him. Although Ji Wan is a naughty child, he is careless, kind, and can be easily taken advantage of." The lady knew Zhang Ji Wan very well. She had watched the child grow up. "I have my own opinion on this matter.

Don't tell Ji Wan, so that he won't misunderstand you."

Chen Ningyu nodded.

A few days later, the lady found a new place for the three members of the Lu family.

Zhao Shi was a little bit unconvinced when she heard this. She smiled and said to Lu Yun, "My cousin has arranged a house for us, right on the back street. It's not good for us to live here. Others will think we are staying here for free and look down on us. Now we have our own yard, which is always a good thing."

Lu He had always wanted to be independent, and said with a smile: "It should have been done a long time ago. When I have achieved fame and success in the future, we will buy that yard. It may be a little small, but at least it is our own home."

Only Lu Yun had a gloomy face.

Seeing her like this, Zhao was surprised: "What's wrong with you?"

Lu Yun forced herself to cheer up: "When are we going?"

"We'll go today. We've asked someone to help us move our things."

"So soon!" Lu Yun was a thoughtful person and always felt that something was wrong. They had been living well together and the lady had never asked them to move out before. Why did it suddenly become like this? Was it because she rejected the marriage proposal?

"But is the lady angry?" she asked.

"How could that be? My cousin is very considerate and even asked your aunt to help you again."

Lv Yun sneered. If it was really that good, why did they remove all the maids? Never mind. She didn't believe that if she didn't live here, she would never have a good life in her life! She didn't say anything else. When the servants who moved the house came, she followed Zhao and Lv He to say goodbye to the lady.

The lady looked at her and smiled, "Even if they live outside, they are still our relatives. If you want anything, just tell us. Don't keep it to yourself. We will know about it sooner or later, and it will make you sad."

There was something else behind these words. Lu Yun raised her head and looked at the old lady, but saw that her eyes were cold and her face turned red all of a sudden.

Zhao smiled and said, "We are sorry to bother you, cousin. We just hope that He'er will be well and can repay you."

"You're welcome." The lady said, "Let's go now. It will be dark soon after we pack up."

The three Zhao family members said goodbye and left.

Zhang breathed a sigh of relief, she had always disliked them, luckily this time the lady somehow knew to ask them to leave, but it was still very frustrating that they had occupied a small courtyard for nothing.

But never mind. It's easier to invite a god than to send him away. Finally he's gone!

She immediately sent someone to clean up the place where Zhao and his family had lived and restored it to its original state. Zhang Jiwan naturally didn't know the ins and outs of the matter, and she told Chen Ningyu that it would be best for them to move out so that when others asked about it, they wouldn't have to say that they were still living under someone else's roof. This way, perhaps Lu Yun could marry into a good family.

Chen Ningyu only agreed with a few words and secretly felt fortunate that Zhang Jiwan had never fallen for Lu Yun, otherwise this would have been a big deal and the Zhang family would have been in turmoil. However, with Zhang Jiwan's personality, he would definitely stand up for the girl he liked. In a way, this was one of his strengths.

In mid-April, Madam Yang invited the lady to go to Lingquan Temple to burn incense. Lingquan Temple is located at the foot of Lingquan Mountain and has a history of more than 400 years. There are many eminent monks in the temple and the incense is very popular. Rich people in Beijing often like to go there. Not only can they make a wish, but even taking a walk on the road and just looking at the beautiful scenery is

refreshing.
The lady had been very worried about her granddaughters recently, and thought it would be nice to go there to pray for a smooth life. She was willing to do so. She asked someone to inform Zhang, Jiang, and the three girls that Cao Xiangmei was pregnant, so it was not convenient for her to go.
As a result, Zhang also said that she was not feeling well.
The lady did not force her and told her to stay at home.
Chen Ningrou said softly to Chen Ningyu, "Fourth sister, look at how well Third Sister is dressed today. She almost wears all her belongings, but she is still a million miles away from you!"
Chen Ningyu ignored her. What Chen Ninghua thought had nothing to do with her.
But today, Chen Ninghua really put in some effort.
Several people took a car to Lingquan Temple.

☆, Chapter 30 Old Hatred
This was not the first time that Chen Ningyu had gone to this temple. In the past, on the birthday of Guanyin, the lady would find time to go there. However, it seemed that the lady only believed in Guanyin and was not particularly interested in other Bodhisattvas. If it had not been for Madam

Yang's invitation today, the lady would not have gone easily.

The three girls were sitting in the same car. Chen Ninghua said nothing and sat upright. But Chen Ningrou could not sit still. When they got to the official road, she would lift the curtain to look out from time to time. Suddenly, she said to her two sisters, "I wonder if Marquis Wu Ding will come."

This was a sensitive question, Chen Ninghua pretended not to hear it. Chen Ningyu said, "He should come. He has been away for the past few years. It is rare for Madam Yang to come to Lingquan Temple. I am afraid she will accompany him."

Chen Ningrou nodded: "Fourth sister is right." Then she looked at Chen Ninghua, "Third sister, this dress is really beautiful, but what about the extra ones I made for you last time?"

Chen Ninghua replied perfunctorily: "Yes."

Chen Ningrou chuckled: "It's no wonder you come to my mother's place so often."

Chen Ninghua's face immediately turned pale. Chen Ningyu had long been tired of this kind of drama. To be honest, she didn't like it either. Chen Ningrou was just relying on her status as a legitimate daughter to bully her concubine sister. She leaned back and said lazily, "Let's take a rest. We have to go up the mountain and worship the Buddha again soon."

Although Lingquan Temple was built at the

foot of the mountain, it was still at a certain height. One had to walk up the stone steps to get there. If one took a sedan chair, it would be disrespectful to the Bodhisattva. It was said that even the emperor had to walk up, let alone them.

The two men stopped talking.

When they arrived at Lingquan Mountain, everyone got off the bus one after another.

Mother Hu pointed forward and said with a smile, "That's the carriage from the Marquis of Wuding's mansion. I'm afraid Madam Yang is waiting for you."

The lady said, "Let's go and take a look."

The people in front were indeed from the Wuding Marquis Mansion.

Today, Madam Yang came with Madam Tang, Yang Yanling, Yang Yankang, and Yang Fu. Seeing Madam Yang, she smiled and said, "Finally you are here. My dear sister, you are so slow."

"You are not as impetuous as me." The lady laughed.

Several younger generations greeted their elders, exchanged greetings, and then walked forward.

Madam Yang and the Mistress Tai walked in front.

Unlike the Yang family, which had no sons coming, Chen Xing of the Chen family had difficulty walking, and Chen Xiu no longer wanted to come to the temple due to the death of his first wife. As for Chen Li, Cao Xiangmei was pregnant, and he stayed at home with her on his rare day off. There was not a single son at all.

Therefore, Yang Yanling only went with Yang Yankang.

Tang looked at Chen Ninghua and thought to herself, if she dressed up well, she would be nice, but it was a pity that she was a concubine's daughter, who would like her? I'm afraid her efforts today were in vain.

Sure enough, when Chen Ninghua greeted her, she called Yang Yanling "Marquis", but Yang Yanling didn't even look at her. He just nodded slightly, and was very cold.

Chen Ningrou sneered beside him.

However, when Chen Ningyu went to see Yang Yanling, there was a smile in his eyes.

Others didn't pay much attention to this.

When they arrived at Lingquan Temple, there were young novice monks to greet them. Actually, they came here quite often, so soon a middle-aged monk came, who must be the deacon of the temple, and personally led them to burn incense.

When it was her turn to worship the Buddha, the old lady knelt down, kowtowed respectfully, and muttered something. Chen Ningyu heard some of it and was deeply moved.

When she made a wish, she also had some sincerity in her heart.

Yang Yanling stood not far away, and seeing her so pious, he couldn't help but raise the corner of his mouth. Could it be that she was praying to the Buddha to give her an obedient man?

But he doesn't believe in ghosts and gods.

Madam Yang asked him to go, but he refused. After finishing these tasks, Madam Yang and the other lady went to listen to a lecture, while the girls went to the south side of the temple to see the pagoda.

There is a world-famous tower in Lingquan Temple, which is eleven stories high. Different patterns are cast on the sides of each floor. The tower is covered with Buddha statues, and there are two majestic Vajra statues cast on the top of the tower. Under the sunlight, it is extremely majestic and awe-inspiring.

Danqiu had just gone to the toilet and just came back. She didn't look very well and was panting. It was obvious that she had run. She and Gu Qiu were whispering.

Soon, a shadow was cast over Gu Qiu's face as well.

Chen Ningyu was just marveling at the craftsman's skills. When he turned around and saw the two men in this state, he couldn't help but feel surprised and asked, "What's the matter?"

Gu Qiu came up and whispered, "Dan Qiu just said that he saw the Third Prince, and he seemed to be coming this way."

Chen Ningyu suddenly felt as disgusted as if he had eaten a fly.

How come I met him again?

Although Li Changluo has not taken any action during this period, she still thinks about him from time to time and is worried. As a result, she goes to Lingquan Temple and they meet again!

Does he really want to marry me?

Her interest in viewing the tower was gone in an instant.

Chen Ningrou suggested at this time: "Actually, there's nothing much to see in the tower. Let's go and see the moon laurels. They should all be bearing fruit."

Several people had no objection and turned back.

On the way, he met a young man. Judging from his clothes, he must be from a wealthy family. But his words and actions made people despise him. He stared at Chen Ningyu and almost drooled.

Originally, the girls were watching the pagoda and had asked the young monk to guard it earlier, but this man was able to come here, and it seemed that he was not a young man from an ordinary family.

An old woman questioned the young monk, and the young monk hesitated.

The young man ignored her, smiled lasciviously, and asked Chen Ningyu: "Whose family are you from?"

"We are from the Marquis of Wuding's Mansion. If you know what's best for you, you'd better leave quickly." A maid tried to scare him away by using the name of the Marquis' Mansion.

"Marquis Wuding's Mansion?" The young man's eyes lit up, "No wonder, I've heard of the good reputation of the fourth young lady of the Chen family, but I didn't expect it to be like this!" He walked straight over and said with a smile, "In fact, we are relatives, Fourth Young Lady Chen, I'd like to invite you to visit my mansion someday, okay?"

relative?

When Chen Ningyu thought of Li Changluo, he couldn't help but take a few steps back.

The young man saw that she was getting further away from him, so he walked faster and scolded her, "All of you go away. I'm just talking to my cousin. Cousin Chen, to be honest, my name is Yan Yuan, and I'm the son of Princess Huaying..."

Princess Huaying is the emperor's biological sister, so this person is Li Changluo's cousin.

Chen Ningyu's heart moved, and he no longer retreated: "Are you telling the truth?"

Yan Yuan was indeed the son of Princess Huaying. When he saw Chen Ningyu speaking, he thought she was looking at him differently, and said with great joy, "Yes, how could I lie to you, cousin? We are really relatives, we should get closer!"

Others came closer.

Unexpectedly, Chen Ningyu took a few steps forward and slapped him, shocking everyone around him and staring with their eyes wide open.

"You scoundrel, you have the audacity to pretend to be the eldest princess's son.

Get out of here!" Chen Ningyu shouted.

Yan Yuan had never been beaten since he was a child, and the only time he was beaten was really too serious. But this time, he was slapped by a girl, a girl he liked. How could he endure such a great humiliation? He jumped up immediately.

But Chen Ningyu went to the back again, and several strong women blocked her way, making it impossible for him to move forward.

"What are you all standing there for?" Yan Yuan shouted, "Catch this bitch!"

He also brought an entourage, but they were few in number, only two servants.

Seeing that the maids were all tall and strong, the servant was already scared. What kind of family is this Wuding Marquis's mansion? They all practice martial arts. If they go up, won't they be beaten? But Yan Yuan ordered, so he had to obey, and he had to fight for his life.

The result was just as they expected. In a short while, they were knocked to the ground by several old women and the whole place was in chaos.

Seeing that he could not take revenge, Yan Yuan cursed: "You little bitch, wait for me, I won't believe in Yan until I strip you naked!"

Chen Ningyu just looked at him and sneered.

She had wanted to slap this man in the face a long time ago. Now that he came to her door, how could she refuse? Not to mention that he could be of any use, it was a pity that she only slapped him once, which was too little!

Chen Ninghua also looked at Chen Ningyu in surprise. It was not the first time that Chen Ningyu encountered such a thing, but it was the first time that she slapped someone in the face, and in this way. If it were usual, she would just ignore it and would never take the initiative to meet it. Could it be that she originally wanted to... But why?

Chen Ninghua was puzzled.

☆, Chapter 31 Beauty is the root of trouble

There was a lot of noise here, and soon several people came. Yan Yuan saw one of them and shouted as if he had found a rescuer: "Third Prince, I have been looking for you everywhere but couldn't find you. Now you finally appear. Lend me some guards. I want to catch that bitch!"

Among the people who came was Li Changluo, but not only him, there were also Yang Yanling and Yang Yankang.

Actually, they met in the guest hall. Since the two old ladies went to talk, the Yang Yanling brothers had nothing to do, so they were drinking tea in the guest hall. They happened to meet Li Changluo, who said that he wanted to see the tower and invited them to go together. Yang Yankang was willing to go, and Yang Yanling gave him face, so they went together.

The result was this scene.

When Li Changluo heard the word "bitch", he frowned and asked, "Who are you talking about?"

"She!" Yan Yuan pointed his finger at Chen Ningyu, "She just hit..."

He suddenly stopped, too embarrassed to say it out loud, and could only grit his teeth, wishing he could eat Chen Ningyu.

Li Changluo's face darkened and he said calmly, "Jingzhou, they are the girls from the Marquis of Wuding's mansion. What nonsense are you talking about? Go quickly, or I'll tell Aunt Huaying that you've gotten into trouble again."

"What trouble? It was obviously that bitch's fault. I didn't touch her at all. Third Prince, just lend her to me." Yan Yuan refused to leave. He originally came to Lingquan Temple to find Li Changluo.

But how could Li Changluo agree to do so? Hearing Yan Yuan scolding Chen Ningyu as a bitch, he was already very angry and said in a stern tone, "What do you mean by lending it to you? It's good enough that I didn't arrest you. This is a quiet place in Buddhism, why don't you leave?"

Under normal circumstances, the two of them would have been on good terms and would often hang out together, but today Li Changluo refused to help him, and Yan Yuan couldn't help but feel strange.

At this time, Chen Ninghua said, "Forgive me for being so nosy. I'm afraid there is a misunderstanding. It was only because this young man said something rude that my fourth sister slapped him. I'm afraid she was really angry."

It turned out that it was Chen Ningyu who beat someone up. No wonder Yan Yuan refused to leave!

Li Changluo knew Yan Yuan well. In his opinion, Yan Yuan was extremely lustful. With his personality, it was not difficult to understand why Chen Ningyu would hit someone. It must be that Yan Yuan said something unpleasant to offend her.

But it is surprising that she has such a fierce side.

Li Changluo wondered what the scene was like at that time. She raised her jade hand, and I really didn't know what kind of style it was!

His eyes were a little blurry for a moment.

Yang Yanling was standing next to the two of them, and couldn't help but raise his brows.

How could he not see that it was all Chen Ningyu's beauty that was causing the trouble?

No wonder they say beautiful women are the root of trouble, as can be seen today.

Li Changluo said: "It's just a misunderstanding, Jingzhou, for my sake, let's just let it go."

"What?" Yan Yuan yelled, "She hit me, and

that's it? I told her my identity before, but she insisted that I was pretending. Who is she to dare to hit me?"

"Are your actions today in line with your status? You have brought this upon yourself. If you continue to persist, I will go back and tell my father!" Li Changluo was very serious.

The title of Princess Huaying is not scary, but the title of the emperor is scary. Yan Yuan's face changed immediately. The last time he was beaten in his life was by the emperor himself, and he almost broke his butt.

"Okay, I'm a magnanimous man!" Yan Yuan glared at Chen Ningyu fiercely and walked away angrily.

Li Changluo looked at Chen Ningyu with concern: "Ms. Chen Si, are you okay? Jingzhou is a bit reckless."

Chen Ningyu thought, aren't you reckless? She glanced at him, lowered her eyelids and said calmly: "I'm fine, thank you for your concern, Third Prince."

Just a casual remark made Li Changluo's heart beat faster.

The person in front of me exudes beauty in every move. Her delicate facial features are not painted in any way, but they are gorgeous and bright, like fireflies at night, and will never be ignored.

Li Changluo's eyes were glued to her, unable to move away. He looked at her and his voice became a little gentler: "I didn't expect you would come to see the tower. Speaking of which, this tower is really interesting. Have you been up there to take a look?"

The other three girls could see that Li Changluo was not asking them, so they remained silent.

But Chen Ningyu didn't want to chat with Li Changluo, so he replied, "The tower is too high, it's not convenient for us to go up. Third Prince, please take your time to look at the tower. We've been here for a while, so we have to go back."

This made Li Changluo very uncomfortable. Every time he wanted to get close to her, she avoided him. This time was no exception. But there were so many people around her, how could he take advantage of her?

After the people left, Li Changluo looked at Yang Yanling and said, "You two families are on good terms. What do you think of this Fourth Miss Chen?"

Yang Yanling told the truth: "She is very beautiful."

Li Changluo's face changed slightly, and he said with a fake smile: "Could it be that you have taken a fancy to her? It seems that it is not difficult to say that you, Marquis Wuding, want to marry her. I heard that your two families have this intention, but?"

Yang Yanling said: "It's just a visit to each other."

This answer is half-hearted.

Li Changluo's heart was filled with alarm. He took two steps and said slowly, "Miss Chen Si is really attractive at first sight."

Yang Yanling paused for a moment, smiled and said, "Who wouldn't be attracted by a beautiful woman?"

Li Changluo's breath was stuck in his throat and his face was as black as the bottom of a pot.

Yang Yankang broke out in a cold sweat.

I really don't know if his elder brother understood what Li Changluo meant. If it were him, he would definitely say that it was a blessing for Miss Chen that the Third Prince liked her. Isn't this the best strategy?

After Chen Ningyu returned, he was in a very bad mood.

This third prince is like a ghost that lingers around!

She couldn't even eat the delicious vegetarian food.

But Chen Ningrou came closer and whispered, "Fourth sister, the Third Prince is really a good person. Look, not only does he stand up for you, but he also speaks so gently and doesn't put on airs at all."

Chen Ningyu laughed twice and did not answer.

Chen Ningrou said to Chen Ninghua, "Third sister, don't you think so?"

Chen Ninghua thought for a moment, then looked at Chen Ningyu, who was picking up rice grains like pearls, and said, "It seems that he made a better impression than last time. After all, he is a prince, and I heard that the emperor likes him."

What is this? Chen Ningyu was surprised. Even Chen Ninghua spoke well of the Third Prince?

She threw her chopsticks on the table and said, "I'm full, you guys eat."

She stood up and left.

If Chen Ninghua or Chen Ningrou were in her current position, she would definitely not speak for the Third Prince!

At this moment, Chen Ningyu was really disappointed.

Mother Hu was reporting to the Madam Dowager. When she heard the words "Third Prince", the Madam Dowager's heart skipped a beat and she asked, "What did you say?"

"No, I came here with Marquis Wu Ding and Third Young Master Yang."

The lady comforted herself, "It must be a coincidence." Then she asked, "Did Ning Yu really slap that Master Yan?"

"Yes, those old women said they were dumbfounded. They had never seen someone as powerful as the fourth young lady. With one slap, Master Yan seemed to see stars and almost couldn't stand." Mother Hu was also surprised when she heard this.

Although Chen Ningyu does not give people the impression of being weak, she has a very good temper and always smiles like a spring breeze.

The lady sighed: "It's not her fault."

Only then did Mother Hu realize something.

"The Fourth Miss, the Eldest Princess, and the Second Master Fu have a very good relationship." She suddenly realized.

The lady stretched out her hand and pinched her brows: "I'm afraid that if her actions today were to be spread out, people would gossip about her."

Mother Hu said, "I told them to watch their mouths."

The lady nodded with satisfaction.

After returning to Furong Garden, Chen Ningyu sat by the pond and told Bai Tao to go to the kitchen to get some steamed buns to feed the fish. She could look at this in her spare time and her mood would be better.

Bai Tao came back after a while, looking unhappy.

"Is it not allowed to take some of this?" Chen Ningyu was surprised.

Bai Tao shook her head and hesitated for a while before saying, "I just went there and heard a few maids talking about the girl. It turns out that the girl beat Master Yan last time and the news has spread. People say that the girl is fierce and some say that they don't know what the master did to the girl."

Chen Ningyu didn't react much and just took the steamed bun.

Bi Tao said angrily: "Is there such a thing? It's obviously that Master Yan who is disrespectful and deserves to be beaten!"

"Yes, I wanted to beat him!" Danqiu said, "Why are these people talking nonsense? There are other people at the scene. What can Master Yan do? He just speaks dirty words."

Chen Ningyu threw the small piece of steamed bun into the pond and watched a group of fish swim over to grab the food: "It is true that I passed it, so it is not surprising that they passed it on."

"That will damage the girl's reputation!" Gu Qiu was anxious, "It must be some old woman who spread it. I don't believe that Master Yan would spread such a shameful thing!"

The Yang family would definitely not spread this rumor. Enemies sometimes come from within. Chen Ningyu shook off the debris on his hands and said, "Everything has a price. I hit someone in the heat of the moment, and I have to bear the consequences."

She walked in slowly.

Several maids looked at each other.

☆, Chapter 32 His Thoughts

The lady was also troubled by this matter. Logically, Mama Hu should have already given instructions to the servants, so how could outsiders know about it?

Could it be that someone from the Yang family spread the news? Or was it the Third Prince?

Just as the lady was thinking about it,

someone from the Princess's Mansion came and said they wanted to take Chen Ningyu over.

The princess must have also found out about it, so the lady-in-waiting went to call Chen Ningyu over.

"Do you want to go now?" she asked.

Chen Ningyu nodded: "My aunt is here to pick me up, so I will go." She sat down next to the lady and apologized, "I was wrong last time. I shouldn't have caused trouble. Grandmother, please don't be angry."

The lady sighed, "You have always been a cautious girl, but you ruined your reputation because of that playboy. I feel sorry for you."

"If a reputation is really that easily ruined, what's the point of coming? Besides, everyone in Kyoto knows what kind of person Yan Yuan is," Chen Ningyu said, "Grandma, don't worry."

The lady nodded and gave her a few more instructions.

Chen Ningyu went to Princess Huiying's mansion.

The lady sighed, leaned on the couch, and said to Mother Hu, "We still have to marry Ning Yu off. We can't be too picky now. If there is a suitable one, we have to decide quickly."

"But the third girl hasn't decided yet."

The lady pinched her brows and said, "Ning Hua is going to get married, and I have been looking for someone for a long time. Now, we can just do it together with Ning Yu. It's okay for two girls to get married in the same year. Ning Hua will be married a few days earlier."

Mother Hu said: "That's right, it's a double happiness."

The lady went to call Zhang.

Chen Ningyu arrived at the eldest princess's house. When the eldest princess saw her, the first thing she said was: "Did you really beat that bitch?"

"Yes." Chen Ningyu smiled, "It's a pity that the blow was not hard enough."

"Okay, well done!" The eldest princess was very happy, "You are indeed worthy of being my niece!"

Fu Cheng reminded: "Madam, that's not what people say outside."

"Why do you care about those brainless people outside? How can Ning Yu still be married?" The eldest princess smiled and patted Chen Ningyu's hand, "Don't worry, my aunt will make the decision for you who you want to marry."

Chen Ningyu has always been impressed by the eldest princess's toughness.

Fu Chaoqing came in and saw Chen Ningyu with complicated eyes.

"Second cousin." She smiled at him.

"Ayu, does your hand hurt?" he asked.

"What?" Chen Ningyu didn't understand.

"Don't hit people randomly next time." Fu Chaoqing said seriously, "He's like this, why dirty your hands."

Without waiting for Chen Ningyu to answer, the princess said, "Why dirty your hands? That damn thing, I wish I could kill him! But when he saw me, he ran away like a rabbit. I couldn't hit him even if I wanted to."

"It's an old thing, why bring it up again?" Fu Cheng looked at Fu Chaoqing, actually he couldn't hide his anger.

If it weren't for Yan Yuan, Fu Chaoqing wouldn't have been like this. It was said to be an accident, but in fact it was man-made.

But, can they really kill Yan Yuan?

Fu Cheng sighed secretly.

Chen Ningyu didn't want to be trapped in this heavy atmosphere, so she smiled and said, "Aunt, I'll make a few pairs of shoes for you when I have time, you can try them."

The princess smiled and said, "Why do you need to try it? You are the best at making this and it is comfortable to wear. Come, come to my room. I have also got some fabrics that are most suitable for making new clothes for you."

The eldest princess would leave any good things to Chen Ningyu, treating her like a real daughter.

The two talked for a while before Chen Ningyu came out.

Fu Chaoyun did not return until the evening. Like the eldest princess, she praised Chen

Ningyu a lot and then took her to find Fu Chaoqing.

"Shall we go fishing later? I tell you, fishing is better in the evening."

Chen Ningyu laughed: "If I don't come, you won't go fishing?"

"What's the point of being alone?" Fu Chaoyun said, "When you're not here, Chaoqing won't talk to me. He's alone in the study, and I don't know what he does all day. Where can he find so many books to read?"

He didn't like reading and learned martial arts with Fu Cheng when he was young. In his eyes, Fu Chaoqing was just a nerd.

Chen Ningyu said: "If you really want to read all the books in the world, you will never be able to finish them in your lifetime."

"Why do you say the same thing as Chao Qing?" Fu Chaoyun snorted, "I find it boring anyway."

As they were talking, the two arrived at the door of Fu Chaoqing's study.

Fu Chaoyun went straight in and said, "Why aren't you coming out when Ah Yu is here?"

Fu Chaoqing put down the book in his hand: "She just went to talk to mother."

Chen Ningyu rarely came to his study. Looking around, she felt that the number of books was increasing day by day. The study was originally three rooms connected together, all of which were filled with books. Although she also loved reading, she was far inferior to Fu Chaoqing.

It's a pity that he was in poor health, otherwise, with the emperor's appreciation of him, if it weren't for that cold winter and the incident of Yan Yuan pushing him into the water, he might have already been an official in the court!

But now, Yan Yuan was fine, he was just taught a lesson by the emperor himself, and what about Fu Chaoqing? How could he realize his ambitions?

Chen Ningyu's heart couldn't help but ache.

It was not unfair at all that Yan Yuan was beaten by her!

"Ayu, let's go." Fu Chaoyun had already called Fu Chaoqing to go fishing.

Chen Ningyu suddenly remembered the jade mantis and apologized, "Second cousin, the jade mantis you gave me was broken."

Fu Chaoqing was stunned for a moment before he said, "It's okay. I'll take you there next time I see something interesting."

Fu Chaoyun walked a few steps to a shelf in the study, took out a jade mantis and said, "Don't you have another one? Just give this to Ah Yu."

This jade mantis is very similar to the last one.

Chen Ningyu's heart started beating fast.

Fu Chaoqing looked at the Jade Mantis, but he looked calm, and asked Chen Ningyu: "Ayu, do you want it?"

Chen Ningyu didn't know what to say for a moment.

These jade mantises appear to be a pair, one for her and one for him.
Why did he buy two in the first place?
Maybe, it was just an unintentional act?
She shook her head slowly: "Since it's yours to keep, how can I take it away from you?"
"If you like it, just take it. Why are you being so polite to him?" Fu Chaoyun stuffed the jade mantis into her hand and said, "It's just a little thing. I have a lot of them. Why don't you go to my room and take a look. If you like something, take it away."
Chen Ningyu held the jade mantis and his palms felt hot.
Fu Chaoqing looked down at her.
When their eyes met, Chen Ningyu felt that his eyes were like a dark ocean. Her shadow was reflected in his pupils, making her look lonely and a little helpless.
In the past two years, she has never understood his thoughts.
She didn't understand him, so she pretended to know nothing. It didn't seem to matter whether she liked him or not.
Fu Chaoqing said calmly: "It's really just a little thing, not valuable at all, I'll just give it to you."
He found a brocade box and asked her to put the jade mantis in it.
He closed the lid again and reminded, "Keep it safe this time."
She hummed and took it.

The three then went fishing.

Unexpectedly, just as Fu Chaoyun threw the fishing rod into the water, he saw Li Changluo coming towards him not far away.

Fu Chaoyun was shocked and said to Chen Ningyu, "Ayu, go back quickly."

But it was too late, Li Changluo had already walked in front of them.

"Why are you here, Third Prince?" Fu Chaoyun's tone was not as polite as before.

Li Changluo frowned. He had just learned that Chen Ningyu came to the Princess's Mansion, and he could not help but follow her. However, when he saw the Princess, her expression was the same as Fu Chaoyun's, very unwelcome.

What's wrong with this family?

The crown prince hasn't been appointed yet, and he is one of the strong candidates. Aren't they afraid?

Could a girl like Chen Ningyu be more valuable than their future?

Li Changluo raised his chin: "Why, I can't come?"

"Not really." Fu Chaoyun calmed down a little, "But the Third Prince should be very busy. I wonder how he has time to spare. I haven't seen you at home for several years."

Li Changluo smiled and said, "I was negligent in the past. We should still visit each other more often."

His eyes fell on Chen Ningyu's face again.

This face now appears in his mind more and

more frequently, making it impossible for him to sleep at night and he feels extremely itchy!

Fu Chaoqing took two steps forward, stopped Chen Ningyu and said, "Since the Third Prince is here, it is not appropriate to talk here. Why don't we go to the main hall?"

"Yes, yes." Fu Chaoyun also said.

Li Changluo didn't leave.

"Seeing you guys having so much fun fishing, it's been a while since I've had such fun." He walked over, bent down and picked up the fishing rod that originally belonged to Fu Chaoqing, and smiled at Chen Ningyu, "It turns out that the fourth girl can fish, too."

Chen Ningyu already hated him to a certain extent. How could there be such a entangled person! But he was a prince after all. Chen Ningyu knew the importance of his identity and did not dare to act rashly.

She replied: "Not really a good fisherman."

"So we can fish now?" Li Changluo pointed to her position with his eyes, "Sit down."

Sit next to him? How could Chen Ningyu agree?

Just then, the eldest princess arrived. Just now, when Li Changluo heard that the two brothers and Chen Ningyu were fishing in the pond, he ran away. The eldest princess had no time to stop him, and she also ran over in a hurry.

"Chang Luo, why don't you say a few more

words to your aunt?" The eldest princess said with a smile, "It's just fishing, why are you in such a hurry?"

In front of the princess, Li Changluo didn't dare to be too presumptuous, and quickly stood up again: "I was anxious for a moment, but I also wanted to play fishing."

"Your temper is still the same as when you were a child." The princess said, "Chaoqing, Chaoyun, then you can accompany Chang Luo for a while." She looked at Chen Ningyu again, "Ningyu, I have something to ask you, come with me."

Chen Ningyu was rescued by the princess and quickly followed.

Seeing the beauty walking away, Li Changluo was extremely annoyed.

It seems that this method doesn't work!

The princess turned around and held Chen Ningyu's hand, and said softly, "Were you scared just now?"

"Luckily my aunt is here." Chen Ningyu bit her lip. "To be honest with you, I am also worried about this matter. Last time at Lingquan Temple, not only Yan Yuan was there, but the Third Prince was also there."

"What?" The eldest princess widened her eyes. "This damn boy is actually staring at you?"

Otherwise, why would he go wherever Chen Ningyu was?

Chen Ningyu didn't dare to think so at

first, but today, it seems to be the case. She has run into a stalker this time.

"Aunt, what should I do?" she asked the eldest princess for help.

She was really afraid that one day the Third Prince would go to ask the Emperor for help, and the Emperor might even agree. By then, the Emperor's order would be hard to disobey, and her family would have to marry her to Li Changluo. If that happened, would she be able to live a good life?

☆, Chapter 33 The Best of Both Worlds

The eldest princess did not speak immediately.

She was born into a royal family and knew that some things were not as simple as imagined.

If it were an ordinary family, she would only need to go to her brother and the problem would not be difficult to solve. But now, her brother is the emperor, the most honorable person in the world, and no one can disobey him!

She was silent for a long time before she said, "I didn't know Chang Luo was so persistent. I need to think about this matter carefully. Don't be afraid."

Because Li Changluo had not taken any action after the Lantern Festival and the Queen was selecting a daughter-in-law as usual, she thought everything was fine. But now it seems that her nephew is possessed!

Chen Ningyu nodded and said, "It's enough to have your words, auntie. But this matter is unusual, you should be more cautious." She paused, "Auntie, I beat Master Yan last time, maybe you can do something about it."

The princess was startled, then she realized that Chen Ningyu had a lot on her mind, and couldn't help but sigh: "Ningyu, you are so smart, you must not let that damn boy get away with it! Auntie has her own ideas." She patted her hand again and sighed: "I called you here by mistake today, I never thought this would happen, you should go back this afternoon."

Chen Ningyu shook her head and said, "I'd better stay a few more days. I was in a hurry to go back last time. Fortunately, grandma didn't ask any questions. If it happens again this time, I'm afraid grandma will get suspicious. I don't want to make her worry too much. Besides, the third prince has come once, so he won't come again every day."

If so, he must be crazy!

The princess thought for a moment and said, "You are right. Even if you know about this, there is nothing you can do except marry you off."

Chen Ningyu did consider this.

If they were afraid that she would marry into the royal family and were in a hurry to marry her off, it would be a tragic thing if she married the wrong person. In any case, she didn't want to gamble with her life.

Ever since Chen Ningyu left, Li Changluo no longer had the heart to fish, so he just stayed for a while and then left.

Fu Chaoyun threw the fishing rod into the pond and cursed, "How dare he chase someone into my house? If he wasn't a prince, I would have beaten him up long ago! Beat him till his teeth are all over the floor!"

He finished speaking, but no one responded.

Fu Chaoyun looked back and saw Fu Chaoqing staring at the pond, motionless, as if he didn't hear him either.

"Xiao Lan, what do you think we should do?" he asked.

Fu Chaoqing slowly lifted up the fishing rod and said calmly, "You can't eat hot tofu in a hurry."

"Is the Third Prince a hot tofu?" Fu Chaoyun said, "Our Ah Yu is the hot tofu, and now the Third Prince wants to eat her!"

Fu Chaoqing couldn't help but smile: "Brother, let me ask you, if the Third Prince had a way to marry Ah Yu immediately, would he still do this?"

"Well," Fu Chaoyun scratched his head, "probably not. If he could marry A-Yu, he would have done it long ago. After marrying her, he would do whatever he wants..." This was a bit vulgar, so he quickly stopped talking.

But Fu Chaoqing's face still sank, just like the sky that was clear just a moment ago suddenly started raining.

Seeing him like this, Fu Chaoyun frowned and said, "I always say whatever I think, why do you care about it?"

His younger brother had changeable moods and he always accidentally annoyed him.

Fu Chaoqing threw away the fishing rod: "I can't explain it to you clearly."

He stood up and left.

Fu Chaoyun was so angry at him that he was in a bad mood. He returned to the house and threw his coat on the ground.

Yu had been waiting for him since early morning and asked hurriedly, "Has the Third Prince left?"

"gone!"

Yu heaved a sigh of relief, patted her chest and said, "It would be scary if I kept it forever. What would Ning Yu do then?"

Fu Chaoyun slammed the table and said, "I've never seen such a shameless person. Ah Yu obviously doesn't like him, but he still won't let go. He doesn't even look at himself. Ugh!"

Yu said: "The third prince is also quite good-looking."

Fu Chaoyun glared: "You want to make me angry too?"

Yu laughed again: "Actually, I think there is a good way."

"What method?" Fu Chaoyun asked hurriedly.

Yu said: "Why not let Xiao Lan marry Ning Yu? Isn't this the best of both worlds?"

She had noticed early on that there was

something going on between the two of them, but she was still not quite sure. She made this suggestion today, firstly to share some of the burden with Fu Chaoyun, and secondly to test Fu Chaoyun.

As a wife, she doesn't want Fu Chaoyun to really have someone else in his heart.

Fu Chaoyun was stunned for a while before he said, "What nonsense are you talking about? We treat Ah Yu as our sister, and Xiao Lan is the same. How can we marry Ah Yu?"

Mrs. Yu laughed: "You are not Xiao Lan, do you know what he is thinking? My husband, you are a man, not as careful as a woman. I can see that Xiao Lan likes Ah Yu, you really didn't notice it at all?"

Fu Chaoyun fell into silence.

After Yu's advice, it turns out that Fu Chaoqing treats Chen Ningyu differently. He treats her much better than he treats his brother!

But is this a love between men and women? He couldn't tell.

He could have been as nice to Chen Ningyu as Fu Chaoqing was to her, but he was indeed a little careless.

He had doubts: "If Xiaolan liked Ah Yu, she could have married her long ago if she just told her mother. Why didn't he tell her?"

Yu was overjoyed. It seemed that Fu Chaoyun didn't like Chen Ningyu!

She thought for a moment and said, "Maybe it's because of the Chen family. Didn't mother stop associating with the Chen family a long time ago? If Xiaolan marries Ah Yu, then the two families will be in-laws. Maybe he didn't mention it because he was worried about this. Why don't you test him first?"

Fu Chaoyun listened and thought that this was possible. He happily hugged Yu and said, "Madam, you are right. I will ask him when I get a chance!"

Yu felt relieved, and she no longer had to feel jealous when looking at Chen Ningyu from now on.

She is just Fu Chaoyun's sister.

The next morning, Fu Cheng went to the yard to practice boxing. The eldest princess had just finished her meal and was thinking about Chen Ningyu when Fu Chaoqing came to pay his respects.

There was no color on his face, it was so white that it was almost transparent, but his eyes were still shining, brighter than the stars in the sky.

The eldest princess was frightened by his appearance and asked hurriedly, "What's wrong with you? Are you feeling uncomfortable?"

"No, I just didn't sleep well."

The princess breathed a sigh of relief: "Is it because of Ning Yu's matter? I am also very upset."

Fu Chaoqing said: "I have a way, you can try it."

"Oh? Tell me about it quickly." The eldest

princess said, "You have always had many ideas. No one in the family can compare with you."

Fu Chaoqing smiled and said, "Last time I heard from mother, Princess Huaying wanted to be a matchmaker, right? Why don't you go and tell her that the Third Prince has long been interested in Ah Yu and wants to marry her."

The eldest princess was stunned. What did this mean?

"It just so happens that Ah Yu beat Yan Yuan." Fu Chaoqing explained, "I'm afraid Princess Huaying must have been angry a long time ago."

The princess suddenly realized and clapped her hands, saying, "Chaoqing, it seems that you and Ning Yu have the same idea. She also asked me to do something about it yesterday, but I haven't thought it through yet. Now that you're here, I understand."

Fu Chaoqing smiled slightly: "Ayu is very smart."

But he still underestimated her. It turned out that she thought so far ahead at that time.

The eldest princess praised this method as the best. She was naturally optimistic and felt that the problem could be solved before she even started.

But Fu Chaoqing is not such a person. Although he thinks this trick should be useful, when he thinks of Li Changluo and his determined look, he always feels that things may not go so smoothly.

Chen Ningyu stayed in the Princess's Mansion for four or five days before returning.

During this period, Li Changluo never came again.

But that doesn't mean he won't take action in the future, so Chen Ningyu's heart was really in turmoil. Since she came here, this was the first time she felt truly scared, the fear of not being able to control her destiny!

Fortunately, she still had people to rely on, which somewhat reduced her worries and gave her more courage.

As for the eldest princess, she went to the palace early in the morning to get the news. When she heard that Princess Huaying had entered the palace that day, she immediately changed her clothes and went out.

Princess Huaying had just arrived at the Queen's place, and before she had said a few words, the eldest princess also arrived. The two of them had another fight with guns and sticks, which was very boring.

Mrs. Jia got tired of hearing this and served tea to see off the guests.

Princess Huaying was extremely annoyed. She originally wanted to be a matchmaker, but was disturbed by the princess. She was so angry that she glared at the princess and said, "Why did you come to the palace without anything to do?"

The eldest princess raised her eyebrows: "Only you are allowed to come, but I can't come? And you are only allowed to be a matchmaker, but I can't?"

Upon hearing this, Princess Huaying became wary: "Why, you also have a good candidate?"

"I am a very good choice." The eldest princess provocatively said, "You don't need to mention this matter in front of the Queen next time. The third prince likes my niece very much, and will marry her sooner or later. She, don't do this anymore!"

"That fourth girl from the Chen family?" Princess Huaying was furious. "Well, I haven't said anything yet, and you still dare to mention it? That fourth girl dared to hit my Yuan'er! Is there anyone in the family who educates her?"

The eldest princess was amused. "Then go ahead and make a scene. Who knows whose child is so ill-mannered and embarrassed? My niece didn't believe it was your son. Who wouldn't beat him for such behavior? If you don't accept it, let's go to the emperor to reason with him."

Princess Huaying's face turned red and white, and she was very embarrassed.

In fact, she really had no choice but to refrain from making trouble. Otherwise, with her personality, she would have gone to the Yongchun Marquis' Mansion long ago. But it was a Marquis' Mansion after all. If the news got out and the Emperor found out, what would happen if Yan Yuan was used to getting into trouble?

She could only let Yan Yuan swallow his anger.

But unexpectedly, the third prince actually fell in love with Chen Ningyu!

Princess Huaying was very nervous.

Why was she so diligent in matchmaking? Wasn't it because she wanted to place her own people with the Third Prince? Now, one of the Second Prince and the Third Prince must be the Crown Prince, and she thought that she had to build good relations with both sides.

After the princess finished speaking, she walked away arrogantly.

Princess Huaying spat at her from behind and went back.

But these past few days, she has been feeling a little uneasy.

Chen Ningyu's reputation had long been rumored in the capital, but their mansion was very low-key and seldom let the girl go out, so many people had not seen her with their own eyes. Princess Huaying thought about it and called Yan Yuan over.

Yan Yuan picked up a fruit and ate it.

Princess Huaying said, "Stop eating. I want to ask you, what does Miss Chen Si look like?"

Yan Yuan was stunned: "Why are you asking this?"

"You go ahead and say it."

She said in a delicate voice, "Madam, I

have learned a new song and will sing it for you."

Chen Ningyu was so shocked that she almost fell down.

What kind of dream is this!

She wiped the cold sweat from her forehead and let out a breath.

Unexpectedly, a hand reached out and touched her waist. Chen Ningyu was still thinking about the dream and screamed in fright.

"What's wrong?" Yang Yanling was frightened and sobered up. He stood up, hugged her from behind and asked, "Why are you sitting here?"

"Nothing." Chen Ningyu turned sideways and lay on his chest. His body was warm, and she finally regained a sense of security. She whispered, "It was just a nightmare."

"Are you scared?" Yang Yanling hugged her tighter.

"I dreamed about Yinling." She pulled up the quilt, revealing half of her head, and tilted her head to look at Yang Yanling, "How do you think Yinling died, sir?"

"There should be a result tomorrow. Manager Luo and the others are still interrogating them." He stroked her hair and coaxed her, "Go to sleep quickly. It's still early. I'll hold you. Don't be afraid."

But Chen Ningyu couldn't sleep, and she kept moving in his arms.

"What's wrong? Why don't we get up and eat something before going back to sleep?" Yang

Yanling asked.

"No need." Chen Ningyu drew a few strokes on his chest with her fingers, "I want to ask you something, Lord Marquis."

Yang Yanling laughed: "If you want to ask, just ask. Why are you being so shy?"

"But I'm afraid the Marquis will be angry again."

"You're asking me something. How can I be angry?" Yang Yanling was surprised. "Go ahead."

"Oh?" Madam Yang said, not seeming to take it too seriously. "You are in charge of this matter. Why do you want me to decide? Just do it yourself. I am not kidding when I leave it to you."

"But it's not just that." Chen Ningyu said, "Over the years, the income of the manor alone has been reduced by 70,000 to 80,000 taels, and it's not all taken by the managers."

Madam Yang was shocked: "So many?"

"That's all. Most of them were taken by..." Chen Ningyu lowered her head slightly. "My mother and Second Aunt took them."

Although Madam Yang had expected that the two must have something going on, she had never expected that they would secretly take so much money! She immediately became furious and sent someone to call Tang and Fan.

When Tang and Fan arrived and saw Yang Yanling and Chen Ningyu, their hearts skipped a beat.

Mrs. Fan was the first to laugh and said, "Oh, you two, one just came back from Yingzhou, and the other just came back from the farm, why don't you take a rest?"

"Even if you take a break, you still have to deal with things." Chen Ningyu replied calmly.

Tang asked, "What's the matter?"

"The annual income of the manor is several tens of thousands of taels of silver short. We have to settle the accounts." Chen Ningyu ordered, "Bring all the managers up here."

The two of them turned pale when they heard this.

Madam Yang looked at them and asked, "Do you have anything to say?"

"Those stewards are too greedy. Not only do we support them in our mansion, but we also give them generous monthly allowances, yet they are still not satisfied?" Fan shouted, spitting out her mouth. "They should be punished. I think we should just sell them off. People like them cannot be kept in our mansion."

He acted really hard, and Chen Ningyu watched coldly.

Tang said the same thing.

Mrs. Yang became more and more disappointed with them.

As soon as the managers came up, they knelt down and kowtowed.

Madam Yang said, "Tell me, what happened?"

Tang and Fan stared at them intently.

Manager Wu was the first to give instructions, and he was also the first to answer: "In the past, the first and second wives were in charge. Every time they came back, they asked me to tamper with the account books, and the extra money was given to the two wives."

Fan was so angry that she wanted to jump up: "You blind man, when did I ever tell you that? Are you trying to frame me? Tell me the truth, was it someone who instigated you to say that?"

The person who instigated this must be Chen Ningyu.

Manager Wu shook his head: "Even if you said that, I dare not speak nonsense. Please let the Madam make the decision! I was also forced to do so. The Madam was often away from home during those years, so I had to obey the two ladies in everything."

Fan refused to admit it: "Mother, I didn't do that. These villains are just fence-sitters. They will say whatever you want them to say. Where can I put all this money? Mother, you know me well..."

She was just about to show her ability to deny her mistakes, but she was stabbed in the back. Tang said, "Mother, I was confused for a moment and listened to my sister-in-law. I feel really guilty now. I shouldn't have been so foolish as to let my sister-in-law persuade me!"

"What, what did you say?" Fan's eyes widened.

She thought that Tang and she were on the same front, but it turned out that Tang had already made plans.

"You, you are accusing me too?" Fan pointed at Tang's nose, but didn't know what to say. She couldn't say that Tang also took a lot of money, wouldn't that be the same as admitting it?

Mrs. Fan was so anxious that she almost died.

At this moment, Yang Dongping arrived with two girls.

Madam Yang frowned: "Jing'er, Fu'er, go out first."

Mother Sun asked the maid to take Yang Fu and Yang Jing to the next room.

Yang Dongping said, "Mother, my wife would never do such a thing. Someone must have planned this, otherwise why would she stay in the village for so many days? I don't know how many evil schemes she has come up with. Besides, these stewards are not that hard to bribe."

When enemies meet, their eyes turn red. Yang Yanling sneered, "Second uncle has been recuperating at home all day, so he must not know what Second Aunt did. Could it be that these tens of thousands of taels of silver disappeared out of thin air? Ning Yu hadn't married yet, and I was not in the capital. Whoever swallowed it, only knows!"

Yang Dongping's face suddenly showed anger:

"How dare you say that about your second aunt?"

"Whoever took it is the bitch. Why, Second Uncle admits it now?" Yang Yanling stood up and sat in the seat of honor next to Madam Yang, and said in a deep voice, "The country has its laws, and the family has its rules. If the thief is not removed now, there will be no peace in the family in the future! Now that the evidence is conclusive, I think Second Aunt should admit it, so as to avoid physical pain later."

Fan was so scared that she sat down on the ground.

Are you going to force her to confess?

Yang Dongping was furious: "Don't push your luck!"

"What's wrong with me being too demanding? Why don't we take it to court and let the officials judge the case?" Yang Yanling raised his eyebrows.

Yang Dongping knew that Yang Yanling would never give in, so he went to ask Madam Yang: "Mother, you must not believe what these managers say! Which farm doesn't rely on the weather for food? How can you say that the income is the same every year? Mother, when you are not in the capital, you have to take care of me and raise the children. It's not easy! I have been useless all these years, and only you are with me. Mother, please think twice!"

After hearing this, Madam Yang did have some reaction.

Although Fan was wrong, she did work hard. While she was hesitating, Tang suddenly called out, "These past few days, my sister-in-law has been busy moving money around. Mother, they've put it all in a big yard on Jixian Street. That yard was also bought by my sister-in-law. If you don't believe me, ask someone to search it."

Fan almost vomited blood. She got up from the ground and pointed at Tang and said, "How much better can you be? You have a yard in the capital, don't you want me to count them for you?"

"No matter how much I have, it's not as much as you. It was you who instigated me that day, saying that since our mother was not around, we didn't have to be restricted. Wasn't that what you said? I swear to heaven!" Tang pointed to the sky.

It's really a dog-eat-dog situation, both of them end up with a mouth full of fur.

Chen Ningyu also understood why Tang wanted to turn against them. Someone had to take the blame. Anyway, she had investigated the matter thoroughly, and Tang must have known in his heart that he could not escape.

Upon seeing this, Madam Yang hurriedly asked people to search.

Fan was desperate and knelt down with a thud: "Mother, please forgive me this time for my many years of service. I will hand over all the money. Please consider that our three children have not yet started a family."

Madam Yang sighed deeply.

Yang Yanling said coldly: "I can spare you, but you need to move out tomorrow. You will get every penny you deserve, but you will never set foot in this place again."

"What!" Yang Dongping was shocked.

Even Chen Ningyu did not expect that Yang Yanling would propose separation at this time.

Madam Yang also looked at Yang Yanling in surprise.

"Yanling, isn't this a bit..." Madam Yang advised, "They are your second uncle and second aunt. Our family has never had this practice of dividing the family."

Yang Yanling said sternly, "Grandma, please move."

Madam Yang then went with him to the inner room.

Yang Yanling then said, "It's not that I have to split up the family, but my second aunt has become a traitor and my second uncle is restless. They will definitely drag down the Marquisate in the future, and then it will be too late."

Madam Yang was surprised: "What do you mean?"

"Didn't my second uncle want to get back on his feet? Grandmother, do you know who he went to find?" Yang Yanling sneered, "Uncle Gongshun."

Madam Yang's face changed drastically.

This Earl Gongshun is the elder brother of the third prince's biological mother. When the concubine gave birth to the third prince, the emperor conferred her brother the title of Earl Gongshun. Later, after the concubine passed away, Earl Gongshun was quite capable and accomplished several things in the past few years. The emperor still valued him. But Madam Yang was originally worried that their mansion would be involved with the third prince. Now, one concubine is not enough, and even the second son has started to get confused!

"Grandma, I am thinking about the whole Yang family. If you don't believe me, you can ask my second uncle's followers." Yang Yanling was very firm. "If grandma really doesn't agree, maybe I will be the only one to move out."

Having said that, Madam Yang also believed that Yang Yanling was not lying.

Madam Yang nodded and walked out.

At this moment, she seemed to have aged a few years.

"Mother!" Yang Dongping could see it and couldn't help but feel anxious.

Madam Yang said calmly, "Dongping, at your age, you should support the family on your own. Let's separate in a few days. I won't bother with the second daughter-in-law. You two should live your life well."

The outcome has been decided.

Yang Dongping was dejected.

Back in the yard, Chen Ningyu looked at Yang Yanling again and again.

Yang Yanling smiled and said, "Why, do you

think it's so sudden?"

"Yeah, I haven't even thought about proposing a separation right now!"

"You did a good job. It wouldn't have been easy if it hadn't happened today." Yang Yanling held her shoulders and said, "I said you are a good wife. Even if I'm not in the capital, you can still help."

Chen Ningyu smiled and said, "You are the one who asked me to do it. But what did the Marquis say to Grandmother? Is Grandmother willing to divide the family?"

"You want to know?"

"Of course!" Chen Ningyu was very curious.

"It all depends on your performance tonight."

Chen Ningyu was speechless for a moment, and slapped him on the arm with his hand: "You are so bad, and you are still keeping me in suspense!"

Yang Yanling laughed out loud.

"In fact, I sent people to keep an eye on Second Uncle. I knew he wouldn't be so quiet, so I told Grandmother just now that he went to see Earl Gongshun." Seeing Chen Ningyu's expression as if he was wondering who Earl Gongshun was, Yang Yanling explained, "He is the biological brother of the Third Prince's biological mother."

Chen Ningyu suddenly realized: "It seems that Second Uncle really wants to help the Third Prince win the position of Crown Prince! If he..."

Seeing her pause, Yang Yanling raised his

eyebrows.

"If Second Uncle knew about you and the Third Prince, it would be bad. He would definitely help the Third Prince deal with you!"

Yang Yanling hummed, "Indeed, so I have to get him out as soon as possible to prevent him from doing anything behind my back."

Chen Ningyu breathed a sigh of relief: "Fortunately it worked. The more I think about it, the scarier it gets."

"What are you afraid of, I'm here with you?" He lowered his head and pecked her rosy lips.

Chen Ningyu naturally put her arms around his neck and tilted her head back to kiss him on the lips.

Yang Yanling looked at her picturesque face close before him, and for some reason he suddenly thought of what Fu Chaoqing had said, and he felt a little bad. It was not difficult to understand what Fu Chaoqing said, as it was obvious that he liked Chen Ningyu.

He also warned him to be nicer to Chen Ningyu!

But she was his wife, did she need others to warn her? Besides, wasn't he good enough to her?

Yang Yanling was upset.

He frowned and asked Chen Ningyu: "Do you think I treat you well?"

Chen Ningyu was stunned.

"Answer me." Yang Yanling was very serious.

Chen Ningyu said: "It will be fine naturally."

In her opinion, Yang Yanling met the requirements. She didn't have high expectations for this marriage, but Yang Yanling was obviously satisfactory. However, she was a little puzzled as to why Yang Yanling asked this question.

"That's all." Yang Yanling tapped her head. "You still have a conscience, but remember, you can't lose it in the future."

What are you talking about?

Chen Ningyu was still confused.

The next day, Yang Yanling went to court early. After getting up, Chen Ningyu went to pay her respects to Madam Yang. As soon as she arrived, she found Yang Dongping and his wife there. When they saw her, there was undisguised hatred in their eyes.

It looks like he's here to beg for mercy again.

But there was no way Madam Yang could take back what she said yesterday.

The two men had no choice but to leave again in dismay.

Madam Yang said to Chen Ningyu, "Yanling is the Marquis after all. Even if the family is divided, the first share will still be his. However, your second uncle is still idle and has not found a job. In the future, Yanshou will start a family, and Fu'er and Jing'er will also get married. We need to prepare those betrothal gifts and dowries, which will be quite expensive."

Although the second house disappointed Madam Yang, she could not be harsh on her son. Chen Ningyu said, "Grandmother, please divide it as you see fit. As for the Marquis, I will persuade him."

Now she just wants the separation to go smoothly, and doesn't want to care too much about anything else.

How could a family like them be short of money?

Madam Yang nodded.

Chen Ningyu came out and met Yang Fu again.

Yang Fu saw that she was not in a good mood either, and complained: "I thought my sister-in-law was a good person, but I didn't expect her to be so unscrupulous! We are also close friends on weekdays, is my sister-in-law so heartless? Now that the family has been divided, my father's leg has not healed yet, how can my mother and our three children live?"

If they separate, everyone will know that they are not on good terms with Marquis Wuding, which means they are leaving this mansion and will have to rely on themselves for everything in the future.

Chen Ningyu sighed. It was something that was clearly known to her, and she didn't want to explain it.

It was normal for Yang Fu to behave like this after such a sudden change. She left without saying a word.

Tang and Yang Yankang saw this and walked over from the side. Tang walked in front of her and said, "Daughter-in-law, you are really amazing this time. I did something wrong, but I don't blame you. We will still be a family in the future."

"A family is a family. I just hope my mother won't make the same mistake again."

Tang Shi was in a difficult situation now, so he didn't dare to put on airs. He just kept his anger to himself and smiled, "Of course."

Chen Ningyu also smiled, said goodbye and left.

Tang then said viciously: "It's just a moment of complacency, we'll see what happens in the future!"

Yang Yankang quickly covered her mouth and said anxiously, "Mom, please be patient. Do you still want to offend my brother and his wife at this time? If it weren't for me this time, I don't know what I would do!"

Fortunately, she has a cunning son. Tang sighed, "I can't help it when I see her face. It's as if she is the most innocent in the world and we are all mud in the ground. How can your eldest brother fall in love with her and marry a debt collector?"

Yang Yankang didn't know what to say, so he just said, "No matter what, mother, you should just keep your tail between your legs and behave yourself. Mother, don't want us to be kicked out too, right?"

"I am his mother, how can I chase him away?"

Yang Yankang said with disdain: "You speak

as if Big Brother is your biological son. Besides, even if he is, Big Brother has such a temper. Even if he is your biological mother, do you think he wouldn't dare?"

Only then did Tang stop talking.

When Yang Yanling went to court this time, the emperor really gave him another reward. He brought back a box of gold. When Chen Ningyu heard about it, he thought he had made a fortune again, but there was so much money that he didn't know what to do with it.

But who would have thought that Bai Tao would stammer and look strange.

Chen Ningyu glanced at her.

Bai Tao then spoke: "I heard that the Marquis brought back two beauties."

☆, Chapter 60 Promise

However, Chen Ningyu did not see the beauty, only Yang Yanling alone. She smiled and asked, "Didn't you give the beauty as a reward? Why didn't you bring her here for me to see?"

Yang Yanling raised his eyebrows: "Do you really want to see it?"

"Look, why not? No one in my family has ever been admired by a beautiful woman since I was a child. Isn't this strange?"

Yang Yanling was quite happy to hear that she was a little angry.

He is already quite jealous, so why not let

Chen Ningyu feel a little jealous too?

"Bring the man here." he ordered.

The beauties came soon. One had almond eyes, rosy cheeks and a graceful figure. The other was even prettier, with fair skin and delicate features. In a word, both of them could be called beauties.

"It's really good." Chen Ningyu said, "Is it also a reward from the emperor?"

"No, it was given by the Empress." Yang Yanling paused and added, "Nominally, the eunuch in charge said, but in fact it was given by my aunt."

This made Chen Ningyu even more annoyed.

Concubine Shu might have sent someone away to please her nephew Yang Yanling. Of course, there were other reasons as well. But in her opinion, this was very sinister. Wasn't it destroying the relationship between other people's husband and wife?

She asked calmly, "What does the Marquis plan to do with it?"

"These two are both good at singing and dancing. They were given by my aunt. So let them stay."

Chen Ningyu chuckled twice: "Okay, since the Marquis said so, then I'll stay."

She ordered Danqiu to prepare two side rooms and asked the two beauties their names. One said her name was Zhichun and the other's name was Yurong.

Bitao came over to lead them downstairs.

Yang Yanling said, "No need, let them serve you later."

Chen Ningyu twitched his lips.

Well, he's showing off already. She snorted secretly, sat down and picked up the soles to make shoes. She pierced the needle with extra force, and didn't even mention helping Yang Yanling take off his official uniform. She just pretended not to see him.

Yang Yanling just thought it was funny, changed into casual clothes, sat down leisurely and said: "Please keep these gold, silk, and jade articles well. Oh, pick out some jewelry tomorrow."

"Why?" Chen Ning paused.

"See that Zhichun and Yurong have nothing on their heads. After all, we are a marquis' mansion, even maids shouldn't be like this."

Isn't this too much?

Chen Ningyu suddenly felt strange. Even if Yang Yanling really had no interest in her, there was no need for him to treat her like this, right? She looked at Yang Yanling suspiciously, and saw that he was smiling with the corners of his mouth raised. She immediately understood.

This is just teasing her again!

Chen Ningyu threw the sole of his shoe on the table and said, "If the Marquis wants to send it, he won't do it himself. I don't have the time!" After saying that, he went into the inner room.

Zhichun and Yurong were somewhat frightened. Although they were sent by Concubine Shu, and she hoped that they would be favored by

Yang Yanling, it would definitely not be a good thing to offend the mistress.

Yang Yanling didn't react at all.

Gu Qiu couldn't help but remind him, "My Lord, it's not easy to coax the Madam back."

Is it really a good idea to make such excessive demands?

Gu Qiu was really worried about Yang Yanling.

Chen Ningyu only appeared again when it was time for dinner.

Seeing Zhichun and Yurong serving dishes to Yang Yanling on both sides, although this was teasing her, it was a bit too much.

Chen Ningyu raised her eyebrows and said, "If the Marquis really likes them, why not raise them as concubines?"

"This is a good idea." Yang Yanling agreed.

"Then I'll arrange a date. Is tomorrow okay, sir?"

"Of course, the sooner the better."

"How about tonight? We can carry them together. It will be a great joy to serve the Marquis."

Yang Yanling finally couldn't hold it back anymore, he burst into laughter and waved his hands: "Alright, all of you go down."

Zhichun and Yurong left in a hurry.

Chen Ningyu asked, "Why is the Marquis not satisfied? How about I pick out some jewelry for them and let them wear for you to see, and then you can call them back. I'll make two new clothes for them tomorrow, and they will be even more beautiful. I'll take them to pay respects every day, and it will be glorious. The two concubines are from the palace, and ordinary people can't have them."

"You, keep talking." Yang Yanling pulled her over to sit on his lap, "Are you really angry?"

"It's the Marquis' turn now. Isn't the Marquis angry?"

He had already gotten over his anger. Yang Yanling asked, "What would you do if I really made them concubines?"

"What can I do? Being a wife is just like fish on a chopping board. If the Marquis has fifteen or sixteen wives, what can I do? I can only pack up and leave. Fortunately, I still have some money, so I won't starve to death. It will be difficult to get married again in the future, but you don't need to worry about it. I will find a way..."

"Nonsense!" Yang Yanling was just having fun at first, but now he was angry because of what she said. He said with a straight face, "If I really get a concubine in the future, will you divorce me?"

"Isn't that good?" Chen Ningyu said, "You want to take a concubine, which means you don't like me anymore, so why should I stay with the Marquis?"

Yang Yanling's face darkened.

In fact, for a family like theirs, having one or two concubines is nothing. Now that he has no one and treats her very well, she can say such things.

I really don't miss it at all.

Yang Yanling was unhappy again.

"Eat!" He put her down.

Chen Ningyu didn't want to coax him. These were all her real thoughts. She hoped that Yang Yanling could think about it carefully. If that day really came, the two of them could go their separate ways without dragging things out.

Neither of them enjoyed the meal well.

In the evening, Yang Yanling went to the study and did not come back until very late. She did not wait for him and went to bed first.

As a result, the next day, before dawn, she was awakened by Yang Yanling.

In the past, he had told the servants not to light the lights out of consideration for her, and he also took very small actions. But today, he was obviously doing it on purpose. Chen Ningyu opened her eyes with difficulty, thinking that he must be seeking revenge for what happened yesterday. Small-minded man!

Seeing her unhappy face, Yang Yanling reached out and pulled her out of the bed, shouting, "Why don't you get up and serve me!"

Chen Ningyu almost swore.

She grabbed the quilt and said, "My Lord didn't want me to serve him in the morning before."

"That was in the past." Yang Yanling grabbed her blanket and said, "You will be the only one by my side from now on. Shouldn't you serve me more? Do you really want me to let someone else do this job?"

Chen Ningyu was stunned.

What is he saying?

Will she be the only one from now on?

She tilted her head and asked, "Really?"

Yang Yanling really wanted to beat her up at this moment.

Chen Ningyu quickly got up and dressed Yang Yanling with a smile on her face: "As long as the Marquis likes it, it is not difficult for me to get up and serve you every day, but I have to go to bed early at night."

Yang Yanling's face darkened again.

You can choose not to get up early, but you cannot go to bed early!

It was a rare occasion that the two of them had breakfast together on a day other than a holiday.

Chen Ningyu brought him the official hat and put it on.

Yang Yanling reached out and grasped her hand, saying sternly, "I never make promises easily, but once I say something, I will do it. I treat you like this, so how can you treat me?"

He is willing to be with her for the rest of his life, but what about her?

Chen Ningyu was stunned.

Do you really have to make this kind of

confession so early in the morning?

But she didn't avoid it, because she was not a person without conscience.

"Of course I am willing to stand by you through thick and thin, and share life and death with you, sir!" she said very seriously.

"Is that all?" Yang Yanling raised his eyebrows.

Chen Ningyu thought for a moment and said, "I will never keep a lover secretly."

Yang Yanling chuckled and knocked her head: "What are you thinking about? I'll settle the score with you when I come back!"

Chen Ningyu smiled and saw him off.

Danqiu asked: "Madam, what should we do with those two? What should we tell them to do?"

"Don't worry about it for now, we'll talk about it later." There is still one big thing that has not been resolved, and that is the division of the family.

She went to pay her respects to Madam Yang.

Madam Yang was the first to say, "Those two were given by the Empress. It would be a shame if Yanling didn't bring them back. Don't forget them."

Probably because he heard what happened in the evening, when the two of them had a quarrel.

Chen Ningyu said, "I know. I had dinner with the Marquis this morning."

Madam Yang breathed a sigh of relief: "That's good." She showed her the detailed list of the division of the family property and said, "You can tell Yanling about it when the time comes. I haven't been in much energy these days."

She was unwilling to divide the family property, but her son and daughter-in-law were both troublesome, and the old lady felt uncomfortable.

Chen Ningyu agreed immediately and asked, "Where will they live in the future?"

"We live in the courtyard on Jixian Street. It was bought by your second aunt. It's very big." Mrs. Yang became angry again and didn't want to say anything more.

Chen Ningyu didn't mention it again.

When Yang Yanling came back, she showed him the list: "Although it's a bit much, but after all, Second Uncle is Grandmother's biological son, and the legitimate son. Second brother, eldest daughter, and second daughter are not married yet. I think we should do it this way, and don't make Grandmother sad anymore."

Yang Yanling took a look and frowned slightly.

In his opinion, it would be better not to give it. After all, the second house had secretly taken so much money, and now they were giving it back. However, since Chen Ningyu said so, he thought it was better to have less trouble than more, so he let it go.

After a few days, Yang Dongping and his family moved to Jixian Street.

At the same time, Yan Yuqing was suffering from wave after wave of impeachments. The emperor wanted to protect him, but there was solid evidence for many of his crimes, so he had to strip Yan Yuqing of his title of Marquis of Anji. Not only that, Yan Yuqing was also sentenced to exile.

Princess Huaying was devastated and went to the palace to ask for an audience with the emperor that same day.

Looking at his own sister, Li Shiyu was also very disappointed and reprimanded: "It's not just one or two years. I reminded you earlier to restrain your behavior and not to disregard the law. Today, he has brought this upon himself!"

If he insisted on preserving it, it would probably cause dissatisfaction among the officials.

Princess Huaying cried, "It's not a big deal. Please, Your Majesty, take back your order and at least don't exile me!"

"The emperor is guilty of the same crime as the common people, let alone him?" Li Shiyu said coldly, "Today's incident should be regarded as a punishment. You go back and teach Yuan'er well, don't follow his father's old path."

Princess Huaying wanted to beg, but Li Shiyu didn't want to listen and ordered the eunuch to take her out.

The wind in the palace was particularly cold at this moment, and Princess Huaying's eyes were red and swollen from crying.

Concubine Ning came over and said, "Lingzi, what happened?"

Princess Huaying cried even harder: "Sister, please persuade the emperor for me. My husband didn't mean it."

"Oh, it's about this." Concubine Ning said, "Come sit with me first."

The two of them went to Rui'an Palace.

Concubine Ning comforted her: "The emperor is just angry for a moment, don't worry. Although this is exile, who dares to harm the prince consort? It's just a show, and he may be back in a few months."

"But how can he bear this kind of suffering?" Princess Huaying wiped her eyes.

Yan Yuqing was also the son of a wealthy family. He was very handsome and elegant. Princess Huaying fell in love with him because of this. Although Yan Yuqing was not very capable, he was very good at serving his wife.

Therefore, Princess Huaying also really likes him.

Concubine Ning sighed, "After all, it's still the officials who impeached him. It's not a particularly vicious thing, but they have to hold on to it. I heard that it was all the work of Marquis Wu Ding who was behind it."

Princess Huaying immediately showed her anger: "I know it must be him!"

It's a pity that although she knew it, she couldn't stop it. Marquis Wu Ding had no leverage over her, so she could do nothing about it.

Concubine Ning said, "He and Concubine Shu have a good relationship. Concubine Shu often speaks well of him in front of the emperor."

Princess Huaying frowned.

Given the relationship between the two, Marquis Wu Ding would definitely stand on the side of the Third Prince in the future. However, she had not originally decided which prince she would support. She just wanted to not leave any one behind. Now, it seemed that her feud with Marquis Wu Ding was set.

She glanced at Concubine Ning and said, "Speaking of me, my sister is much more considerate. Concubine Shu is just a face, what else can she do? Chang Luo is also a brainless man, and he will not be able to handle important tasks in the future."

Concubine Ning smiled with satisfaction.

As soon as October came, the weather became colder day by day. By the end of the month, it was unbearable to live in the house without a charcoal brazier. But even so, Chen Ningyu never left home without a hand warmer and wore very warm clothes.

Fortunately, Yang Yanling no longer lets her serve him breakfast in the morning, otherwise she would really feel resentful.

"Tell the kitchen to cook more winter nourishing dishes later. Don't make them too light." She instructed Gu Qiu, "Mutton or something like that would be best. Bring some over every few days. The Marquis is always away from home, so he's not like other people."

Even such a strong man sometimes comes back with his face blue from the cold, so naturally special attention must be paid to his food.

Gu Qiu responded.

"And what I said last time, have you thought about it?" Chen Ningyu smiled, "I think the eldest son of the Wang family is good."

The Wang family is one of the accompanying rooms, and now they are in charge of some work in the outer courtyard.

Gu Qiu blushed: "It's all up to the young lady."

This meant that she had agreed. Chen Ningyu was very happy. She had prepared her dowry for her. "I'll let you go for a few days after the wedding. You can come back later and do some housekeeping. You can take care of what the kitchen buys."

Gu Qiu nodded.

A few days later, Chen Ningyu married her off. A banquet was set up in the yard and the servants were delighted.

When Gu Qiu came back, she was a young woman and looked good in every way.

After all, she was the head maid beside Chen Ningyu. The Wang family treated her very well and did not dare to offend her at all. Naturally, she lived a comfortable life. Chen Ningyu promoted her to be a manager and gave her two taels of silver more in monthly salary than before.

"The madam wants the young lady to come over." Danqiu came to report.

Madam Yang seldom invited her to visit unless there was something important. Chen Ningyu hurriedly put on her cloak and went out. When she got there, she saw an old doctor with a white beard in the main hall. She recognized him as Doctor Li, who was usually employed by Madam Yang.

Actually, it was Doctor Li, but because of his old age, he had left the palace and usually did not see patients unless he had an old acquaintance with them.

Chen Ningyu met Madam Yang and Doctor Li.

Madam Yang smiled and said, "I tend to get sick easily in the winter, so I asked Doctor Li to come. Then I thought of you. Although you are young, you don't need to worry too much, but it's always good to see you. I'll prescribe a paste for you to take, which will also nourish your body."

Chen Ningyu smiled and said, "Doctor Li is known as a miracle doctor. It is an honor for him to see my daughter-in-law."

Doctor Li said, "What kind of miracle doctor? Don't listen to their nonsense." He looked at her face again and said, "You look good. Come on, give me your hand."

Chen Ningyu stretched out his hand.

Doctor Li took the patient's pulse very seriously and nodded from time to time.

Madam Yang was a little nervous.

After a while, Doctor Li finally let go of her hand and said, "You are a young man after all. I don't need to worry about you. But your body needs to be taken care of. If you take good care of it when you are young, you will not be prone to illness when you are old, and you will live a long life."

Chen Ningyu agreed: "You are right. It is the same as 'If you don't work hard when you are young, you will regret it when you are old'. If you change it to 'If you don't take care of yourself when you are young, you will regret it when you are old.'"

Doctor Li smiled and said, "Yes, yes, Madam is very perceptive."

Chen Ningyu smiled: "Thank you for the compliment."

Doctor Li prescribed her a paste prescription containing more than thirty kinds of medicine.

Although any doctor can prescribe ointments, famous doctors are different. Sometimes, the prescriptions prescribed for the same patient are completely different. This is the difference in the level of their skills.

Chen Ningyu thanked Doctor Li again.

After Chen Ningyu left, Madam Yang asked Doctor Li, "How is my daughter-in-law's health?"

"It's no big deal."

"Then why haven't you gotten pregnant yet?" Madam Yang was worried about this. Chen Ningyu had been married for almost eight months, and apart from the fact that Yang

Yanling was fighting outside, it had been six months.

Doctor Li smiled and said, "It's not that easy to have a baby. She can get pregnant whenever she wants. But I think her health is a little poor. She is afraid of cold and heat."

"What?" Madam Yang was shocked. "How could this happen?"

"Did you get hurt when you were young?"

Madam Yang thought about it and shook her head: "It seems not."

She didn't know that Chen Ningyu had once fallen into the water and lost his life.

She hurriedly asked again: "Is it serious?"

"Let's wait and see. It shouldn't be a big deal, but we can't be sure." Doctor Li said, "But Madam, many newlyweds give birth only after one or two years. You are too impatient."

"Yes, I am in a hurry!" Mrs. Yang admitted, "Can't I invite you to come?"

The eldest wife has only one grandson, who is already 27 years old. If she is not anxious, who will be?

In the future, this marquisate will be passed down from generation to generation.

Doctor Li comforted her, "How about this, if you still don't get pregnant after a year, I will come back again, how about that?"

Madam Yang said, "That's the only way."

When Yang Yanling came back, Madam Yang called him over.

"Today, I asked Doctor Li to check Ning Yu."

Yang Yanling asked quickly: "Why, is she sick?"

"No, hey, you kid!" Madam Yang said angrily, "Why aren't you anxious? Isn't Ning Yu pregnant yet? I asked Doctor Li to check her out. Pregnancy is not a good thing, but it's a pity that she is not pregnant."

"Why are you in such a hurry, grandma? She is only a few years old. I am in my prime, so why should I be afraid of not having children in the future?" Although Yang Yanling also wanted Chen Ningyu to give birth to a child for him, he was not in a hurry.

Madam Yang didn't know what to say: "Just a reminder to you, Doctor Li said her health is not very good."

Yang Yanling hummed.

Madam Yang asked again, "What are you going to do with the two girls? They are still lying in the yard."

"Why don't I give it to you? It's good at singing and dancing, and it's good for killing time."

"I want to listen to music, so I will call Jin Ling and the others." Madam Yang stretched out her hand to pinch her brows and sighed, "Your aunt is bewitched. She actually gave someone to you. Do you think two beauties can buy you off? Even if she gave it to you, our mansion can also be given away."

"Oh? Mother wants to send them away?"

"It's all over now. It's always unsafe to keep it at home. What do you think?"

"It's my own thing. I was planning to give it to my grandmother."

Madam Yang said, "Tomorrow I will ask Steward Luo to send her to a farm far away. She is still ours anyway, so I think the palace won't have much to say. They can't force you to marry her."

Yang Yanling nodded: "Let's do as grandma said."

He said that and went back.

As soon as I entered the house, I smelled the strong aroma of mutton.

"Eating mutton again?" he asked, untying his cloak and putting it over his arm.

Chen Ningyu took his cloak and put it away for Gu Qiu, asking, "Are you tired of eating this, my Lord? If you are, I will ask them to cook something else. I just think that eating mutton is the best today. It nourishes the body and helps to resist the cold."

"You ordered me to eat it, how could I get tired of it?" Yang Yanling pinched her face, "I see you really like it."

Chen Ningyu smiled and said, "There are so many varieties. Even though it's all mutton, it tastes different every day."

Yang Yanling looked at her and smiled, and then he remembered what Madam Yang had just said, and said, "Wait for me to rest in the future, and I will go out to practice boxing, and you can follow me."

"Ah?" Chen Ningyu was stunned. "Why?"

"To keep fit." Yang Yanling said, "You only know how to eat and don't know how to move. How can you be healthy in the future?"

"Why don't I move? I used to go to the garden often, or..." She couldn't remember. In fact, she was getting lazier and lazier, especially in winter, when she didn't have to pay her respects every day and would stay in the house all day.

Yang Yanling said: "After reading it, I can't even say it myself."

Chen Ningyu said perfunctorily: "Whatever the Marquis says is what it is."

As a result, when the court had a holiday, Yang Yanling really dragged her outside.

Chen Ningyu curled up into a ball and begged, "My Lord, can you wait until the weather is warmer before coming out? I'm freezing here!" What she feared most was the winter here.

However, Yang Yanling seemed particularly grim at this moment, and said seriously: "Stretch out your hands, make a fist, and squat down."

Chen Ningyu looked at him with pitiful eyes. Yang Yanling was not soft-hearted at all and said, "If you don't practice, you still have to get up early every day to serve me meals tomorrow."

"..."

Chen Ningyu had nothing to say.

It seems that practicing boxing after

getting up is better than being forced to get up early in the morning.

Besides, exercise does have benefits!

After comforting himself, Chen Ningyu stretched out his hand.

Yang Yanling shouted, "Stand up straight, with your back straight!"

Chen Ningyu shuddered and looked at him, only to find that this face was no longer the same as usual, it was so scary.

She stood up straight at once.

His voice echoed for a long time in the cold wind.

☆、Chapter 61 Something Different

Because of Yan Yuqing's matter, Princess Huiying sent a huge gift. Chen Ningyu didn't know about it at first, and she was going to be happy when she found out. However, she fell ill and was lying in bed, with a runny nose from time to time.

Gu Qiu quickly ordered the servant to call for a doctor.

Although they could hire an imperial physician in their mansion, they would not easily apply for a doctor unless it was a serious illness, so they usually hired doctors from the capital's medical clinic.

After the examination, the doctor prescribed a prescription for Chen Ningyu.

"It's nothing serious, I just caught a cold. It will be fine after taking the medicine for a few days."

Gu Qiu thanked him and sent the doctor out.
Chen Ningyu was so angry that her teeth were itching, thinking that this must be because Yang Yanling forced her to go out and learn boxing last time!

Madam Yang knew about it and also came to see her. This was the first time Chen Ningyu fell ill since she married into the Yang family, so Madam Yang was naturally worried. She ordered several maids to take good care of her and told her to recuperate and not to come to pay her respects for the entire winter.

Chen Ningyu complained to Yang Yanling: "I caught a cold when I followed the Marquis out to practice boxing."

"There's still this matter?" Madam Yang frowned. "Yanling is a bit ignorant. Why is he practicing boxing in the middle of winter? You don't have the same body as him. How can you bear it? I'll talk to him when he comes back."

As soon as Yang Yanling arrived home, Madam Yang called him over.

Hearing that Chen Ningyu was ill, Yang Yanling was surprised: "It hasn't been long, how come he got sick?"

"She was spoiled in the Chen family, how could she not get sick? You, don't do this next time. If the wife of your parents-in-law finds out, she won't blame you."

Yang Yanling said a few perfunctory words and returned to the yard.

Chen Ningyu was still lying there, covered

with a thick quilt, with only her face showing, and her nose was red.

"How is it? Are you still feeling uncomfortable?" Yang Yanling sat on the edge of the bed and reached out to touch her forehead, which was not hot.

"It hurts. My nose hurts." Chen Ningyu pointed at her nose. "It's scratched."

"Let me take a look." Yang Yanling leaned down and said after a while, "Yes, it is a little broken. Just bear with it. It will be fine after taking medicine."

"My throat hurts too." She blinked.

Yang Yanling turned around and asked, "How are you serving me? Why don't you give me more water?"

Danqiu was startled and hurried to get it.

"The doctor said I caught a cold," Chen Ningyu said, "and told me not to get cold again."

"I heard from my grandmother that it's my fault. I should proceed step by step. Next time, I should practice for a shorter period of time and take it slow." Yang Yanling still did not give up this decision. "You can't stop practicing just because it's cold, right? There's still summer to come. If you don't practice when it's hot, how can you practice well?"

Chen Ningyu was sweating. She thought that if she acted a little coquettishly, Yang Yanling would let her go, but she found out that she had thought too easily.

Chen Ningyu pouted and turned over with her

back facing him.
Seeing this, Yang Yanling took off his coat, got into the quilt, bent down and kissed her on the mouth.
Chen Ningyu said hurriedly: "I will give it to you."
"Didn't I make you sick? I'll get sick once too. It's no big deal." He smiled.
"Who wants to be sick?" Chen Ningyu turned his head away. "Being sick is not comfortable."
Yang Yanling hugged her tighter and said softly, "Don't be angry with me. A rich lady like you should actually exercise more. I asked you to spar with me for your own good. I don't want you to..." He paused and sighed, "My mother passed away when I was four years old. The doctor said that you were born with a bad body, and then you suffered from childbirth. The last time Doctor Li saw you, he also said that you were not in good health. And your mother passed away early, too. How can I not be worried?"
Chen Ningyu was also a little scared after hearing what he said.
The medical technology here is really backward. Giving birth to a child is no less than going through the gates of hell. She thought for a while and said, "Then I'd better fight with you."
She would definitely rather suffer a little than lose her life.
Yang Yanling patted her head and said,

"That's good. Practice once a day in the future, and your body will become strong soon."

From rest days to daily life, Chen Ningyu thought of the way he taught her and said hurriedly, "Can you not be so fierce next time? It's so scary! It's as if you will kill me if I don't do as I say."

Yang Yanling touched his nose and said, "Isn't it?"

"Of course not, it's like they want to eat people."

Yang Yanling laughed: "Maybe you are used to it. I will pay more attention next time. But don't expect me to be soft-hearted. You have to practice as you should. Otherwise, it will be a waste of effort if you fish for three days and cast the net for two days."

Chen Ningyu was a little scared. She didn't like sports in her previous life, so she had almost no perseverance in this area. But she really didn't want to die young, so she nodded obediently.

After she recovered from her illness, Yang Yanling urged her to practice boxing with him whenever he had time. After two months, she became very proficient in it, and Yang Yanling also taught her some sword skills.

But the sword is a weapon after all, and if she is not careful she can hurt herself, so she learns very slowly.

Just like this, the New Year is here before we know it.

That day, Steward Luo brought a gift list to Chen Ningyu and said, "Young Madam, do you know this family? I see that they don't have any dealings with our family, but I don't know why they sent such a valuable gift."

Chen Ningyu looked over and saw Jiang Family, Jiang Chuntang written under the signature.

She couldn't remember who it was.

As far as I can remember, the Chen family didn't seem to have any dealings with the Jiang family.

"Then this..." Manager Luo frowned. There were a lot of social interactions during the New Year. He had to write down what each family gave and then send something in return.

Chen Ningyu asked Gu Qiu: "Do you remember who this Jiang Chuntang is?"

Gu Qiu shook his head.

Danqiu said, "Is he Miss Lu's husband? I remember his last name was Jiang, and I think his name was Jiang Chuntang."

Chen Ningyu was reminded by her and remembered it.

When Lu Yun got married, as her cousin, she also sent a gift, but she didn't attend in person and didn't care much. However, she still knew the name. That was more than a month ago.

But Jiang Chuntang actually sent a holiday gift at this time.

Chen Ningyu said, "Let's put it aside for

now."

Because she hadn't been back to the Chen family for a while and didn't know what kind of dealings the Chen family had with the Jiang family, she didn't deal with it for the time being and only sent a maid to see the lady.

The lady had just woken up from a nap when she heard someone coming from the Marquis Wuding's mansion and called her in.

The old woman bowed before saying, "The young lady sent me here."

"What is it?"

"The young lady said that she received a generous gift from the Jiang family and asked the lady what to do with it."

The lady didn't ask who it was, and directly asked, "Is it Jiang Chuntang?"

"Yes." The woman replied.

The old lady immediately showed a look of disgust, she also received gifts from Jiang Chuntang, and if it wasn't for Zhao's face, she would not have been willing to accept them at all. But who would have thought that Jiang Chuntang sent them to the Marquis of Wuding's Mansion!

Does he also want to curry favor with the Marquis of Wuding?

"Tell your young lady to return it intact."

The old woman replied, "The young lady asked how the old lady was, and said she would come to see her after the New Year."

The lady smiled and said, "Okay, okay, tell her to take care of herself."

The old woman said goodbye and left.

The lady pinched her brows and said to Mother Hu, "This Jiang family is too outrageous. They are so long-reaching. What kind of relatives are they to the Wuding Marquis Mansion? They even gave gifts. Now I understand. No wonder they spent a lot of money to marry Yun'er. It turns out that they have other intentions. The Jiang family has only one son, Jiang Chuntang, who is now a juren, but he didn't pass the jinshi exam this year, so he has to wait for another three years..."

Before he could finish, someone else came in. Upon asking, it turned out to be from the Zhang family. He also said that Jiang Chuntang had sent a holiday gift to the Zhang family.

The lady was really angry.

When Chen Ningyu heard about the old woman's return to the mansion, he asked Manager Luo to return the things to the Jiang family.

The Zhang family quickly retreated.

Jiang Chuntang's face suddenly turned grim upon hearing this. He quickly found Lu Yun and started to scold her, "What's going on? Are the two families so disrespectful to each other?"

Lv Yun was puzzled and asked, "Husband, what are you talking about?"

"What are you talking about? I sent festival gifts to the Wuding Marquis' Mansion and the Zhang family today. We are relatives after all. Why did you reject them all? Aren't you looking down on our Jiang family?"

Lu Yun's face turned slightly pale. She wanted to get angry, but she held back and said softly, "Why do you need so many gifts, my husband? They don't usually visit each other. If you suddenly give them gifts, they must feel embarrassed to accept them."

"I'm sorry, but I can't return the gift?" Jiang Chuntang raised his eyebrows and clenched his fists, "You're giving it back now just to embarrass me! Your mother always said that the lady was kind to you, caring about you all the time, and treating you like her own granddaughter. It turns out that it was all fake!"

Lu Yun took a deep breath and said, "Madam Tai is very kind to us, otherwise she wouldn't have allocated a courtyard for us to live in. Didn't Madam Tai give up now?"

Jiang Chuntang snorted.

"My dear, you didn't mention these things when you married me. I'm marrying you now. We are husband and wife, so what can't we solve?" Lu Yun advised, "The Wuding Marquisate and the Zhang family don't like to make friends with others. Just withdraw."

After hearing this, Jiang Chuntang suppressed his anger for the time being and softened his tone.

"I was a little abrupt this time, my lady, please don't blame me. I also want to build good relationships with your relatives. Even if we don't visit them now, we may visit them in the future. How about we visit them in person next time? What do you think?" Jiang Chuntang put his hand on Lu Yun's shoulder and bent down to kiss her cheek. "I know you are the most considerate person. I married you because I like this about you. You should know that."

Lu Yun frowned slightly. What did she know? If she had known this earlier, she would have reconsidered it.

It's a pity that time will reveal a person's true character!

"It's not impossible to visit." Lu Yun smiled and said, "But you have to pick a good time. You can't just go any day."

"Of course, everything is up to you."

After Jiang Chuntang finished speaking, he hugged her and went to the inner room.

☆、Chapter 62: Happy

That day, a palace maid came to report that Yang Dongping and Fan were waiting outside the palace gate, so Concubine Shu summoned them in.

Shufei also knew about the last division of the Yang family. Yang Dongping asked for a meeting at that time, but Shufei never met him because she didn't want to interfere in the division of the family. But Yang Dongping did not give up. She met him again and again, and this time she met him.

The two of them bowed to Concubine Shu.
Concubine Shu gave him a seat.
"Your Highness looks younger now." Fan said flatteringly as soon as she arrived. "I saw you a few years ago. You are even prettier now than you were then."
Concubine Shu smiled and said, "Are you living in Jixian Street now?"
Fan's eyes suddenly turned red, and she said aggrievedly, "How can it be good? I have to buy everything from scratch, and I have been busy for many days. As for the original Marquis' Mansion, I have spent a lot of effort, but in the end, it is divided just like that."
Concubine Shu was unmoved: "Dividing the family is a common thing. The family of Minister of Works Lu also divided the family a few days ago. It will be more peaceful if each room is passed on to another room."
Fan didn't dare to refute, she forced a smile and said yes, then thought about the purpose of the visit and said, "Yanling's personality is actually not bad after the separation. The Queen gave him two beauties out of kindness, but who would have thought that they would be sent to the manor in the blink of an eye? He just doesn't know how to appreciate other people's kindness. The Queen treats him very well, but he doesn't seem to care about others."
Concubine Shu narrowed her eyes slightly.
Her nephew was a hateful one, but she was

her aunt after all. She gave him this gift because she saw that he had no concubines around him. He was quite good. Shufei glanced at Yuanniang, and Yuanniang quickly reached out and picked up a piece of freshly boiled pear and put it into her mouth.

After eating, Concubine Shu said calmly, "He has always been like this, but not being interested in women is also an advantage."

Yang Dongping interrupted, "Is disrespecting elders a virtue? I'm still his second uncle, how does he treat me?" He raised his eyebrows, "I'm not saying that if he can treat me like this, he can treat you like this in the future."

They are siblings, so they are more casual when talking to each other.

Concubine Shu looked at him and asked, "What does brother mean?"

Yang Dongping's coming today must not be without purpose. As a family, Concubine Shu also wants to see what he is going to do.

Yang Dongping said, "I think this Marquisate will be destroyed by him sooner or later. He has no business skills and only knows how to lead troops to fight. I think Your Majesty should reconsider. Who can't be the Marquis of Wuding?"

It turned out that he was blatantly asking for the title. Concubine Shu smiled and said, "It was because my eldest brother passed away that the emperor gave the title to Yanling. Now he is doing well. What can I do?" She glanced at Yang Dongping and said, "Besides, my brother has been recuperating at home for many years. What achievements have you made? You can say this, but I can't."

Yang Dongping's face changed, and he said angrily: "That kid just relied on luck. If I hadn't been injured, I wouldn't have returned to Beijing that year. If you give me another chance, I will definitely let the queen know my ability."

"Is your leg injury healed?" asked Concubine Shu.

"almost."

Concubine Shu nodded and said, "In that case, I will talk to the emperor next time and have you reinstated."

"You don't have to worry about this, my lady. I have already met Lord Gongshun."

By saying this, it was shown that she was of the same mind as Concubine Shu, and both supported the Third Prince to become the Crown Prince in the future.

However, Concubine Shu frowned.

Although she kept trying to win over Yang Yanling, he was her own nephew, so she kept a low profile in other things. As for Earl Gongshun, she had not met him for several years because she was afraid that the emperor would become suspicious. But who would have thought that Yang Dongping had met him in private.

Seeing that Concubine Shu looked unhappy,

Yang Dongping and Fan looked at each other.

"Brother, don't go to see Duke Gongshun again." Concubine Shu warned, "Otherwise, if this continues, who knows who will destroy the Yang family. So let it go. I am tired too."

She served tea to the guests.

After being ridiculed in the end, Yang Dongping felt humiliated.

Throughout his life, he was suppressed by Yang Dongyuan and could not make any progress. After Yang Dongyuan died, the title was given to Yang Yanling. As the second uncle, he began to be suppressed by Yang Yanling again.

Now even Concubine Shu looks down on him.

Yang Dongping said angrily: "When I become successful in the future, I will make them regret it!"

Fan sighed, "I didn't expect the queen to still side with that brat."

He originally thought that since Yang Yanling had offended Concubine Shu, Concubine Shu might vent her anger on him, so he was willing to find ways to give the title to Yang Dongping so that they could help each other. However, Concubine Shu did not have this intention.

Yang Dongping said coldly: "I might as well come up with a solution myself."

After the two left, Concubine Shu rubbed her forehead and felt a headache. Her second brother had never made any progress, so she never counted on him. Now it seems that as long as he doesn't cause her trouble, it's good enough.

"Your Majesty, Concubine Chen is here." The palace maid came to report again.

Shufei invited her in.

Chen Ninghua smiled and greeted, "I just went out for a walk and passed by the garden. I saw wintersweets in bloom. They were really beautiful. I picked some for you. Please don't dislike them, Your Majesty."

At this time of year, only wintersweet can bloom beautifully.

The maid brought in a bunch of golden winter plums. Concubine Shu took a look and nodded: "I love winter plums too. Unlike other flowers, they are noble and aloof, but they can withstand the winter, which is something that other flowers cannot compare to."

"Yes, I think so too. This is a unique one."

Concubine Shu asked someone to put up the winter plums: "It's so cold, you should not go outside often, or you will catch a cold."

"I know, thank you for your concern."

Concubine Shu asked her to sit next to her. The two of them had been close for some time. Chen Ninghua was quite liked by Concubine Shu. The palace was quiet and sometimes one needed someone to talk to. This was how the time passed.

Soon after the spring came, it was February.

Chen Ningyu got up this morning and was just about to eat when Madam Yang came over with a doctor.
"Call the doctor quickly." Mrs. Yang smiled.
Chen Ningyu was puzzled and asked, "I'm fine now, why do I need to see a doctor?"
"Silly child." Madam Yang laughed, "Your baby has been postponed for several days, how come you don't realize it? I didn't know it before, otherwise I would have called a doctor for you a long time ago."
"It's only been a few days." If it was just a few days, it didn't necessarily mean she was pregnant. If it was half a month, she might have thought in that direction, but who knew that Madam Yang was so anxious and couldn't sit still when she heard about this.
Chen Ningyu also followed her wishes and stretched out his hand for the doctor to feel his pulse.
The doctor carefully felt her pulse. After a while, he smiled and bowed to the two of them: "Congratulations, Madam, congratulations, Madam, the Madam is indeed pregnant!"
Mrs. Yang didn't know how to show that she had gotten what she wanted, so she hurriedly asked someone to bring a large ingot of silver to the doctor.
Chen Ningyu was stunned. She didn't expect that she really was pregnant!
For a moment she didn't know what her mood was. She seemed happy, but not particularly

happy either. She had a strange feeling as if she had fallen from the sky and had to live an honest life from then on.

"Are you stupid?" Madam Yang said angrily, "Yanling will be back soon, and you don't know how to be happy. You should listen to the doctor and know what you can and cannot eat. Don't be willful and be patient."

Chen Ningyu hummed.

The doctor gave a lot of instructions, but Chen Ningyu didn't need to listen personally. Gu Qiudanqiu and the others took out paper and pen and wrote down every instruction neatly.

Madam Yang was very satisfied: "You have put so much effort into everything around you. I don't need to send anyone else."

She also instructed the cook to take good care of Chen Ningyu's body from that day on. She also planned to return to work and be the housekeeper again so that Chen Ningyu would not have to work so hard and could rest assured to take care of her pregnancy.

Chen Ningyu said hurriedly, "That's not necessary, Grandma. These things are all well managed now. I don't need to worry too much. Grandma, you are old. If you get hurt, it will be worrying. How can I take care of the baby? Let's just do it like this. I will be more careful."

Madam Yang did not force it.

When Yang Yanling came back, someone told him the good news on the road, and he strode back to the yard.

Chen Ningyu was leaning over to read a book. When she saw him, she wanted to get up, but Yang Yanling came up to her, put one hand on her belly, and smiled like a fool: "Are you going to give birth to a child for me?"

Chen Ningyu frowned: "What is born for you, is also born for myself."

Yang Yanling laughed, "You are the mother of the child, right?" He stroked the child with his hand and asked curiously, "How come you didn't know it was already there? When did it happen?"

How to explain this? Chen Ningyu was speechless. The winter did not dampen his passion. They had sex frequently. How could he guess on which day she would get pregnant? And it seemed impossible to accurately determine the day of conception by taking the pulse.

"Male or female?" he asked again.

Chen Ningyu stared at him in disbelief, a little annoyed: "What's the matter, Lord Marquis, do you still favor boys over girls? Do you dislike your daughter?"

"No way, I'm just asking." Yang Yanling glanced at her, "Why are you so impulsive? Does your temper get worse when you're pregnant?" He remembered that she seemed to have started like this a few days ago.

That day, he just wanted to change his position, but she almost kicked him off the bed.

Chen Ningyu coughed and said, "Yes, it is a little bit, so please bear with me, my

Lord."

Now that there is a ladder, she must climb it up. This way, it would be understandable if she bullies him a few times in the future.

How could Yang Yanling not agree? Although he was not in a hurry, it did not mean that he did not want to do it. Now that he had achieved his wish, he was overjoyed.

"Take good care of your baby, and don't hit me like that. But you still have to walk, and don't be lazy, do you hear me? Ask for whatever you want to eat, and tell me what you like."

Chen Ningyu pulled his sleeve and said, "My Lord, I want the moon. It will be brighter if I hang it over the bed at night."

Yang Yanling laughed and scratched her nose: "Okay, I'll pick it for you tonight. Now I'll ask someone to build a ladder. You can go with me later to open your eyes. You can pick the moon and the stars."

Although it was just a joke, his doting tone made Chen Ningyu feel sweet and satisfied.

Unfortunately, the good times did not last long. At the end of the month, Yang Yanling was appointed Governor-General of Shaanxi by the Emperor and was ordered to set out to wipe out the Shaanxi rebels within two days.

As for these rebels, they have not been causing trouble recently, but have been going on for three or four years. It's just that the previous governor was incompetent and failed to suppress the bandits. Instead, he allowed the bandits' ranks to grow stronger. He has now been dismissed and replaced by Yang Yanling.

However, Chen Ningyu believed in Yang Yanling's ability and asked with a smile, "Will the Marquis come back soon like last time?"

Yang Yanling was stunned for a moment before he said, "Yes, you stay at home and take good care of your baby. Don't worry about me."

But that moment of hesitation still made her discover it.

She paid close attention to Yang Yanling, and saw that he was indeed not as relaxed as last time. He spent most of the day in the study just looking at maps and did not come out at all. When it was time for dinner, others had to call him. It was nothing like last time, when he gave her many instructions and still had time to flirt with her.

Chen Ningyu could hardly eat this meal.

Seeing her moving the rice grains around with chopsticks, Yang Yanling asked, "But the rice is not to your liking? Ask the kitchen to cook a new portion of what you want to eat."

"No, I was thinking about your trip to Shaanxi."

Yang Yanling smiled and said, "What is there to think about? I've already said it's just a small matter."

It's too late to pretend now. Chen Ningyu sighed, "The Marquis and I have been married for almost a year. I can see that the Marquis is worried. Is this time dangerous?"

Yang Yanling put down his chopsticks.

Chen Ningyu asked the maids to leave and said, "If the Marquis refuses to tell me, I will inevitably have wild thoughts and may even go back to the Chen family to ask my father. It would be better if the Marquis tells me so that I can share some of the burden."

Yang Yanling sighed, stretched out his hands and said, "Come here."

Chen Ningyu sat over there.

He put his arm around her waist and asked, "Can you really tell?"

"It's so vivid. Didn't you look at the map? I guess the terrain there is quite complicated. Otherwise, they are just a group of rebels. Why would it take so many years to find them?"

"Yes, you are right." Yang Yanling stroked her hair gently, "I am just worried about other things. Do you know who recommended me to go?"

This was a bit mysterious. Chen Ningyu's heart sank. "Could it be the Third Prince's people?"

"There is also Yan Yuqing." Yang Yanling said, "I am afraid that if I make a mistake, they will catch me and make a big fuss about it."

Chen Ningyu couldn't help but move closer to him.

"Don't be afraid. At least I'm prepared. Just be careful..."

"It's easy to dodge an open attack, but it's hard to guard against a hidden arrow. If you are cautious and restrained, you might delay military operations." Chen Ningyu had other concerns. He curled his lips and said, "Those who love to impeach me are afraid that if you go to the toilet and use some expensive silk, they can use it to make a fuss. Can you really dodge it?"

Yang Yanling laughed at what she said, and then said seriously: "Anyway, no matter what, I will try my best to avoid it."

Chen Ningyu touched his face and sighed softly: "You are good in everything, but you always forget that you are not alone."

"What do you mean?" Yang Yanling raised his eyebrows.

"You have me, as well as relatives from the Chen, Zhang, Xu, and Wu families. Otherwise, what is the purpose of marriage? Isn't it just to help each other?" Chen Ningyu said, "Don't worry, Lord Marquis. I will go back and discuss it with my grandmother."

"This..." Yang Yanling really didn't expect this.

He had been trained on the battlefield at a young age and had experienced many dangers. He learned how to lead troops and how to flexibly apply various military tactics. He was used to relying on himself and becoming a real general.

When he married Chen Ningyu, he didn't think about the family behind her. He just wanted to marry her, so he married her. Now Chen Ningyu's words made him suddenly enlightened.

"Thank you for your help." Yang Yanling accepted her kindness.

By the next day, he would be ready to leave. At this moment he was instructing Chen Ningyu again.

The second separation was different from the first. Chen Ningyu thought that she would just get more and more accustomed to it in the future. After all, she married such a man. She could only become stronger.

Yang Yanling said goodbye to Madam Yang, kissed Chen Ningyu on the face, and whispered, "No matter what, I will come back before our child is born, don't be afraid."

Hearing this, Chen Ningyu really wanted to pull his sleeve and stop him from leaving.

Although she had to get used to separation, she also got used to his kindness to her.

Now that she is pregnant, she would rather he stay with her.

However, eight or nine out of ten things in life are not as we wish.

Yang Yanling rubbed her hair and said, "I will think carefully about the names of our children, one for each boy and one for girl.

You should also think about it. If yours is better than mine, I will use yours."

"Really?" Chen Ningyu was excited.

"Of course it's true. Also, don't forget to go out for a walk every day." Yang Yanling sighed, "You are too lazy. I'm really worried that if you don't move, you won't have the strength to give birth to a child." He looked at Madam Yang again, "Grandma, please urge her!"

Madam Yang said yes with red eyes.

Only then did Yang Yanling turn around and leave.

Chen Ningyu looked at his back and tears started to flow down her cheeks.

Unlike last time, this time, besides being reluctant, she also felt a little pain in her heart. As soon as he left, she already started to worry about his safety.

Seeing her crying like crazy, Madam Yang patted her on the back and said, "Silly child, stop crying. This is not good for the baby in your belly. If Yanling finds out, he will be worried again."

Chen Ningyu nodded and wiped her eyes again. Seeing that the young couple had a good relationship, Madam Yang was also relieved and comforted them, "Yanling will be back soon."

Chen Ningyu looked at her and suddenly said, "Grandma, I want to go see Concubine Shu."

"What?" Madam Yang was stunned.

"Grandma, I want to meet Concubine Shu." Chen Ningyu said it very clearly.

Madam Yang couldn't help but frowned: "How did you think of meeting her? Did Yanling say something? But Yanling didn't tell me about this. Oh, but for those two beauties, I have already sent them to the manor."

"Not really." Chen Ningyu thought for a moment, "Not entirely. I just want to know what my aunt thinks. Please send a message to her, grandmother. I want to meet her alone."

Seeing that she insisted again and again, Mrs. Yang agreed to her request.

☆, Chapter 63 Choice

Two days later, Concubine Shu summoned her.

In fact, Concubine Shu was also puzzled as to why Chen Ningyu wanted to see him, and moreover, after Yang Yanling had left the capital.

"Please sit down. I heard that you were pregnant. I didn't even have the chance to congratulate you, but you came here on your own." When Concubine Shu saw her, she gave her a seat.

Chen Ningyu thanked him and sat down.

Concubine Shu looked at her and saw that she looked good. It seemed that her family treated her well. She reminded her, "Pay attention to your diet on weekdays. You shouldn't come out in weather like this. It looks like it's going to rain. Be careful when you walk."

Before coming, Madam Yang also said the

same thing, but Chen Ningyu felt that she had to come once.

It's because the Third Prince has now put his hatred for Yang Yanling into action.

She wanted to know whether Concubine Shu was clear-headed or not.

Chen Ningyu nodded: "I know, thank you for your concern, madam."

Concubine Shu asked, "How is my mother? She didn't come with you."

"Grandmother has been taking the ointment prescribed by Doctor Li and has not been sick this winter. This time, I asked to see you alone."

Concubine Shu raised her eyebrows: "Oh? What's the matter?"

"It's because of your trip to Shaanxi." Chen Ningyu's face became more serious. "The recommended officials are people of the Third Prince and Yan Yuqing. This trip may be full of dangers, so I want to talk to the Queen."

Concubine Shu was stunned. As a governor, it was normal for Yang Yanling to go out to fight wars frequently, so she didn't think too much about him being sent to Shaanxi this time. She didn't expect that it was related to Li Changluo.

"Your Majesty, I think the Third Prince wants to put the Marquis to death!" Chen Ningyu said seriously, "I wonder what your Majesty thinks about this?"

"No way?" Concubine Shu shook her head. "I raised him, how could he be so cruel? He just wanted to... I definitely wouldn't want to take someone's life. Besides, Yanling is my nephew."

Shufei didn't want to think that Li Changluo was so stupid for doing stupid things just for a woman.

Chen Ningyu sighed. This was the reason why she had to come.

If Concubine Shu did not recognize Li Changluo's true face and still wanted to push him to the position of crown prince, he would not only drag herself into trouble in the future, but also harm the entire Yang family. How could she not worry?

"I hope your majesty will think twice. After all, it's just blood ties. What else can it be compared to? As long as your majesty is willing, I'm sure we can find out." Chen Ningyu stroked her belly. "Now I just hope that the Marquis can come back safely."

She was reminding Concubine Shu that she and Yang Yanling were her relatives, and Li Changluo was just a child raised by Concubine Shu, not her biological child. It was time for her to make a choice.

Concubine Shu frowned.

She never thought that one day Li Changluo would really be irreconcilable with Yang Yanling.

"The Marquis didn't tell Grandmother about this, fearing that she would worry." Chen Ningyu added, "Grandmother has enough things to worry about. It is often said that it is not easy for the Yang family to get to where we are today. Now that we have separated from Second Uncle, we have no one closer to us than the Queen."

After hearing this, Concubine Shu sighed slightly.

She knew how many tears Madam Yang had shed for her since she entered the palace, and she felt quite guilty towards her.

"I'll think about it. It's hard for you to come and talk to me about this."

Chen Ningyu nodded.

After she left, Concubine Shu was in deep thought for a long time.

A few days later, several officials reported to the emperor that Yang Dongping had been reinstated, asking him to allow him to return to his original post. However, Li Shiyu had not made a decision. When he came to Concubine Shu, he mentioned Yang Dongping while talking.

Concubine Shu didn't expect that Earl Gongshun would act so quickly, so she ran around for Yang Dongping.

"The last time my brother came, I saw that he still had difficulty walking. How could he lead the army to fight? I think it would be better for him to rest at home. My brother is not young anymore. I am worried that he will be injured again in the future and it will be even more difficult for him to recover."

Li Shiyu was a little surprised, but also very happy that Concubine Shu was sensible.

Now Yang Yanling is the governor, a first-rank official. If Yang Dongping is reinstated, he will be a second-rank official. The Yang family's momentum is a bit too great.

"Since my beloved concubine has said so, I will do as my beloved concubine says."

"Thank you, Your Majesty, for your understanding." Concubine Shu smiled and snuggled into Li Shiyu's arms.

Those memorials were useless.

When Yang Dongping found out, he was so angry that he almost vomited blood.

Originally, Earl Gongshun had promised himself that he would make it happen. But now, the Emperor did not agree, so he had to think of Concubine Shu as the cause.

She's my own sister, yet she's taking advantage of me at a time like this!

Yang Dongping smashed everything in the house.

Chen Ningyu quickly went to the Yongchun Marquis Mansion.

The lady had only seen her after the New Year, and she felt strange that she came again this time. After all, Chen Ningyu was pregnant, and it would not be appropriate for her to go out unless there was something special.

"It's for the Marquis." Chen Ningyu said directly, "The Third Prince is narrow-minded. This time when suppressing the rebels in Shaanxi, he sent people to strongly recommend the Marquis. I think he must be doing something bad behind the scenes. Wasn't the former governor dismissed?"

The lady knew it was for this reason and asked, "How did you know that? Did the Marquis tell you?"

"Yeah, but I was the one who asked first."

The lady laughed and said, "A husband and wife shouldn't keep secrets."

Chen Ningyu was puzzled as to why he didn't rush to talk about this matter first, but mentioned the relationship instead. She suddenly realized: "So grandma knew it!"

"Silly child, your father is the commander, how could he not know? He told your uncle and me that day that our two families are relatives, so naturally we are paying extra attention. If there is any disturbance, everyone will be able to detect it." The lady comforted, "Don't worry, if there is really a problem, we will work together to find a way to solve it. You still have your two aunts, right?"

Chen Ningyu sighed: "But I'm still a little scared."

The lady took her in her arms, patted her back gently and said, "Everyone goes through this, Ning Yu, you are married now. Although your grandmother can still protect you from the wind and rain, it will take a few years. You have to learn how to be a marquis' wife."

Chen Ningyu nodded: "I know, I met the Concubine Shu."

"Oh?" The lady laughed, "Well, you should try to persuade her."

"I just don't know if it will be of any use." If Concubine Shu thought it through and no longer stood on the same front with the Third Prince, their Yang family would be safer.

"Do your best and leave the rest to fate." The lady said earnestly, "Things in the world often don't go as we wish. We can only do our best. As long as we have a clear conscience, that's all."

Sometimes these storms cannot be avoided, and you can only rely on your faith to get through them. If you fail in the end, face it calmly.

Chen Ningyu sighed softly.

In early April, Yu gave birth to a daughter. Chen Ningyu went to congratulate her. She was more than two months pregnant at this time, but her belly was not noticeable and she could still wear clothes. However, Madam Yang was already in a hurry to ask someone to make large shirts suitable for pregnant women.

The eldest princess was so happy to have a granddaughter that she couldn't stop smiling. She was happier than having a son.

Chen Ningyu smiled and said, "This time, my aunt finally got what she wanted."

The eldest princess smiled and said, "That's right, but you are pregnant, and it would be best if it's a son. I will burn incense and pray to Buddha, and yours will not be missing either. You should take care of yourself, alas, poor child." Speaking of Chen Ningyu's life experience, the eldest princess felt sorry for her again.

When she was in the Chen family, her mother was just a stepmother and could not be relied upon. Now that she married into the Yang family, she became a stepmother-in-law and could not be relied upon either. Fortunately, Mrs. Yang was knowledgeable and sensible and did not do anything to disappoint her.

Chen Ningyu said: "It doesn't matter if it's a son or a daughter, the Marquis said that he likes them all."

The princess smiled and pinched her cheeks. "How can you believe a man's words? He is just trying to make you happy. Who doesn't like sons? Especially in a mansion like theirs, daughters can't inherit the title of marquis."

Yu joked, "Mother, you didn't just give birth to one child."

"That's right. Look at my head. Our Ning Yu should have seven or eight children. They will all be handsome men and beautiful women in the future."

Chen Ningyu blushed: "I don't want it!"

It is easy to give birth to a child, but difficult to raise one, and it is even difficult to raise one well.

Unexpectedly, the eldest princess suddenly sighed: "I don't know when I can hold Chaoqing's child!"

Yu's expression changed a little, and she thought to herself, Fu Chaoqing likes Chen Ningyu, so why would he marry another girl? But she couldn't tell the eldest princess this.

Chen Ningyu asked hurriedly: "What's wrong?"

"No one likes this child. Ah Yu, you happened to be here today, so please persuade him for me." The princess had a headache. Fu Chaoqing was already twenty years old, so he should get married. But he looked left and right and was not satisfied. "A few days ago, he even said that the girl from the Qi family was too dark. At night, people couldn't see her. Look, what did he say!"

The eldest princess pinched her brows and gritted her teeth.

Chen Ningyu twitched his lips.

If Fu Chaoqing really acted like this, it only meant that he didn't want to get married at all and was trying to make trouble for the eldest princess.

"I'll talk to my cousin." She just said perfunctorily.

When Fu Chaoyun and his brother came back, Chen Ningyu congratulated Fu Chaoyun. Fu Chaoyun looked at his daughter with her and said proudly, "I think she looks very similar to me, don't you think so?"

The baby's face was small, and it was hard to tell who the baby looked like, but Chen Ningyu still took a serious look and nodded,

"Yes, they do look alike, so you should treat your cousin's wife well and don't bully her. Giving birth to a child is exhausting."

"Of course." Fu Chaoyun smiled, "I also know that my wife is suffering. I almost fainted." He looked at Chen Ningyu sympathetically, "Ayu, you must be careful when the time comes. I see that you are also very weak."

"Of course I have." Chen Ningyu said proudly, "I have learned boxing and some sword skills." After saying that, he struck a stance and showed off his skills.

Fu Chaoyun was stunned: "When did you learn it?"

"The Marquis taught me." I won't even mention how I learned it. I shed tears when I mention it!

The princess smiled and said, "My nephew-in-law really cares about me." She then gave Fu Chaoyun a look and said, "Look at you, you are so stupid and don't know what to do. I, your daughter-in-law, have suffered a lot because of you."

Fu Chaoyun was shot and went to heal his wounds while groaning as he carried his daughter.

☆, Chapter 64: Courting Death

Chen Ningyu took some time to talk to Fu Chaoqing.

Before she could open her mouth, Fu

Chaoqing asked, "Mother asked you to persuade me again?"

Chen Ningyu was stunned: "How do you know? Is it obvious?"

Fu Chaoqing smiled and pointed at her hands: "Before this, you always liked to shake hands."

Chen Ningyu looked down and saw that his two hands were clasped together!

She smiled and let go: "Then you should know that this is not what I want, but my aunt is worried about you, so I have to come."

"I know." Fu Chaoqing was silent, walked forward for a while, and said slowly, "Ayu, I may never get married in this life. Instead, I need you to persuade mother more in the future."

"What?" Chen Ningyu asked, "Why?"

Fu Chaoqing looked back and saw that her eyes were wide open with surprise on her face.

He didn't know why she behaved like this. He always felt that Chen Ningyu was different from others and she was easy to accept many concepts.

"People don't have to get married, do they?" he asked rhetorically.

Chen Ningyu didn't know why, but when she heard this, her nose felt sore. She could accept that he didn't marry her, but she seemed unable to accept that Fu Chaoqing would never marry anyone else in his entire life.

How lonely would life be then?

He should have a confidante who would listen to him talk about his ideals, grind ink for him on snowy days, and cover him with a quilt even when she wakes him up at night, and they could take a walk together in the sunset in the evening. He should also have a son and a daughter like him, so that he could enjoy family happiness in his old age.

How could he remain single till the end of his life?

Chen Ningyu shook her head: "No, second cousin, this won't work, you can't do this!"

Fu Chaoqing frowned slightly and looked at her.

But she suddenly burst into tears.

It was as if my mind suddenly became clear, clearer than ever before.

It turned out that he had made up his mind not to get married, so he didn't marry her, not for any other reason. It was a pity that she only found out about it now.

Fu Chaoqing was flustered when he saw her crying.

"Ayu, don't cry, don't cry." He was a little incoherent, "I, I just said it casually, you may not take it seriously, look, I'm still young."

Chen Ningyu was still crying, and Danqiu came to persuade her, but she refused to listen.

Fu Chaoqing was anxious and didn't know

what to do. He grew up with Chen Ningyu, and it seemed that he had never seen her cry.

What did he say wrong?

Sooner or later, they would have to be told that they were not going to get married. He just told her in advance. Maybe he should have thought about it before saying it?

"Ayu." He asked softly, "What's wrong with you?" He reached out and gently touched her shoulder, "You are still pregnant, don't cry, I heard from my mother that it is not good for the child."

His voice was so gentle, like a breeze blowing between heaven and earth.

At this moment, she wanted to hug him so much, bury her face in his arms and have a good cry.

But she held back.

Gradually she stopped crying.

That was his decision. No matter what, he must have thought it through carefully. But she still hadn't figured out why. Could it be his body...

She shook her head, not daring to think further.

This conversation did not continue. Chen Ningyu apologized, "Second cousin, I lost my temper. Ever since I had a child, I have always been acting weird. I want to cry for no reason and I can't control it."

Fu Chaoqing breathed a sigh of relief: "My sister-in-law was the same at that time."

It can be seen that when you are pregnant,

you are not as rational as usual.
Chen Ningyu was now full of doubts, so he said goodbye to him and went to see Fu Chaoyun.
"How is my second cousin's health now?" she asked directly.
Fu Chaoyun's face changed.
"Is it true..."
"What do you mean really? I think it's good." Fu Chaoyun said hurriedly.
"Not at all. The last time he came to Tong County, he got sick!"
"This..." Fu Chaoyun stuttered, "Ayu, why are you asking these questions? You know Xiao Lan's body is worse than that of ordinary people."
"He said he would never get married." Chen Ningyu stared at Fu Chaoyun, "Are you hiding something?"
Although it really didn't matter if they didn't get married, as she had traveled through time and space and could accept all this, Fu Chaoqing was not a rebellious person, and she was not someone who would give up love for the sake of her principles. He is not.
Seeing her eyes staring at him, Fu Chaoyun was evasive, "No way, what can I hide from you? Ah Yu, why are you saying all this?"
Fu Chaoyun was a carefree person and not good at lying. Chen Ningyu could tell that he was not telling the truth.
"Then I'll go tell my aunt." She threatened Fu Chaoyun.

Fu Chaoyun was indeed anxious and grabbed her: "Ayu, Ayu, if you have something to say, please say it nicely. Don't be anxious! Go and tell mother. Mother will be worried. Don't go."

"Then tell me what's going on."

Fu Chaoyun was cornered by her and sighed, "Xiao Lan once said that she would not live long. He was the one who lied to the doctor so that he wouldn't have to take medicine every day."

Chen Ningyu was stunned as if struck by lightning.

Although she had doubts just now, she still couldn't bear it when she heard the truth.

"Ayu, I have no choice. I can't tell mom, can I?" He said with red eyes, "Ayu, you have to keep it a secret too. Don't tell anyone."

Chen Ningyu nodded silently.

She didn't say anything else, she just felt that fate was so cruel!

After returning to the Marquis' Mansion, she couldn't eat at night. Thinking of every detail of those years, she felt even more heartbroken. She couldn't help crying for a while and had nightmares at night. She was in a bad mood for several days.

Gu Qiu was worried and advised: "Young Madam, you are no longer Miss Chen Si, you are still pregnant."

Chen Ningyu knew it herself: "It will get better, but I can't do anything about it now."

It's not easy to accept this fact.

This is not a breakup, but a matter of facing the separation of life and death in the future.

Unless she figures it out and realizes that fate is inevitable and irreversible, then everything will slowly get better.

In May, Zhang Jihe was going to get married. The Zhang family had many relatives, so Chen Ningyu did not go, for fear of being seen. He only sent someone to deliver a generous gift. However, a few days later, Madam Yang invited the women of the Chen family to come and visit.

"We haven't talked together for a long time. Let's have some fun and see your granddaughter." Madam Yang also noticed Chen Ningyu's mood, so she asked her to come over.

The lady smiled and said, "I miss her too, but she has you as her mother-in-law, so I don't worry about anything."

When Chen Ningyu saw the lady, she also smiled.

She's gotten much better.

After all, she is a mother and she always has to pay more attention.

But Chen Ningrou didn't come today, and Jiang also had a gloomy face.

Chen Ningyu asked.

The lady sighed, "It's Ning Rou! I can't follow her now, so I'll keep her at home and marry her off to the Liu family in June. Your mother is reluctant, but I think she's crazy. If she continues to be willful, I'll have no choice but to send her to a nunnery. I heard you know about this, too?"

Chen Ningyu was startled and said, "Grandma, please don't blame me. I know she likes my second cousin, but I have also advised her. Could it be that she is still stubborn now?"

"That's right!" said the lady, "She came to me once and said she didn't want to marry anyone else, but how could the princess be interested in her? I went to find out, and the princess only likes girls with both talent and beauty, Ning Rou is no match for them. Besides, the princess would definitely not want to marry her."

Chen Ningyu didn't know what to say.

She also didn't expect Chen Ningrou to be so stubborn.

"But forcing her to marry him doesn't seem to be a good idea, does it? The Liu family will be furious when they find out. Grandmother, please think twice."

The lady sighed again: "What do you say?"

"Why not just let her be? When her infatuation fades, she will get married."

These are your own choices, no one can do anything about it.

The lady did not speak.

Chen Ningyu knew that her grandmother looked gentle and kind, but she was actually a resourceful person. Compared with Madam Yang, her temperament was obviously colder and harder, and she was a person who kept her word. That was why the family was so orderly and everyone had their own duties.

Chen Ningyu did not persuade him any further.

A few days later, after Yang Yanling had arrived in Shaanxi for a while, some officials began to impeach him. Several memorials were submitted today accusing him of abusing his power, being lawless, and taking lives.

When Madam Yang heard about it, she discussed it with Chen Ningyu.

Chen Ningyu breathed a sigh of relief: "Finally I know he arrived safely."

Shaanxi is quite far away from the capital. Even if he sent someone to deliver a message immediately, it would not arrive until now.

Madam Yang said angrily, "Look, these memorials came so quickly, if it wasn't premeditated, what could it be?"

"That's all. The Marquis is the governor. If he doesn't even have the right to kill a few people when he goes to suppress the rebels, how can he do anything? Is it possible for him to report everything to the emperor? As the saying goes, a general is not allowed to obey military orders when he is away from home. Don't worry, grandma. Those people can't cause any trouble." Chen Ningyu comforted her, "Besides, our relatives and friends are not pushovers."

Madam Yang felt more at ease after hearing

what she said, "That's right. He has been away for many years and nothing has happened to him. Now he is just a small rebel and should be easy to catch. I am overthinking it. Don't worry and take good care of your baby."

Chen Ningyu said yes.

But the matter was not resolved so quickly. The Third Prince and Yan Yuqing's people impeached Yang Yanling with all their might, even accusing him of more than a dozen crimes including disturbing the people, collecting money, and abducting women, and requested the emperor to order his dismissal and investigation.

During this period, it was almost one-sided. It was because Yang Yanling had been so successful before. He was straightforward in his work and had offended many people when he was governor. Naturally, there would be people who would take the opportunity to take advantage of him.

However, the Chen family, the Zhang family and others did not make much noise, and apart from a few occasional noises, it was not too intense.

When Chen Ningyu heard this, he felt a little surprised.

The lady has sent someone over now.

"The Madam said she was afraid that the Young Madam would worry." Mother Hu came in person. "In fact, Master Zhang and Master Xu both came here for this matter. The Madam said that it was Master Zhang who suggested waiting a little longer to see what the Emperor thought."

One sentence woke Chen Ningyu up.

What about relatives helping each other? There is no need for that. Even if the official who recommended Yang Yanling last time was loyal to the Third Prince and Yan Yuqing, so what? The final decision was made by the Emperor.

If he doesn't agree, everything will be useless.

But the emperor asked Yang Yanling to deal with the rebels, not to frame him.

Yang Yanling has only been in Shaanxi for a short while, and these people are eager to get rid of him. What will the emperor think? Chen Ningyu was moved, Zhang Zhijing was indeed amazing and thought things through. Fortunately, they did not work hard for Yang Yanling, otherwise it would have aroused the emperor's suspicion. This kind of treatment was the most appropriate.

Now, Li Shiyu was indeed annoyed about this. He didn't keep so many Jinyiwei for fun. Didn't he know who was the mastermind behind the impeachment of Yang Yanling? Yan Yuqing didn't mention it. His third son was the one who really disappointed him!

"At Chang Luo's age, it's time for him to be crowned king." Li Shiyu sighed and said to Wei Yan.

Wei Yan's heart trembled, thinking to himself, it seems that the emperor is going to deprive the third prince of his right to be the crown prince, but he is happy, so the second prince must be the future emperor!

The news soon reached Concubine Ning's ears. She laughed.

Sometimes people are so stupid that they collapse without their opponents doing anything.

She told Lingxin, the person next to her: "Spread this news."

Although it is a simple sentence, it contains mystery, because the emperor only said it to Wei Yan, and now everyone in the palace knows it. What will the emperor think of Wei Yan?

Lingxin was puzzled. Isn't this going to put Eunuch Wei to death?

But she never doubted her master's decision.

Watching Lingxin walk out, Concubine Ning sneered twice.

Wei Yan only provided some information, but his own family had to clean up so many messes for him. Now, it is time for him to come to an end. But I wonder what Shufei will do when she knows the news?

If you are not careful in this action, it will lead to irreparable consequences.

☆, Chapter 65 Abandonment

And Concubine Shu already knew it at this moment.

For more than ten years, she raised Li Changluo, treated him as her own son, and placed many hopes on him. Like all mothers in the world, she hoped her son would become successful.

But now, this dream may be shattered.

Concubine Shu was sitting upright on a chair when she heard the palace servant say that Li Changluo wanted to see her.

She didn't need to guess, she knew why Li Changluo came.

At this time, everyone knows the truth.

When Li Changluo saw her, he knelt down and bowed deeply.

Concubine Shu dismissed the palace maids.

"Mother, is this true?" Li Changluo looked at Concubine Shu pleadingly. He never thought that his father would make a decision so early, and he didn't know why it turned out like this.

Concubine Shu asked him to get up and comforted him, "It's still unknown. Maybe someone spread rumors. Don't worry."

Li Changluo said anxiously, "How could it be a rumor? Eunuch Wei has been arrested. Father has sent people to search his house. They all say that it was Eunuch Wei who leaked it. Mother, what should we do?"

Concubine Shu said: "If things have come to this, Changluo, you should obey your father."

"What!" Li Changluo's eyes widened, "Mother, you can't ignore your son!"

Concubine Shu sighed: "Chang Luo, do you know what you did wrong?"

Li Changluo asked hurriedly: "Please tell

me clearly, mother."

"You shouldn't have framed Yanling." There was disappointment in Concubine Shu's eyes.

Li Changluo was startled: "Mother..."

Concubine Shu said, "Do you think others don't know? Chang Luo, you treat people as fools, and you treat me as a fool too."

"I don't dare!"

"You dare, you are so brave." Concubine Shu said in a sad tone, "I have advised you many times not to go against him, but you didn't listen, and even spent so much effort to deal with him. Chang Luo, he is my nephew!"

In this palace, she was the only one who treated him the best, but he did not hesitate at all when it came to harming Yang Yanling. How could this not make Concubine Shu feel heartbroken?

Even if she tried her best to help Li Changluo become the crown prince, it was hard to say whether there would be a good ending in the end, not to mention that she had to gamble the lives of all the people in the Yang family.

Is it worth it?

This is something she has been thinking about.

Obviously, she has got the answer now.

"Chang Luo, if the emperor really makes a decision, you should just be a good prince." Concubine Shu said the last sentence.

Li Changluo walked out with a pale face.

In the past few days, Concubine Ning has been waiting for news about Concubine Shu.

But Concubine Shu never left the house, nor did she ask for an audience with the emperor.

After all, because of the affection they had for so many years, Li Shiyu went to see Concubine Shu.

Her eyes were red and she looked a little haggard.

Since his words were spread, it was normal for Concubine Shu to behave like this. After all, that was the child she raised. Li Shiyu felt a little guilty and he sat down to comfort Concubine Shu.

Shufei said softly that it was nothing.

"Nothing, you've lost weight?" Li Shiyu held her hand, "If you have anything to say to me, just say it."

Concubine Shu shed tears again: "It's Chang Luo who is not doing well. The emperor originally had high hopes for him. I just thought that he would be crowned a king in the future and we wouldn't be able to see each other for several years. I was always a little sad."

Li Shiyu heard that she had been crying these past few days, which showed how sad she was. But who would have thought that when he came in person today, she had no complaints. Even though her eyes were full of pleading, she didn't say a word of pleading.

Li Shiyu sighed.

He is also a father, how can he not understand this feeling?

"Nianlian, I haven't made a decision yet, maybe..." He looked at Concubine Shu, meaning that maybe she could consider it.

Concubine Shu showed some joy, but the light soon disappeared.

She shook her head and said, "It's all my fault. I didn't teach Chang Luo well. Now that he is like this, he can still reflect on himself. I know that the emperor has given him a lot of patience. What more can I ask for? The decisions made by the emperor are always beneficial to the entire country and the people. I only hope that the emperor will not blame Chang Luo too much. After all, he is still young and has not thought through many things."

Li Shiyu was very pleased to hear this. He held her in his arms and said, "I'm sorry for making things difficult for you."

Concubine Shu shed tears and whispered, "As long as the emperor is by my side, I will have no difficulty. Chang Luo still has a long way to go, but I only have the emperor."

She was in tears and looked very pitiful.

Li Shiyu couldn't help but bent down and kissed her.

Even so, although Concubine Shu had her own little thoughts, she ultimately chose to be loyal to him. She did not have so many twists and turns, nor did she have such courage. Even if she wanted Li Changluo to become the crown prince, over the years she had only tried to win over her own nephew and did nothing else.

Li Shiyu stayed with Concubine Shu that night and stayed for two days.

When Concubine Ning heard this, she was so angry that she couldn't eat properly.

Li Shiyu dealt with the matter quickly and all the officials who had been impeached were dismissed. Fortunately, not many people were implicated, but this served as a great reminder to all civil and military officials.

Don't involve the prince for no reason, be careful about your official hat!

Good news soon came from Shaanxi that Yang Yanling had trapped the rebels in Linhu County, including the bandit leader. It would not take many days for them to be captured.

Madam Yang and Chen Ningyu both breathed a sigh of relief.

Then, he will be back soon.

By June, Chen Ningyu's belly had grown quite big, and she was finally able to wear the clothes that Madam Yang had ordered for her. Madam Yang was very happy and came to see her every day, giving her many instructions.

Chen Ningyu also went out for a walk every day. She did not forget what Yang Yanling said, that she should keep exercising. However, her longing for him grew deeper day by day, as if the baby in her belly grew bigger, and her longing for him became stronger.

That day, she flipped through various poetry collections and picked out names for her children. If it was a boy, he would be named Yang Yushi, and if it was a girl, she would be named Yang Xiu. She liked the word "Xiu" very much because it had a broad and beautiful meaning.

"Sounds good, right?" she asked Gu Qiu.

Gu Qiu smiled and said, "Young Madam is well-educated. I would like to ask Young Madam to marry one for my child in the future."

She is now pregnant too.

Chen Ningyu was very happy: "Okay, I'll think about it."

Bai Tao came in at this moment and said, "Someone from the Chen family is here."

Chen Ningyu was invited in, and it turned out to be an old woman.

The old woman bowed and said, "Madam Tai asked me to come and see that the fifth young lady is here."

"No." Chen Ningyu was surprised. "Why? Is the fifth sister missing?"

Otherwise, why would I come here to look for her?

The old woman said, "Yes, the Madam said she was afraid that she would disturb the Young Madam."

Chen Ningyu was a little surprised.

It sounds like Chen Ningrou ran away from home?

"What happened?"

Madam Chen also told the maid not to hide anything, so the maid told her everything: "Madam has arranged a marriage for the fifth young lady. He is the second son of Mr. Liu, the left minister of the capital. The fifth young lady didn't seem to be dissatisfied and was very well behaved. But yesterday, she sneaked out of the house and has not been found yet. She will get married in a few days."

The mansion is still in chaos. Jiang is crying and shouting, worried that something has happened to Chen Ningrou. Chen Xiu is looking for her everywhere. The lady is anxious and has arrested all the maids and servants who served Chen Ningrou for questioning, but they didn't get much clues. They only know that Baozhu left with Chen Ningrou, and that Baozhu was responsible for luring away the guards at the back door. Chen Ningyu had a headache, wondering how such a thing could happen. But no matter what, the most important thing right now was to deal with the Liu family. The wedding was about to begin, and if the bride went missing, that would be such an embarrassing thing. If things went wrong, the two families would even become enemies! It's no wonder that the lady came to her, after all, she also knew the inside story.

"Did grandma send anyone to visit my cousin?" she asked.

"I've been there," the old woman replied,

"but I didn't find anyone."
Chen Ningyu let her go first.
After a while, Madam Yang came to see her and asked about this matter, thinking that there was something going on in the Chen family. Chen Ningyu did not hide anything and told her everything.
Upon hearing about this, Madam Yang also found it absurd. She frowned and said, "This is not easy to handle. Both families are engaged, and if there is no bride at that time, it will be a great humiliation for the man's family. Even the woman's family will be criticized for not being able to discipline a girl properly."
So, Chen Ningrou's move was quite vicious.
I guess she hated him very much in her heart, so she pretended to be submissive at first. When the two families got engaged, she took the opportunity to slip away to embarrass the lady.
This damn girl really doesn't know whether she lives or dies.
By doing this, she would offend the entire family. Where would she find a place if she were to be found later?
Chen Ningyu said: "It seems too late to tell the Liu family now. They must have told all their relatives. This method won't work, so we can only find the person."
Madam Yang sighed, "Where do you think your fifth sister will go?"
Chen Ningyu didn't know.
Madam Yang consoled him: "Don't worry.

There are so many people in the Chen family. I just came to ask. If you can't think of it, forget it. It's tiring to take care of the baby. The baby in your belly is growing bigger. You should spend less energy on it."

Chen Ningyu agreed.

But she was still worried about the lady.

At this age, her own granddaughter is playing tricks on her. The old lady must be very angry. She doesn't know whether she can find Chen Ningrou. If she can't find her, what will happen to the Liu family in the end.

What a big problem!

She thought about it and asked Madam Yang, "Does our family have any relationship with the Liu family?"

"I am familiar with Madam Liu, but in recent years, I have been out of town so often that we don't see each other much."

Madam Yang also knew what she meant. "If this situation really cannot be resolved, I will talk to Madam Liu when the time comes."

Chen Ningyu nodded, thanked Madam Yang first, returned to the yard, and started talking to the people around him.

"Guess where the fifth sister is hiding? In my opinion, it is impossible for her to leave the city. She is not that brave. She knows that it is dangerous outside."

Gu Qiu asked, "Could it be hidden in the inn?"

Dan Qiu asked, "Maybe she went to her grandparents' house?"

Everyone was talking at once, but it seemed that their guesses were not very good. The Chen family must have searched these places. When it was almost evening, Bai Tao saw a maid coming over. She went over to listen to a few words and said in panic, "They said they found it, but the Fifth Miss, the Fifth Miss has already shaved her head!"

☆, Chapter 66: Breaking off the Engagement

This news shocked Chen Ningyu again. Is Chen Ningrou determined to shock people until she dies?

She came back to her senses and asked, "Is there a nunnery in the capital?"

Even if you want to become a nun, it is not that easy. In a formal nunnery, it is not the case that if you want to become a nun, you can go to the nunnery and the nun will shave your head for you.

Gu Qiu replied, "Madam, there is one in the west of the capital. It was very popular at first, but it became unpopular after a fire. I heard that most of the nuns went to the nunneries outside the city, and only a few are left here."

Chen Ningyu didn't know about this and she frowned.

"I'd better go to Chen's house and take a look."

She went to talk to Madam Yang, but Madam

Yang did not dissuade her this time. Now that Chen Ningrou had become a nun, she would definitely not be able to marry, which was a big deal. So she only told her to be careful and sent a few more people to accompany her.

Chen Ningyu returned to the Chen family immediately.

At this moment, Chen Ningrou had been brought back, of course it was forced. She had refused to leave and was dragged back by several strong old women.

The old lady was sitting there in anger at the moment. She was already old, and the marriages of her two sons, two daughters, and three granddaughters were all handled with great fanfare. Now, there was Chen Ninghua in front and Chen Ningrou behind, both of whom were troublesome!

Chen Ningrou went even worse and caused such a big trouble.

Jiang cried and begged the Madam: "Ning Rou is ignorant, please forgive her, mother."

The lady sneered: "She spared me, didn't she? She shaved her head to save trouble, but I don't know what to do now!"

Zhang also said, "Second brother's wife, I'm not saying anything wrong, but Ning Rou really went too far this time. How are we going to explain this to the Liu family? I heard that there are dozens of tables prepared for the banquet, and some of the distant relatives are here."

Jiang just cried. She didn't know how to

solve the problem. She sobbed and said, "Is Ning Rou possessed by something? She wasn't like this before. How about we ask a Taoist monk to exorcise the evil spirit for her?"

"You're completely shirking responsibility," Chen Xiu rebuked, "I don't know how you raised Rou'er to let her do something like this!"

Jiang immediately cried even more sadly.

When Chen Ningyu came in, she saw this scene and also heard what Jiang said.

"Hey, why are you here?" The lady saw her and asked with concern, "You are pregnant, you should be careful. I just asked someone to ask you, it's nothing."

"Grandma, how can I not come back? I also want to help a little."

The lady sighed.

Zhang said, "We can only ask the Liu family to cancel the engagement."

"It's our family's fault. I'll go and apologize tomorrow." Chen Xiu said with a sullen face, "We'll do whatever they say."

"The Madam said that she has some friendship with Old Madam Liu, so we can go and talk to her." Chen Ningyu paused and said, "But if we tell the truth, I'm afraid the Liu family will resent us."

After all, Chen Ningrou refused at first, but it was the lady who forced her to marry. This is the harmful aspect of marriages arranged by parents and matchmakers.

But Chen Ningyu couldn't say it directly. In this matter, she originally disagreed with the lady forcing Chen Ningrou, but the lady insisted on having her own way, which led to this situation.

Of course, Chen Ningrou herself also had big problems. If she had cried, made a fuss, and even threatened to hang herself before the engagement, other families would have known about it and would not have agreed to marry her. But she chose to do this after the engagement, which was totally wrong.

"I think it would be better to just do as mother said just now and say that Fifth Sister was possessed by evil spirits. Otherwise, if Liu family asks why Fifth Sister wanted to become a nun, it will be hard to explain."

Madam, think so.

"But why would the nunnery allow my fifth sister to be ordained?" Chen Ningyu still had questions. "It should be said that the five roots must be pure, and the nun in the nunnery would have examined it. How could it be so fast?"

Zhang replied, "The nunnery is in such a state of disrepair. Ning Rou went there with money and asked others to shave their heads and give them the money. How could they refuse? They are so obsessed with money that they don't care about the rules."

Chen Ningyu was speechless.

The lady rubbed her forehead and said, "Let's do it this way. I'll trouble your mother-in-law to come with me when the time comes."

"Mom is going too?" Chen Xiu asked.

The lady said, "I was the first one to choose this marriage, how can I ignore it? I have no choice but to sacrifice my reputation."

Jiang lowered her head even lower and asked with a trembling voice, "Mother, how are you going to deal with Ning Rou?"

"What can we do? She wants to be a nun. We'll send her to a nunnery tomorrow!"

"No, mother!" Jiang cried, "She just made a mistake in the heat of the moment, mother, how could she want to become a nun? You should keep her at home." She hugged Chen Xiu's legs again, "Husband, she is also your daughter, can you really bear to let her go to a nunnery?"

In Chen Xiu's heart, Chen Ningrou was also well-behaved and cute, and he really didn't expect this day to come.

"Mother." Chen Xiu also pleaded, "Please forgive Ning Rou this time."

The lady was silent for a while, then closed her eyes and said, "If something like this happens, many people will know about it. Why do you still keep her at home? Even if she is possessed by evil spirits, she should go out to get treatment, right? There are nunneries outside the city that accept girls. Let her stay there first, and wait until she understands and comes back. That's it, and you all should stop talking!"

Hearing that there was still room for maneuver, Jiang didn't dare to say anything more.

The lady was shocked and in a bad mood, so she went to rest later.

Chen Xiu said to Chen Ningyu, "Mother loves you the most. How about you stay here for a few days? I'll go and tell Madam Yang."

Chen Ningyu naturally agreed.

"Don't worry about your son-in-law. I think he will be back soon." Chen Xiu looked at her with concern. "Now that you are pregnant, are you still used to it? When your mother was pregnant with you, it was also very hard, but she didn't like to talk about it."

Chen Ningyu smiled and said, "I was not used to it at first, but after a while, it got better. However, I inevitably had backaches and my appetite was also strange. Sometimes I loved to eat, and sometimes I didn't want to eat at all. But I still had to eat so that the baby in my belly wouldn't be hungry."

"It's not easy to have a child." Chen Xiu sighed, "It's hard for you, Ning Yu, so how are you doing in the mansion?"

"Well, everything is fine. My second uncle and second aunt no longer live here. It's very quiet now. The lady comes to see me every day."

Chen Xiu smiled and said, "It's good that they are devoted to you."

The father and daughter talked for a while,

and Chen Xiu sent her to Furong Garden before leaving.

The next day, she thought of Chen Ningrou and went to see her.

Chen Ningrou really shaved her head. She was sitting in front of the desk, reading a book. When she saw her coming, she sneered and said, "Are you here to laugh at me? I'm telling you, I'm fine now. Anyway, I don't have to marry into the Liu family."

Still very willful, and seems a bit fearless.

Chen Ningyu said, "What's so funny about this? Fifth sister, when it comes to getting married, we are no different. We all obey our grandmother."

Chen Ningrou was stunned.

"It's just that your method of handling it is different. You only think that since grandma is unwilling to help you, you want to make grandma regret it, right? Then what good will you get from doing this? Are you really going to never marry and become a nun for the rest of your life?"

Chen Ningrou put down the book: "I just won't get married. You know who I want to marry. Since I can't marry him, forget it." She looked at Chen Ningyu with a pair of shining eyes. "I'm not afraid to say anything. I only like him. If anyone else wants me to marry him, I would rather die!"

Said it so firmly.

At this moment, Chen Ningyu admired her a little.

Although Chen Ningrou has always made her dislike her.

"If you think this way, I have nothing to say." Chen Ningyu said, "It's always everyone's choice."

Chen Ningrou smiled and said, "Yes, I don't have the luck of my fourth sister. I have to fall in love with someone who doesn't like me, but I don't regret it. I have also realized this time that no matter my father, mother, or grandmother, they all really love me. They only want me to marry someone else. They don't care about my preferences. I have thought it through. Family is nothing more than this."

These words made Chen Ningyu's heart move.

She couldn't help but wonder, if in the past, the lady wanted her to marry a young man, and that young man happened to be someone she really disliked, what would she do?

Would she question the lady's feelings for her?

Will the lady still force her after knowing this?

She suddenly didn't dare to think further.

"Fifth sister, take care." Chen Ningyu took a last look at Chen Ningrou and left Jinxiuyuan.

After a while, Mrs. Yang came.

Yesterday Chen Xiu sent someone to get some news.

"Old sister, I have to ask for your help this time." Mrs. Chen apologized when she saw her, "I'm so sorry."

"What nonsense!" said Madam Yang. "We are relatives and sisters for many years. What does this mean? Let's go now. The longer we delay, the worse it will be."

So they went to Liu's house.

The Liu family had actually heard some rumors and originally wanted to come and ask, but the Chen family arrived first.

When they heard that Chen Ningrou was suddenly possessed by evil spirits and took the money to run to the nunnery to become a nun, the Liu family was shocked. This turned out to be true, and they were naturally very dissatisfied.

The lady apologized repeatedly and said she was willing to make the matter public and tell the people in Kyoto that their daughter was possessed by evil spirits and they felt that the Liu family should not be implicated, so they wanted to ask the Liu family to cancel the engagement.

As for all expenses, they will be borne by the Chen family.

This attitude is considered very good. Although the Liu family feels that it is too unreasonable, they can't do anything about it. They can't possibly want Chen Ningrou anymore. Besides, even if the Chen family takes the blame, it will not affect the Liu family's young master's marriage in the future.

Madam Yang also pleaded with Madam Liu.

The Liu family agreed.

Within a few days, the lady sent Chen Ningrou to a nunnery outside the city.

At the same time, in the palace, Li Shiyu originally wanted to make Li Changluo a prince and send him away from the capital. However, Li Changluo fell ill and could not get up again. The imperial physician examined him again and again but could not persuade him to change, so he could only be treated slowly.

No matter what Li Shiyu was like, he would not watch his son die in front of him, so he temporarily gave up the idea of making him king and let Li Changluo recover from his illness first.

☆, Chapter 67 Return to Beijing

In July, Yang Yanling returned to Beijing. Chen Ningyu's belly was already very obvious. When she heard that he had arrived at the city gate, she could not sit still and kept walking around the house.

Madam Yang came in with a smile and said, "Don't worry, he still has to go see the emperor, and it might be dark when he comes back. Can you stand until then with your belly bulging?"

Chen Ningyu sighed, "He's been gone for too long. I didn't know when he would come back, which would have been better. But now, I can't help it for even a moment."

Madam Yang patted her hands and pulled her to sit down. "It's like this. I'm not here yet. I said I came to persuade you, but I can't sit still. Let's talk and kill time." Chen Ningyu smiled.

"Let me show you these little clothes." Madam Yang called the housekeeper who was in charge of needlework. "I asked for it earlier. Now there are more than ten or twenty pieces of each kind."

The housekeeper brought the clothes and spread them in front of Chen Ningyu.

As expected, everything was already ready. There were not only small shirts and jackets for outer wear, but also inner clothes, which were as big as her palm. Chen Ningyu touched them and found them soft and thick. The outer clothes were embroidered with various patterns, including five blessings patterns, round patterns, and cloud patterns.

"This is great." Chen Ningyu praised, "It's pleasing to look at, and it will definitely be comfortable to wear when the time comes."

The housekeeper smiled and said, "It's all done according to the madam's instructions."

Madam Yang said, "The shoes haven't been made yet. I know you have good craftsmanship, so I've made quite a few for the children. Also, there are small quilts and other things. Children need to cover themselves differently from adults, so I asked them to make several different thicknesses of quilts."

Chen Ningyu thanked Madam Yang: "Grandma, you are so thoughtful."

"That's my great-great-grandson!" Madam Yang paused, "Even a great-great-granddaughter would be just as good."

She was afraid that Chen Ningyu would misunderstand and think that she only cared about boys.

Chen Ningyu smiled and said, "I will be filial to you anyway."

The two talked for a long time.

Seeing that it was getting dark, Madam Yang said, "I'm afraid it's time to go back. I'll go see how the kitchen is preparing."

When Yang Yanling came back, his family naturally had to have a meal together. It was a welcoming banquet, and Mrs. Yang went there in person to show her importance.

Chen Ningyu said, "I'll go with you. My waist is sore from sitting there."

"Why are you going? The road is unclear now, be careful not to fall. Just wait here. I, an old woman, am more agile than you now."

Mrs. Yang went out with a smile.

Chen Ningyu didn't know what to do, so he stood up and looked at the door again and again.

The people around her knew that she was anxious, so when Yang Yanling appeared, Bai Tao shouted from afar: "Madam, the Marquis is back!"

Chen Ningyu was immediately surrounded by great joy and called Gu Qiu: "Hurry, help me out."

Gu Qiu supported her and they both came to the yard.

Although it was night, lanterns had been lit everywhere to welcome Yang Yanling. He walked in wearing a dark blue jacket, with half of his face buried in the shadows, so he could not be seen clearly.

Chen Ningyu shouted: "My Lord..."

She only said two words when her throat became blocked for some reason and her nose felt sore that she wanted to cry.

When Yang Yanling heard her voice, he looked forward and saw her standing not far away, with her black hair half hanging down and her small face looking particularly white in the night, as if it was glowing.

He strode up to her, stretched out his hand and held her in his arms, leaning against her hair and said, "Ning Yu, my lady."

The voice actually seemed a little strange. Chen Ningyu couldn't hold back her tears, which flowed down. She hugged his waist and cried, "Why did you take so long? It's been so long. Look, my belly is so big. It's been half a year."

His heart softened and he quickly apologized, "I won't go there again. I will just stay with you."

Chen Ningyu continued crying, wetting his shirt front.

Yang Yanling patted her back and said, "Okay, okay, stop crying. I'm back now. I'm going to tell the emperor tomorrow not to send me to fight in any wars. My wife won't agree. Is that okay?"

Chen Ningyu chuckled and reached out to hit him: "You are just talking nonsense. The emperor thinks you are crazy."

He grabbed her hand and looked at her with a smile: "It's nothing to go crazy for my wife."

His eyes were filled with tenderness and affection, as if they could melt people.

Chen Ningyu then looked at him carefully and said distressedly, "The Marquis has lost weight."

Yang Yanling pinched her face and said, "My wife has gained weight. Come, show me my child."

He squatted down and looked at her belly.

It was autumn now, and she wasn't wearing thick clothes, so her belly protruded and couldn't be covered.

Yang Yanling reached out and touched it, with a big smile on his face, he leaned forward and asked: "My son, are you behaving well in there? Have you bullied your mother? Grow up quickly and come out to show your father."

Chen Ningyu laughed again.

Yang Yanling pulled her into the house and said, "Be careful not to catch a cold if you stay outside all the time." He asked Danqiu to wrap her in a light cloak and said, "Sit for a while. Let's go see grandma."

Chen Ningyu said, "I'm not tired. I've been sitting with grandma all afternoon. Let's go quickly. Grandma misses you too."

Yang Yanling went with her.

On the way, he was afraid that she might get into trouble, so he never let go of her hand.

Mrs. Yang was happy to see her grandson, but she was afraid that he was hungry, so she quickly asked the kitchen to serve some food.

Tang and Yang Yankang were also there.

The mother and son have been very well behaved recently. Tang was afraid that she would be kicked out of the house like the second wife, so she never went out of the house. Yang Yankang didn't cause any trouble.

The family had a harmonious meal together.

Mrs. Yang knew that the two of them were feeling happy after a short separation, so she said she was tired early and told them to go back.

Yang Yanling went to wash up. He had been traveling these days and had no time to take care of these things. When he got home, he felt unwell all over. Chen Ningyu was sitting on the beauty couch reading a book.

The baby is due in three months. When the baby is born, she has to be a good wife and mother. But being a good mother is not something that can be done by just talking about it. She has to teach the child.

However, she had no experience and was still a little worried. So she decided to recharge herself by reading various books.

Yang Yanling came in, picked up the book in her hand and looked at it, then said with a smile: "The Analects? What's the matter? Have you changed your taste when I was away? Did you like to read vernacular novels before, or some kind of fantasy novels?"

"Yes, I didn't have any children before." Chen Ningyu glanced at him.

Yang Yanling flipped through the books on the low table next to the couch and saw books on military affairs, geography, biographies of famous officials, etc. He then picked up a volume, sat next to her and said, "You are right. I am not at home most of the time. The child needs your education. You are a girl... you should read more books. When the child grows up, if he is a boy, send him to the academy early."

"What if it's a girl?" Chen Ningyu asked.

"As for my daughter, you can teach her however you want. As long as she is like you, everything will be fine." Yang Yanling said with a smile, "Can I still expect my daughter to achieve great things in the future? I will be satisfied if she finds a good son-in-law."

Chen Ningyu smiled and took his arm: "I will be satisfied only if you find someone like the Marquis, but it would be best if he doesn't have to go to war like the Marquis, or if he is like my uncle, but his personality cannot be the same."

She felt that Zhang Zhijing was also an ideal husband. He was capable, smart, filial, and would not take concubines. His only shortcoming was that he was too strict. If he had a gentler personality, he would be truly perfect.

Yang Yanling gnashed his teeth and pinched her face: "As soon as I came back, you dislike me?"

"I don't dislike you, Lord. I just dislike that you're a general." Chen Ningyu snuggled into his arms, her face pressed against his chest, and said with her eyes slightly closed, "How could I dislike you? Lord is so kind. I just don't want to worry about you. I don't want my daughter to be in fear in the future."

Yang Yanling sighed slightly and hugged her tightly.

The two were silent for a while, and Chen Ningyu suddenly said, "My Lord, the Third Prince was originally going to be crowned a king, but he claimed to be seriously ill and is now staying in the palace."

Yang Yanling also heard about this today.

He had always been very alert to Concubine Shu and the Third Prince. Hearing this, he sneered and said, "They will definitely cause trouble." He smiled at her and said, "You also made a contribution when you went back to see Aunt last time."

"Auntie, you still have to figure it out yourself."

Yang Yanling's face turned serious again: "But it was my aunt who raised the Third Prince. If anything happens to him, I can't escape the blame."

Chen Ningyu agreed very much after hearing this: "We need to keep an eye on them. My Lord, why don't you meet my cousin Fu tomorrow? He is in the Jinyiwei, so it will be more convenient for him to do things."

Yang Yanling hummed, and said in a gentle tone: "You are really worried. I will take care of it. You don't have to worry about these things in the future. I am here. You just need to give me a baby."

But the next day, he still listened to Chen Ningyu and went to meet Fu Chaoyun.

Fu Chaoyun was a deputy captain in the Embroidered Uniform Guard and often went to the Meridian Gate for inspection. He was quite surprised to see Yang Yanling.

Yang Yanling told him the purpose: "We are not going to monitor the Third Prince. After all, he is in the Imperial City. Even if you are a Jinyiwei, you cannot come and go freely. Therefore, we only need to keep an eye on his followers. He also has a few confidants."

Fu Chaoyun understood and said, "Okay." He then asked him about Chen Ningyu.

"When the baby is born, I will invite you to have a drink." Yang Yanling smiled.

Afterwards, he went to find his long-time friend, who was serving as the commander of the imperial guards in the capital.

The imperial guards, the people who guard the emperor, empress, crown prince, and concubines, are the key in Yang Yanling's opinion. If the third prince makes any unusual moves, it will certainly not escape their eyes.

He just reminded them to be more cautious and not be careless at all.

After doing all this, he felt relieved and went to see Concubine Shu again.

Since Concubine Shu has abandoned the Third Prince, she is still his good aunt.

When Concubine Shu saw him coming, she was filled with joy, for that was her nephew whom she had lost and found again.

As a result, Yang Yanling warned her as soon as he arrived: "Aunt, no matter how seriously ill the Third Prince is, if he wants to see you, you should not go."

☆, Chapter 68: Martial Arts Examination

Concubine Shu frowned. Li Changluo was about to be crowned king, and he was still thinking about this.

"Yanling, he's leaving the capital soon, what else could it be?" She smiled, "Don't worry about it. You're going to be a father soon, so you should be more open-minded and don't hold the past in your heart."

Yang Yanling laughed: "Aunt, do you think I am holding a grudge against him? I am just afraid that he will take advantage of you!"

Concubine Shu asked: "How to use it?"

Yang Yanling said calmly, "My nephew is a bystander. How can such a coincidence happen in the world? He is seriously ill just when he is about to be crowned as a king? He is in a bad mood because he did not get what he wanted. It is normal to have a minor illness, but this illness makes him unable to move. How can people believe that he had no symptoms before? The emperor and aunt have feelings for him, so they think it is true."

Concubine Shu's face darkened.

Because it's really chilling to hear these words.

The child she raised with her own hands would not be like this. She even pretended to be sick to deceive others.

"Aunt, don't forget how he treated me. Fortunately, the emperor is wise." Yang Yanling narrowed his eyes slightly. "It is said that you won't cry until you see the coffin. Some people are like that."

Concubine Shu slowly exhaled, clasped her hands together and said, "Since I have already made my attitude clear to the emperor, it will remain the same in the future. No matter what Chang Luo does, I will not help him."

This is considered a promise.

Yang Yanling nodded: "I know that my aunt is in trouble, but I am offended only for the sake of our Yang family."

"How could I not know that it is not easy for you to support the Marquis' Mansion alone." Concubine Shu sighed, "I don't count on your second uncle anymore. Last time, Earl Gongshun wanted to help him revive, but I stopped him. Yanling, how can I not think about the Yang family? I have been doing this for Chang Luo all these years because I am afraid that the second prince will have a hard time in the future... Our Yang family will also have a hard time!"

Concubine Ning has always been a thorn in her side, so the Second Prince must be the same. If he ascends the throne in the future, one can imagine what will happen to the Yang family. She is just preparing for a rainy day.

Yang Yanling said calmly: "Nephew naturally understands, but I think it is too early to talk about this. If the enemy does not move, I will not move either. Nephew thinks it is the best strategy."

If the second prince really becomes the crown prince in the future and then threatens the Yang family, he will not sit idly by. However, if he reveals his intentions at the beginning, he will be easily caught.

Concubine Shu finally understood what he meant. She bit her lip and said, "Why didn't you say so earlier?"

Yang Yanling sneered: "Auntie, do you think you can convince the Third Prince? To be honest, he was not up to the task in the first place, and now it's like this, it's only a matter of time!"

Concubine Shu leaned back dejectedly. It was she who had placed too much expectations on Li Changluo. Fortunately, she came to her senses in time.

"I understand now, you don't have to worry anymore." She said to Yang Yanling, "Take good care of mother. I, as her daughter, have really let her down."

Yang Yanling nodded, said goodbye and left.

In August, it was the time for the military examination. Zhang Jiwan did not waste his efforts over the past few years and passed the exam. He was so happy that he finally didn't have to go back to study!

Zhang Zhijing was both angry and happy.

What made him angry was that Zhang Jiwan succeeded and ultimately did not obey his father. What made him happy was that at least his son was not a useless person and could still be of some use.

Chen Ningyu was also very happy. She thought that she had supported Zhang Jiwan in pursuing his ideals. This guy did not lie and really put it into action. It was just that her belly was too big and it was inconvenient for her to go out, so she did not go to congratulate him in person. But giving a gift was also a headache.

It's not a marriage, nor is it a Chinese imperial examination, otherwise it would be easier to choose things.

Seeing that she was troubled, Yang Yanling took out a small cowhide booklet.

Chen Ningyu was puzzled. What was this thing? It didn't look like a book and didn't look valuable.

Yang Yanling opened the booklet and showed it to her: "It's not ordinary. It contains my father's experience and what I have discovered in the past few years. Although it is not valuable..."

"How can it not be valuable!" Chen Ningyu shouted, "It is a priceless treasure."

Yang Yanling smiled: "Do you think so?"

"Yes, this is much better than those military books. Most of the information in the books is dead. Even if you learn it, if you don't know how to use it, it's just learning in vain. The Marquis gave him the most precious one. My cousin will definitely be very happy. He originally wanted to be a general."

Yang Yanling smiled and said, "Since you are satisfied, just send him off. I think this guy is quite determined."

It took only three years to pass the military examination. That showed real effort.

After Zhang Jiwan received it, he was indeed very happy. He came to the mansion the next day to express his gratitude in person. Later, he joined the Five Military Commanders' Office and worked under Yang Yanling.

Madam Yang came to talk to Yang Yanling again that day.

"Your brother is already grown up. You can't really ignore him. After all, he is born to the same father."

Although Yang Yankang was a playboy, he

actually just loved to eat, drink and have fun. He had never gotten into any big trouble. After the second wife was kicked out last time, he had been idle at home.
Madam Yang couldn't stand it anymore.
How can I get married in this situation? After all, he is her grandson and Yang Dongyuan's biological son!
Yang Yanling couldn't resist, so he found a job for Yang Yankang as a minor official in the Wucheng Bingmasi.
He was an official, but Tang didn't take him seriously. She said unhappily, "You are the son of a marquis, and your elder brother is a first-rank governor. Why do you only serve as a clerk? I think I should talk to your grandmother about this."
Yang Yankang stopped her in a hurry: "Oh, mother, please stop making trouble, okay? I am a clerk, what can I do with my limited ability? I am just a gangster, even if you make me a high official, I can't do it."
Yang Yankang had this great advantage: he was quite self-aware.
Tang was angry: "Why can't you do it? You and he have the same father!"
"Not the same mother." Yang Yankang blurted out.
Tang was so angry that he wanted to hit him. Yang Yankang begged, "My son was wrong, but it's also the truth, isn't it? Mother, we should live in peace now. We don't see how miserable Second Uncle and Second Aunt are. Second Uncle can't even be a minor official

now, right? Second Brother has a hard time finding a wife, don't you want to live like them?"

Tang remained silent.

She also knew the current situation of the second house and could only sigh.

As long as her son lives a stable life and can marry a wife, it would be good enough!

Fu Chaoyun had been keeping an eye on the Third Prince's people recently. When he came back from work that day, he saw Fu Chaoqing's carriage in front. He hurried to catch up, and the coachman stopped the carriage when he saw him.

He lifted the car curtain and bent down to get in.

Fu Chaoqing was sitting and dozing off. He opened his eyes slightly and said, "It's quite early today."

Fu Chaoyun said: "There haven't been many things going on recently, and the officials have been quite quiet. They are afraid that the emperor will get angry and move against them again."

"Oh, then you should go home earlier and spend more time with your father and mother."

"But the Third Prince is restless." Fu Chaoyun came over and whispered, "Didn't Marquis Wu Ding come to me last time? I sent someone to watch him. Two of his followers came out today. They looked sneaky. Do you know what they did?"

"What are you doing?" Fu Chaoqing became a

little interested and felt a little better, so he sat up straight.

"I asked someone to buy medicine, but what I bought was not good medicine, it was poison. If you take it, you will die."

"how do you know?"

"How could I not know? I have been a Jinyiwei for such a long time. I don't know which brothels in the capital are visited by officials the most, which gamblers are the most aggressive, and which are the most vile places for people to buy and sell. The person they are looking for may not be conspicuous, but he sells many things that others cannot get. This poison is not sold in ordinary pharmacies. Only he can get it at a high price."

Fu Chaoqing groaned: "They are trying to poison the emperor to death."

Fu Chaoyun looked a little nervous, and his voice became even lower: "No, he doesn't want his head anymore? If he can't be the crown prince, at least he can still be a prince. Is he that depressed?"

"So what do you think he bought it for?"

"This..." Fu Chaoyun said, "Maybe the second prince was poisoned to death?"

Fu Chaoqing said, "The emperor suspected him of poisoning the second prince, didn't he? It's useless." He paused, "I think he should have other plans, maybe he wants to launch a coup."

Fu Chaoyun couldn't help laughing and said sarcastically, "With just the number of people he has, how can he rebel? He can't even defeat the imperial guards alone."

"What if his people are the Imperial Guards?"

Fu Chaoyun was stunned: "If it is the Imperial Guards, it will be a bit troublesome."

Unexpectedly, Fu Chaoqing shook his head again: "Forget it, don't bother with him."

"Don't worry about it?" Fu Chaoyun said with eyes wide open, "This is going to affect the emperor, how can we just ignore it?"

"Look at his current situation. The emperor is about to make him a king. He has lost his power. Who would be willing to work for him? Others are not fools. Besides, what can he do with his brain? If he really had something to do, he wouldn't have fallen to this point. The two princes are the same, not much different, but it's only been a few years and he can't help it."

He was rash, thoughtless, impulsive, and had no virtues whatsoever, so he deserved to fail.

Fu Chaoyun argued: "There have been cases of this happening in history, but it's hard to say."

"If you're worried, just keep a close eye on it." Fu Chaoqing said lightly.

Fu Chaoyun nodded.

Fu Chaoqing asked again: "How is Yan Yuan doing?"

When mentioning this person, Fu Chaoyun's

face was full of resentment, and he rubbed his hands and said, "Of course I watched. My name is Feng Wei, and Li Xianghong takes turns. But there is no big problem for now, otherwise I will kill him!"

"His father was exiled, so he is naturally a frightened bird and it is not easy for him to make another big mistake." Fu Chaoqing was not as emotional as him.

Fu Chaoyun said viciously: "This day will come eventually."

"Let's think of a solution together. Starting tomorrow, you tell me what he does and when." Fu Chaoqing looked a little strange, indescribably odd.

However, Fu Chaoyun didn't notice it and said happily: "That's good."

Fu Chaoqing stopped talking, closed his eyes and went to rest.

☆、Chapter 69 Children

Li Changluo really wanted to poison the emperor. He had a good idea at first. He had enough money to bribe the imperial guards around the emperor. Then he would find a chance to subdue the emperor and order the emperor to issue an edict to the world, making him the crown prince. Then he would poison the emperor.

In this way, he can legitimately become the new emperor!

However, his life was destined to be tragic. Everything has not yet unfolded, and Zheng

Xie, who should have been the most loyal person around him, betrayed him.

He was the first to seek an audience with the emperor and informed him of Li Changluo's plan in detail.

Li Shiyu was furious.

The consequence of this anger was that Zheng Xie was beheaded first.

Li Shiyu hated those who sold out their masters for personal gain the most.

When the news reached Li Changluo's ears, his eyes rolled back and he fainted. When he woke up, the entire hall had been searched and the poison that Zheng Xie had mentioned was indeed found.

The two followers who were buying medicine were also summoned obediently, without missing a word.

When Li Changluo saw Li Shiyu, he couldn't open his mouth. He just knelt there, shaking all over.

Looking at his own son, Li Shiyu felt only sadness.

Born in a royal family without family affection, Li Shiyu had a deeper understanding of this sentence at this moment.

"As we are father and son, I will not kill you. You may leave the capital now."

Li Changluo collapsed to the ground.

Although he was not killed, the price was heavy. He was driven to a bitter and cold land and could never return to the capital. Of course, he could no longer be a prince and lived in poverty all his life.

Concubine Shu couldn't help crying again.

She couldn't believe that this was the child she raised. She had seriously failed in her duty!

She did not ask Li Shiyu for forgiveness, but only asked to live in Jingyue Temple outside the city for a while.

Li Shiyu agreed.

Concubine Ning was secretly happy. Since the Third Prince was like this, then the position of Crown Prince would undoubtedly be her biological son, and he would definitely become an emperor in the future, because Li Shiyu had no other suitable child.

As a result, she was happy too early. Just when Concubine Shu was about to leave for Jingyue Temple, she suddenly felt unwell. She called the imperial physician for a check, and found out that she was pregnant.

Even Concubine Shu herself couldn't believe it.

She had thought of so many ways to have another child, but none of them worked. She had given up thinking about it a long time ago. Who would have known that God would have mercy on her and let her wish come true.

Lost one, gained another.

Li Shiyu was also very happy when he heard this.

During that period, he did stay at Concubine Shu's house for a few days, but of course, he never thought about having a child.

"You don't have to go to Jingyue Temple." Li Shiyu said, "At your age, if you get hurt, you can still live in the palace."

"But." Concubine Shu said with red eyes, "I am guilty of harming Chang Luo."

Li Shiyu sighed, "It's not all your fault. I've thought about it. If I hadn't refused to appoint a crown prince, he wouldn't have had these thoughts. Everyone has greed. He was originally a well-behaved child. Besides, he's not your biological child, so he's pitiful. You're lucky that no one treats him sincerely."

He saw everything about other people in the palace. If Concubine Ning didn't say anything, then the Queen would just be watching the show. She never cared about Li Changluo. If he was not born to them, then he was not their child. But no matter what, he was his son!

Concubine Shu sighed: "It's still my fault that I didn't do it well. Now this one, I will definitely teach him well."

She reached out and gently stroked her belly.

Li Shiyu smiled and said, "You must take care of yourself. I have children in my old age."

When she heard that Concubine Shu was pregnant and would not go to the nunnery anymore, Concubine Ning felt so irritated that she felt like fire was burning in her heart.

It's really like one wave has just subsided, another wave rises!

Chen Ningyu was also thinking, what's good now, Concubine Shu now has her own child, but she doesn't know whether it's a boy or a girl.

If it's a girl, it's okay, she's just a princess. The emperor will love her very much and there will be no problem getting her married when she grows up. But if it's a boy, the emperor is still young and he can wait for him to grow up.

Chen Ningyu has a headache.

Madam Yang also sighed: "It would be nice if it was a daughter."

We are a family and there is nothing to be shy about when talking to each other.

Yang Yanling said: "Whether it's a son or a daughter, it won't be good for us if the second prince ascends the throne in the future."

The implication is that he still hopes it is a son.

Chen Ningyu was stunned.

Madam Yang was also looking at him.

"Let aunt teach you well this time. If you need me, I can help out." The third prince was helpless. Li Changluo was only a few years younger than him. He couldn't help even if he wanted to. Everything was already done and couldn't be changed.

Neither Madam Yang nor Chen Ningyu said anything.

On the way back, Chen Ningyu whispered, "Are you serious?"

"Of course it's true. It's just teaching my nephew, isn't it normal?" Yang Yanling said in a light tone.

"I mean what the Marquis said before." Chen Ningyu said, "Now that I think about it, I am also afraid. The Third Prince is not doing well, but it has brought us a lot of trouble. If the Second Prince really wants to be the emperor in the future, our family will be in trouble."

A new emperor appoints his own ministers!

Yang Yanling hummed: "It's still a little early. I'll only say this once today. Let's not mention it again in the future."

They both know it well.

Chen Ningyu nodded.

By November, Chen Ningyu will give birth to a baby.

Madam Yang had invited a midwife early on. But she hadn't made any movement in the past few days, and Chen Ningyu was worried: "Could it be that the date was calculated wrong?"

"How could that be? Don't think too much. Grandmother has remembered it. She is more worried about this child than you are. She must be right." Yang Yanling comforted her, "Don't be afraid. You are in better health now. I believe you will be fine."

"Really?" She was still worried. "I heard that many people got into trouble."

She was really scared. She hadn't given

birth to a child yet. There was no caesarean section, no anesthesia, nothing. What if she goes?

Yang Yanling pinched her little arm and said with a smile: "Look, you have muscles. It's not for nothing that I taught you boxing before."

"I got pregnant after only practicing for a short while, and I didn't practice anymore. What's the point?"

"Don't you walk often?"

"What's the point of just walking? Everyone walks."

Yang Yanling was anxious: "Don't let your imagination run wild. Try your best, do it. Do you hear me? If you don't give birth to the baby safely, I won't forgive you!"

Chen Ningyu was startled by him and stared at him.

Yang Yanling sighed again, hugged her in his arms and said, "I am just worried, my lady, please stop saying these discouraging words. I will accompany you, and you will be fine."

But his expression still changed.

The great general who fought bravely in the battlefield would one day be said to be afraid.

"Okay, I won't say anything more. When the time comes, I will do my best." Chen Ningyu promised, "I won't let the Marquis worry."

But in fact, she still had no idea.

She is indeed a rich lady. She has never done housework or exercise since she came here. She just eats and drinks every day. Now she regrets not exercising well because she is not strong enough.

Yang Yanling touched her head and said softly, "Don't tell me not to worry, my lady. That's your life. You have to take care of yourself for your own sake!"

When Chen Ningyu heard this, her eyes suddenly turned red.

At the same time, her stomach began to hurt. Yang Yanling hurriedly called the midwife.

The midwife then brought in four women, all of whom were experienced in many cases.

"My lord, please go out." The midwife had already instructed the maids to arrange the things they brought everywhere.

Yang Yanling was reluctant to leave Chen Ningyu alone, so he held her hand tightly and said, "The baby hasn't been born yet, why would I go out? Let's talk about it after the baby is born."

Giving birth will also be painful for a while. It doesn't mean that you will give birth as soon as the pain starts. Some people are better off and the pain lasts for a few hours, while others may last for one or two days.

The midwife had no choice but to stop talking.

Seeing her eyes full of tears due to pain, Yang Yanling said with guilt: "It's hard for you to suffer all this for me."

Chen Ningyu was touched when his hand was held. She had been married to Yang Yanling for more than two years and she knew that he truly loved her, which was why he could pamper her and care about her so much.

Now, even if she faces this fear and gives birth to their two children, it is worth it.

She said seriously, "It doesn't hurt that much, Lord. You treat me so well, it's nothing. Besides, the child is ours. You just said it was for my own sake, how can you blame Lord for it all?"

Yang Yanling bent down and kissed her: "I will treat you well for the rest of my life."

Chen Ningyu felt a little guilty, after all, she didn't have much sincerity when she married him.

"My Lord..." Her eyes flickered.

Yang Yanling interrupted her, looked at her and asked, "I know you treat me the same way, right?"

Chen Ningyu said without hesitation: "Yes."

Yes, during the time he was away, she knew that she loved him just as much, even though they had not known each other long enough and did not understand each other well enough. However, fate had tied them together and they could not live without each other.

From now on, they will have more children.

When Yang Yanling heard this, he kissed her on the forehead and said, "Well, you deserve it. From now on, I will only treat you better. You are the mother of my child."

Chen Ningyu's tears fell.

There is joy and there is pain.

She finally couldn't bear the pain anymore!

Madam Yang also hurriedly pulled Yang Yanling away, and the two of them waited outside together.

Not long after, Chen Xiu and Zhang Jiwan also arrived.

"Don't worry, it will take a while." Chen Xiu comforted Yang Yanling as a person who had experienced it, "Even if she screams miserably, it's nothing. Don't rush to push the door in, it will only make things worse."

He knew Yang Yanling's temper, so he made it clear early on.

Sure enough, Chen Ningyu soon screamed.

Yang Yanling's heart almost broke when he heard this.

Zhang Jiwan pulled him further away and said, "I'd rather not get married. It's too scary."

Yang Yanling said: "Giving birth to a child is scary, but how can marrying a wife be scary? If you don't marry a wife, you will never know this joy."

Zhang Jiwan twitched his lips.

Yang Yanling started walking around outside again, wandering east and west.

Zhang Jiwan was dazzled by him.

Fortunately, the process didn't take long. A servant came running over and shouted, "My Lord, my Lord, the young lady has given birth to a boy! He weighs seven pounds!"

Zhang Jiwan exclaimed: "Wow, seven pounds! No wonder her belly is so big. I heard that when I gave birth, I only weighed six pounds..."

He wanted to talk to Yang Yanling, but Yang Yanling disappeared like a gust of wind.

☆、Chapter 70: The Third Day

Chen Ningyu felt like she was going to die. She just kept trying harder and harder, but she was in a daze and her soul seemed to be flying to the sky. She only came to her senses when the midwife told her that the baby was out.

When I woke up, I felt pain again and tears started streaming down my face.

Madam Yang was outside. She came in first and held the child to her. She smiled from ear to ear and said, "Look, look, it's a son!"

Chen Ningyu tilted her head slightly and saw a little baby with wrinkled skin. Although the baby was not pretty, her heart immediately felt at peace, as if it was filled.

Madam Yang put the child closer and said softly, "Newborns are like this. Don't worry, he will be a handsome boy in the future. You should have a good rest. You can look at him later when you feel more comfortable."

Chen Ningyu hummed, and Madam Yang wiped her eyes with a handkerchief: "It won't hurt so much in a few days, just bear with it and get more sleep."

Yang Yanling also came at this time, rushed to Chen Ningyu, held her hand and said: "How is it, is there anything wrong?"

"Everything is fine, Lord. Everything went smoothly. Nothing serious. Madam will be fine after a few months of rest." The midwife said with a smile, "Madam is in good health. It won't take long."

Yang Yanling breathed a sigh of relief and asked someone to give the midwife a big red envelope and send it away.

Chen Ningyu just looked at him and moved her hand in his palm.

Seeing that she didn't even have the strength to speak, Yang Yanling's nose suddenly felt sore.

She had been married to him for so long and had never experienced anything like this before. It showed that having a child was really scary!

"We won't have any more children in the future. We'll just take care of this one." Yang Yanling said, "So that you won't have to suffer anymore."

When Mrs. Yang heard this, the corners of her mouth twitched.

Although she also felt sorry for her granddaughter-in-law, as the elder in the family, she naturally hoped that the Yang family would expand and have as many children and offspring as possible. How could she not want the one child she had

just given birth to?
But she didn't say anything.
Chen Ningyu felt relieved.
It seems that my husband is very good to me. Normally, everyone wants to have many children, but he only wants one.
Chen Ningyu said softly: "In fact, it's better to have given birth."
The implication is that if you have had one, there will be no problem with the second one.
Mrs. Yang was happy again.
My grandson's wife is a sensible person.
Yang Yanling frowned and said, "Don't talk anymore. I'll stay with you. You can sleep for a while."
Chen Ningyu listened to him, closed her eyes, and soon fell asleep.
When I woke up again, it was already dark.
She turned her head and saw Yang Yanling was still beside her. When he saw her open her eyes, he smiled and asked, "Are you hungry? What do you want to eat?"
Chen Ningyu asked: "Where is the child?"
"At my grandmother's place, the nurse has fed me."
Rich families like theirs were used to having wet nurses, and biological mothers did not need to breastfeed. Chen Ningyu was against it at first, but Madam Yang gave a long speech, and one of her sentences touched her heart.
Madam Yang said that the wet nurse they hired was in good health, so her milk

supply was guaranteed, and she would be able to take care of the baby. Chen Ningyu thought that her own health was not so good, so her milk supply might not be good either, and she would not be able to take care of the baby. To be honest, she didn't even know how to hold the baby after feeding it with milk, so she followed the trend.

"I just went to see him, he was asleep." Yang Yanling said, "Eat something, you must have been hungry during the day."

But Chen Ningyu didn't have much appetite: "Just drink some porridge."

"How can porridge be okay? It's not very nutritious. How about some chicken soup? The kitchen has already made some. Or fish soup? Don't you like fish? It's made with fresh mullet."

Chen Ningyu said, "Let's drink the fish soup. Has the Marquis eaten yet?"

"No, I'm just waiting for you." Yang Yanling leaned over and picked her up, put a soft pillow behind her, and ordered dinner to be prepared.

Chen Ningyu suddenly remembered something: "The child hasn't been named yet, Lord Hou, what do you think he should be called?"

Yang Yanling did not hesitate: "Since you have worked so hard, I will call you Yang Yushi."

Chen Ningyu shouted happily: "Really? You used me to get it?"

"How can I lie to you? Going with the times, this name is not bad either."

Chen Ningyu was delighted: "Thank you, Lord Marquis." He added, "I will give birth to another child and name him after you, Lord Marquis."

Yang Yanling burst out laughing: "What are you talking about? You have to give birth to a child just to give me a name?"

"If the Marquis likes it, it's okay to have one more child." Just based on his behavior, as long as he is willing, she is willing to have another child. She doesn't care about anything at this moment.

Yang Yanling sighed and held her in his arms: "No more children, what's the point? I'm so worried. This is the only one. I'm not lying. If you raise it well, one is enough. If you don't raise it well, the more children you have, the more trouble you will have."

Chen Ningyu was surprised: "My Lord, are you worried that you can't take good care of it?"

"Why not? Look at our home."

After hearing his honest words, Chen Ningyu stopped talking. She wasn't actually very sure about raising a child, after all, she had no experience.

Well, let's just give this one a try and see what happens.

Two days later, it was time for the third day bath, a ceremony that must be held on the third day after every child is born. It is to wash away dirt and avoid disasters, so the Yang family made preparations early.

On this day, the house was filled with guests.

Everyone from the Chen family came, including the two aunts of the Chen family and their husbands, as well as Zhang Jihe and his wife. From the Wu family, only Wu Jian and Chen Ningan came, and as for Princess Huiying, needless to say, her whole family also came.

The relatives of the Yang family usually don't interact much because of Yang Yanling, so few people come, but the lady of the Duke of Weiguo's mansion did come.

Mrs. Chen first held her little great-grandson in her arms to look at him, and everyone came over to praise him.

The princess said to Chen Ningyu: "That's good. Now that we have a boy, you don't have to worry anymore. Tomorrow I will fulfill your wish and give you some more money for the incense."

"Thank you, auntie." Chen Ningyu smiled and asked, "How is Hui'er? She didn't bring her here today, and I missed her."

The daughter born to Yu was named Yu Hui.

The eldest princess' face was immediately filled with love: "If it wasn't so cold, I would have brought her out. She can eat and sleep well, and she is plump and cute, like a meat ball. We all call her Tuan Tuan."

round and round……

Chen Ningyu laughed: "It's a good name, but you can't call her that when she grows up."

The eldest princess also smiled: "You will

definitely be just as likable in the future."

After a while, the midwife outside had prepared everything and called everyone to go.

Chen Ningyu was in confinement and couldn't get any air, so it was not convenient for her to attend. Unexpectedly, Bai Tao came in and said, "Madam, Jiang Chuntang and Lu Yun are here."

Chen Ningyu naturally disliked these two people, but he didn't expect that they would actually come.

"You go out and watch them." Chen Ningyu ordered, and asked Bitao to ask why they were let in.

Bi Tao quickly replied, "They came with the second young master of the Zhang family."

Chen Ningyu was speechless for a moment.

I didn't expect that Lu Yun is still using Zhang Jiwan, and so is this cousin. But never mind, it's just a small matter. Even if they just come here, it's okay to ignore them.

In fact, the lady also felt disgusted at this moment. Several of their families had rejected Jiang Chuntang, but he still had the nerve to come. However, it was not convenient for her to say anything during the ceremony, so she could only pretend not to see it.

However, Jiang Chuntang was very happy. As Zhang Jiwan came in smoothly, he thought that he could take this opportunity to make friends with these people, so he went to greet and talk to them one by one.

Everyone was like the old lady and just said a few perfunctory words.

Lu Yun secretly pulled Jiang Chuntang's sleeve and said, "Let's do this for now, and we'll talk about it later."

Jiang Chuntang listened, but when it was their turn to add water to the basin, he threw in a large ingot of gold, which made a clanging sound and made everyone frown.

Who is he to the Yang family? Why would he send such a large amount of gold?

The eldest princess raised her eyebrows. Even hers was not that big!

Is this a gift?

However, everyone could not disturb the ceremony and continued to pretend not to see it.

Yang Yanling was very angry and turned around to ask Chen Ningyu: "What does Jiang Chuntang do? He just talked to me and was talking nonsense. I don't even know him!"

He really didn't know him. Even when Jiang Chuntang sent a holiday gift last time, he was not at home.

As for Lu Yun's marriage, he had no idea about it. It was Chen Ningyu who arranged and sent the gift, and it was also out of respect for the Zhao family.

Chen Ningyu said, "He's not just anyone."

She told him about the relationship between the Chen and Lu families.

Yang Yanling was even more disdainful and

called the servant over: "Return the gold ingot to Jiang Chuntang now! Tell the gatekeeper that whoever lets him in in the future will not be allowed to stay in the mansion anymore."

The servant hurried away.

Chen Ningyu felt that his action was a bit too radical. Just as he was about to say something, Yang Yanling said, "He just mentioned the vacancy of the Tong County Magistrate. You know what he means, right? This kind of person is as greedy as a mosquito seeing blood when he sees benefits. Even so, he still expects me to find him this position?"

"Then he deserves it." Chen Ningyu immediately felt that Yang Yanling did a great job.

Jiang Chuntang is too impatient.

Who was Yang Yanling, that he could easily find a job for him? It was Yang Yankang, his own brother, whom he disliked but didn't let him get rid of.

You deserve it!

Jiang Chuntang was still trying to get close to Xu Ke over there. He probably realized that Zhang Zhijing was too scary. Compared to Zhang Zhijing, Xu Ke was much gentler.

But Xu Ke was also impatient. Just then, a servant came and stuffed the gold ingot into Jiang Chuntang's hand, saying loudly: "The Marquis' Mansion doesn't need this little money. Please take it back, Master

Jiang. Our Marquis said that the Marquis' Mansion doesn't welcome Master Jiang either. I don't know how you got in."

Jiang Chuntang's face immediately turned red, so red that blood seemed to drip out. He felt that everyone's gazes had turned into arrows, shooting towards him one by one.

He couldn't stay any longer and ran away.

Lu Yun hurriedly followed him, shouting, "Husband, listen to me..."

Jiang Chuntang turned around suddenly when he heard her voice.

When Lu Yun saw his ferocious face, she couldn't help but take two steps back.

"Bitch!" Jiang Chuntang took out all his anger on her. He felt that it was all Lu Yun's fault, which was why those people looked down on her. He slapped her in the face.

☆, Chapter 71: Death of Yan Yuan

The force was so great that Lu Yun fell to the ground.

When Zhang Jiwan saw Lu Yun being beaten, he became furious. If it wasn't for Lu Yun's sake, he wouldn't have invited them to come along.

He rushed over and punched Jiang Chuntang in the face.

Jiang Chuntang was no match for him. He just glared at Lu Yun and cursed, "Don't let me see you again, bitch!" He covered his face and ran away quickly.

Lu Yun sat on the ground and cried.

Zhang Jiwan didn't know what to do.

The lady sighed and asked a maid to help Lu Yun up.

Chen Linzhi didn't want her son to be involved, so she called him repeatedly.

Seeing Zhang Jiwan walk aside, Lu Yun felt very upset.

Thinking back, she shouldn't have had that thought in the beginning, and was driven out of the house by the lady-in-waiting. Later, she shouldn't have trusted Jiang Chuntang wrongly, thinking that he was devoted to her. But it turned out that she was wrong. All he cared about was her relationship with the Chen family. How could he really like her?

But she wanted to let it go. Jiang Chuntang was a juren after all. He just had a quick temper. Maybe she could make him change his mind and the young couple could live a good life. But who would have thought that he was so reckless and a hopeless person!

At this moment, Lu Yun wished there was a crack in the ground so she could crawl into it!

The lady did not expect her to be so embarrassed.

But after all, she lived in the Marquis' Mansion back then, and the Madam Dowager would not add insult to injury, so she asked the maid to help Lu Yun go inside to rest, so that she would not be seen by others. She felt uncomfortable, and everyone saw this and said nothing more.

The lady went to see Chen Ningyu later and told her about this matter.

Chen Ningyu had heard about it before: "I never thought Jiang Chuntang was such a bastard. I know that the Marquis returned the gold ingot to him just to teach him a lesson, but it ended up humiliating Cousin Lu."

Although she didn't like Lu Yun and felt that she had only herself to blame, it was too cruel for her to be beaten in public by her own husband.

The lady said, "Yes, I'm afraid she can't go back to the Jiang family now."

"It's okay to divorce a husband like this." Chen Ningyu felt extremely disgusted.

The lady nodded and sighed, "I am also somewhat responsible for her behavior. I shouldn't have just stood by and done nothing. Yun'er is still young, and my cousin has no opinion. What good choices can she make? I should have stopped her from marrying."

"How can I blame grandma?" Chen Ningyu said hurriedly, "It's also cousin Lu's own fault. If she didn't have feelings for my second cousin, I wouldn't have told grandma."

The lady waved her hand: "Forget it, let's not talk about it. You just gave birth to a child, so don't talk about these things."

She held Chen Ningyu's hand and said, "Take good care of yourself. If something happens during this confinement period, your health will never be well. But I'm not worried. Just listen to your mother-in-law. If she says not to do something, you just don't do it, and then everything will be fine."

They are all experienced people, and Chen Ningyu just needs to obey. Besides, she gave birth to a son, and Madam Yang was so happy that she treated her like a treasure. The Madam was really relieved.

Chen Ningyu smiled and said, "I know. My mother-in-law comes here once a day because she's afraid that I'll get too hot or too cold."

"Isn't it?" The lady hugged her and smiled, happy for her.

Outside the house, Fu Chaoyun glanced at Fu Chaoqing and said, "Why don't you go in and talk to Ah Yu?"

When they came over, they just said hello. Fu Chaoqing didn't even see Chen Ningyu's face clearly before he left.

He shook his head: "What's so good about it? As long as Ah Yu is fine, that's all."

Fu Chaoyun felt sad after hearing this.

As the two were talking, they heard Chen Ningyu say from inside: "Big cousin, second cousin, why are you just hanging around outside? I haven't seen you for a long time!"

Fu Chaoyun smiled and said, "Look, you can't not see it."

He pushed Fu Chaoqing in.

Chen Ningyu felt heartbroken when she saw

that he seemed to have lost some weight. She now understood his thoughts. Although she felt regretful, she could only blame it on the unfairness of fate. What else could she say? She could only accept this arrangement.

As soon as Fu Chaoyun arrived, he joked: "Ayu, I think your boy is pretty good, why don't you let him be my son-in-law in the future."

Chen Ningyu suddenly laughed when she heard this: "Cousin, you are really thinking too far ahead. How old are they? Are you planning to arrange a marriage for them?"

"It's a good idea to arrange an arranged marriage. We are already close, and after we get married, it will be an even closer relationship. Isn't that good?" Fu Chaoyun smiled.

Chen Ningyu ignored him: "No, let's wait until they grow up. If they like each other, it's natural. If not, we naturally don't even mention it."

From now on, she will never use the concept of parental orders to control her children's marriage.

Her son would naturally marry a girl he liked.

Fu Chaoyun curled his lips and snorted: "Your boy will definitely like Hui'er when he sees her in the future. Who wouldn't like my Hui'er?"

The person he treasures most now is definitely his daughter.

Chen Ningyu laughed and joked, "Yes, yes, your Tuantuan is the cutest! If my boy doesn't like her in the future, it's because he has a problem with his vision. It's definitely his fault. Cousin, are you satisfied?"

Only then did Fu Chaoyun feel happy.

Fu Chaoqing just laughed when he heard this.

Chen Ningyu asked him: "Have you seen my son?"

"I see. He will definitely look like you in the future. I heard his name is Yu Shi?" Fu Chaoqing asked.

Chen Ningyu was proud: "I took it!"

Fu Chaoqing hummed: "This is a good name. If we were to give him a courtesy name, we would call him Xingzhi."

"Do it? Go with the times, do it." Chen Ningyu clapped his hands, "Okay, okay, when he grows up, I will tell him that your second cousin has given him a name."

"Ah, that will probably be more than ten years later." Fu Chaoqing said leisurely.

I don't know if he was still there at that time?

When he said this, the expressions of the other two changed.

Chen Ningyu thought that he was alone and would die alone in the future. The more she thought about it, the more she couldn't bear it. An idea slowly emerged in her mind. After all the guests had left, she brought up the matter with Yang Yanling.

When Yang Yanling heard her say that she

wanted her son to recognize Yu Chaoqing as his godfather in the future, his original fear emerged again, and his face naturally looked very unhappy.

Chen Ningyu knew what he was thinking about and said, "My second cousin won't live long. He won't marry in this lifetime, so I want Yu Shi to worship him as his adoptive father."

Yang Yanling was surprised: "How did you know?"

"My eldest cousin once told me that my uncle and aunt don't know yet, but they will know in the future." Chen Ningyu sighed, "My second cousin is so pitiful, Lord, he is like my own brother in my heart now. I just feel sorry for him, what else is there?"

Yang Yanling's thoughts disappeared immediately.

What was there for a dying man to be jealous of? Even though he knew that Fu Chaoqing liked Chen Ningyu, at this moment, he only felt deep sympathy.

If this were not the case, Fu Chaoqing would have married her long ago, so how could it be my turn?

And if he is not a man of high character and would rather be alone than marry Chen Ningyu, then it will not be my turn either.

Yang Yanling nodded and held her in his arms: "In that case, then let's do as you say."

Chen Ningyu hugged him tightly, thanking

him for his magnanimity.

The Chinese New Year was approaching, and because Chen Ningyu was in confinement after giving birth and Mrs. Yang was old and could not catch a cold in the winter, she left all the matters to Mrs. Tang.

The Tang family has been silent for so long, and finally there is a time for them to come to the fore.

She began to demonstrate in front of her servants, acting bossy and bossy, in order to vent her anger at being oppressed for a long time.

Gu Qiu told Chen Ningyu.

Chen Ningyu smiled and said, "Let her be. I just gave birth to a child and need to rest. The family depends on her a little bit."

Gu Qiu asked, "Will the Madam do anything?"

"Ask Danqiu to keep an eye on it." Chen Ningyu looked at Gu Qiu's big belly, "You are about to give birth, so don't overwork yourself. Go home and rest after a while."

Gu Qiu was still worried.

Danqiu frowned: "You still don't trust me? What will you do when you are in confinement after giving birth? Why do you bring the child with you and come here to run around?"

That's all Gu Qiu said.

That day, Yang Yanling came back, took off his official uniform, and held his son in his arms. The more he looked at him, the more he liked him: "My son is so well-behaved. He doesn't even cry at night. When

I talked to my colleagues about this, they often said that their children would cry."

Chen Ningyu said: "That's because those children are full during the day, so they don't sleep much during the day. They always keep their eyes open and only cry when they are hungry. Naturally, they have no energy at night."

However, she also felt that her son was well-behaved, because she had heard that some children were difficult to raise, but her son was not difficult at all, even the wet nurse said so.

The two talked for a while, and Yang Yanling remembered something and said seriously, "Yan Yuan is dead."

Chen Ningyu paused and asked in surprise, "How did he die?"

Although she had hoped that Yan Yuan would die early on, it was just a thought after all, and it could not kill Yan Yuan.

Yang Yanling said: "He died in the river. It was the coldest time of the year and the river was frozen, but there was a big hole in the ice..."

He didn't tell the details of the death so as not to scare Chen Ningyu.

He told Chen Ningyu the news to let her know that she had hoped to punish Yan Yuan earlier.

Chen Ningyu was silent.

Died in the river...

Is this called tit for tat?

Yan Yuan pushed Fu Chaoqing into the river

in the first place, and this time he also fell into the river.

But, for some reason, she couldn't seem to be happy.

It turns out that even if the bad guy dies, your mood may not necessarily improve. You will just think, how good it would have been if Yan Yuan had not done that bad thing. Now that he is dead, it cannot be undone.

Chen Ningyu sighed and asked, "Do you know how he fell in?"

In any case, there are accidents and human factors.

Yang Yanling glanced at her and said, "I don't know. The emperor ordered a thorough investigation today, and even the Jinyiwei was dispatched."

It was because Princess Huaying fainted from crying in front of the emperor.

☆、Chapter 72 Threat

Yan Yuan died, and his relatives were sad and his enemies were happy.

Princess Huiying was very happy now and drank half a jar of wine in the evening.

In her opinion, this is what Yan Yuan should have become.

However, Fu Chaoyun frowned. It was not that he was unhappy, but he just couldn't understand how Yan Yuan died. He had clearly asked two of his trusted aides to keep an eye on him all day long, yet such a thing happened right under his nose.

What is the whole story?

He is careless in other areas, but not in official business.

Now the Jinyiwei has also participated in the investigation of this case. Fu Chaoyun went to ask the coroner the next day, but the coroner could not tell when Yan Yuan died.

Because he had been frozen, this seriously affected his judgment. As for the people from Yan's family, they said that he often did not go home, and it happened that he was not at home on those days.

After some investigation, it was discovered that Yan Yuan had recently fallen in love with a popular girl in Fangyue Tower. Unfortunately, that popular girl didn't like him. Even if he spent thousands of gold, it would be useless. Yan Yuan had been drinking in Fangyue Tower a few nights ago. The river there was often filled with holes from being smashed by naughty kids.

Nothing else was found.

In the end, they could only say that Yan Yuan accidentally fell into the river after drinking.

As for the two attendants, after entering the brothel with their master, they drank some wine and were unconscious. Naturally, they had no idea where Yan Yuan was.

Princess Huaying refused to accept this result. She insisted that it was someone from the Fu family who did it, just because

Yan Yuan had once pushed Fu Chaoqing into the pond.

But how could the emperor listen to her? That incident happened many years ago. Why did the Fu family take action at any other time? Why did they have to do it now? Fu Chaoqing was still an official. Why did he ruin his future? Besides, he had not found any connection between this incident and the Fu family.

Fu Chaoyun has been busy these past two days, and there is evidence to prove it. Fu Chaoqing's daily attendance at court is also normal, so the emperor would not suspect Fu Cheng.

He married the eldest princess to Fu Cheng because he valued his simplicity.

The emperor told Princess Huaying not to think too much about it and said it was God's will. Princess Huaying's husband was exiled and her son died, and she was devastated and never even set foot in the palace again.

Fu Chaoyun couldn't find out anything either. His two confidants said that there were many people on the streets before the New Year and it was common for someone to run away accidentally. So they just thought it was God's will.

He picked up the wine and drank by himself to celebrate. He did not go to find Fu Chaoqing as he did not want to talk about his sad story.

However, he didn't know that Fu Chaoqing

was also drinking at this moment.

A bowl of sake was placed in front of me, and the bright moon in the sky fell into the wine cup.

Life is like a dream. After planning for so many years, he got his revenge and escaped unscathed. He should feel happy. However, that happiness could not fill the gap in his life.

He watched Yan Yuan drown in the river, as if the entire winter had entered his heart.

Now, his hands were stained with blood and he had no scruples from then on.

Whether it is for his lifelong ideals or for the people he loves, he can go on by any means necessary.

He picked up the wine cup and drank it in one gulp.

In the blink of an eye, it is spring and summer.

The flowers in the garden were in full bloom, which should have been a joyful day.

However, Concubine Ning was upset because she heard from the imperial physician that Concubine Shu was pregnant with a boy. This meant that if Concubine Shu gave birth to the boy, he might become a rival for the crown prince.

Of course, it is still a long way from this. After all, the second prince is already twenty-two years old.

At least a crown prince should be appointed. But the problem is that the emperor is still young and he may not be able to wait until the child grows up.

So, it is hard to say who will eventually become the emperor.

It's not that Concubine Ning looks down on her son, it's just that Concubine Shu is too favored. It's nothing that she didn't have a son before, as Li Changluo was not hers after all. But now she has her own son, and which mother in the world would not fight for him?

Even if Concubine Shu tried her best, Concubine Ning felt that she might not win.

She called Chen Ninghua to Ruian Palace.

Before Chen Ninghua arrived, he had already sensed the danger and his whole body was on alert.

She saluted and stood straight.

Concubine Ning smiled and said, "Don't be shy, just sit down."

Chen Ninghua said: "I dare not, may I ask what your Majesty wants me to do?"

"I'm just free, so I asked you to come and talk to me. What's the big deal?" Concubine Ning dismissed the people around her and ordered her to sit down again.

Chen Ninghua had no choice but to sit down.

Concubine Ning asked, "Concubine Shu, how is she doing recently?"

Previously, under the instruction of Concubine Ning, Chen Ninghua often went to Concubine Shu to get some information. Over time, his relationship with Concubine Shu became better and better, and he rarely came to Concubine Ning.

Hearing Concubine Ning's question, Chen Ninghua said calmly, "Your Majesty is fine. She is busy taking care of the baby."

Concubine Ning raised the corner of her mouth.

"I heard that she will eat the food you cook?" Concubine Ning asked again.

Chen Ninghua nodded.

After all, Chen Ninghua was from the Chen family, and the Chen family was related to the Yang family, so Concubine Shu did not suspect her much. Moreover, every time she ate, a palace maid would try the food on her behalf first, so what danger could there be?

Concubine Ning smiled and pointed at her: "You are good, you have the trust of Concubine Shu."

Chen Ninghua immediately said: "It's not trust, just a casual conversation."

Concubine Ning could see her nervousness and sighed, "I know it's not easy for you. There are many young girls in this palace, and none of them are easy to deal with. I heard that you and Concubine Liu had some disputes a few days ago?"

Chen Ninghua forced a smile: "It can't be considered an argument."

Concubine Ning smiled, "It's human nature. She just entered the palace, yet she dares to bully you. You really should teach her a lesson, but..." She smiled more gently, "It was wrong for you to use aphrodisiac on the emperor. This is not what we concubines should do."

Chen Ninghua was stunned: "What, what aphrodisiac? I have never given it to the emperor."

"Of course there is nothing. If you don't believe me, go back to your room and take a look. There must be something." Concubine Ning comforted her, "For the sake of our past relationship, I will not expose you."

Chen Ninghua stood up suddenly and said sternly: "I have never given the emperor any aphrodisiac!"

Concubine Ning giggled and said, "I haven't told the emperor yet, what are you afraid of? Why don't you sit down? You are not a newcomer to the palace, and you are so startled. People will just think that I have done something to you."

Chen Ninghua couldn't remain calm at this moment. She asked, "What does the queen want from me?"

Concubine Ning looked disdainful, picked up the cake and put it in her mouth, glanced at her and said, "What can you give me?"

"Then what does Your Majesty want me to do?" Chen Ninghua was not a fool. She naturally knew that Concubine Ning was threatening her and wanted her to do something.

Concubine Ning raised her eyebrows: "You are so smart, you really don't know? Concubine Shu's belly is getting bigger and bigger."

Chen Ninghua's face suddenly lost all color.

☆、Chapter 73 Finale

Concubine Ning wants her to take action against Concubine Shu!

How could Chen Ninghua agree?

Concubine Ning was so anxious this time. Needless to say, Concubine Shu must be pregnant with a son, otherwise she would not want to get rid of Concubine Shu's child.

This guy is really crazy!

Chen Ninghua said with a trembling voice: "My lady, I'm afraid I can't do it."

Even if she succeeded, she would still be dead.

It's the same death, why should she take another life?

Concubine Ning narrowed her eyes.

"Do you know the consequences?" She said calmly, "Forget it, go back and think about it carefully."

Chen Ninghua left.

She now lives in Heyu Palace, not alone, but with Liu Zhaoyi and Hu Jieyu.

"Your Majesty, what did Concubine Ning say to you?" the maid Yulan asked softly, because Chen Ninghua looked so distraught that she was really worried. She thought that something bad must have happened.

Chen Ninghua rubbed his brows and said, "You and Bai Lan search everywhere in the palace."

Yulan and Bailan were both very surprised,

but they did as they were told.
As a result, they found a jade bottle under her pillow. When they opened it, they saw three pills inside.
Chen Ninghua's heart was shocked.
It turns out that Concubine Ning is serious about this.
She knew best whether there were any pills under her pillow. Of course there were none, but now this appeared out of nowhere.
Chen Ninghua's fingertips trembled slightly. Concubine Ning wanted to let her know that as long as she wanted, it would be easy to frame Chen Ninghua no matter how.
There must be Concubine Ning's people around her.
Which one is it?
Chen Ninghua looked at Yulan and Bailan and felt that she could not trust either of them.
"All of you get out." She said in a deep voice.
She needs to think carefully.
It's spring now, and Chen Ningyu no longer has to stay in confinement after childbirth and can get up and go out for a walk.
During these two months, she almost suffocated herself. Madam Yang came every day and asked her to pay attention to this and take things carefully. She was not even allowed to go out, and had to do everything in the house. She felt like she had grown a lot of weight all of a sudden.
When I looked in the mirror today, I was

shocked to see that my cheeks were so chubby.

I definitely need to lose weight.

Chen Ningyu doesn't want to be a fat beauty. Her aesthetic view is still that thinness is beautiful.

She went to the yard and did a set of boxing.

The whole person feels refreshed.

The nurse came over with her son in her arms and said with a smile, "Young Master just finished eating, and he is very energetic now."

Chen Ningyu leaned over to take a look. The little fellow was indeed smiling with his eyes open. His little red tongue was exposed. He looked so naive. She liked him just by looking at him. She held him in her arms, rocked him gently and said, "Shi'er, what are you so happy about? When can you speak to me?"

Yang Yushi's nickname, so she called him Shi'er.

Shi'er raised his hands and moved them, looking confused and naive.

Chen Ningyu sighed, children grow up so slowly!

He really couldn't wait to hear him call for his mother. When he could speak, she would teach him to read, and she had many stories to tell him!

"Grow up quickly, Shi'er." She bent down and kissed him on the cheek.

Shi'er smiled again, his eyes moving around,

and he looked full of curiosity about the world.

Madam Yang also came to see Shi'er. Compared with Chen Ningyu, she doted on this great-grandson even more. As soon as she arrived, she asked the wet nurse how Shi'er was doing, whether he drank a lot of milk, and whether there was any difference compared to before. The questions she asked were also quite professional.

"Now that you are well, I think I should leave the household to you." Mrs. Yang also had something to say today.

She had no choice but to let Tang manage the inner house at that time, but this eldest daughter-in-law's work was really not to her liking. She treated chicken feathers as a token of authority and made all the servants complain. Now it was time to take back the power and give it back to Chen Ningyu.

Chen Ningyu did not refuse. She learned from Danqiu that Tang was not well managed. Perhaps she had been pent up with resentment for a long time and could not get any money, so she took it out on her subordinates.

If this goes on, the servants will surely become resentful. How can they do their jobs properly?

"Okay, but has Grandmother told Mother?" she asked.

Madam Yang said, "That's what I just said. She was unhappy. I told her not to manage the farm, and she was willing."

"Mother is going to live in the farm?" Chen Ningyu was surprised.

"Yes, I was also surprised at first, but it's good that she is willing."

Chen Ningyu thought about it and seemed to think it was a good idea.

After all, Tang is still the eldest lady in name, but in reality, she has no power as the eldest lady. Madam Yang no longer trusts her, and she cannot make the decisions at home. She has to act according to Yang Yanling's wishes. I'm afraid she doesn't want to live here anymore.

After all, she was the master of the manor and could not see them.

"Mother is also willing to give up my third brother?"

Madam Yang smiled and said, "It's not like she won't come back after she leaves. Your third brother is not idle now. She told me to watch over him. When Yankang is getting married, she will come back naturally."

Chen Ningyu nodded.

In a few days, Tang will go to the village.

Yang Yankang was also surprised: "Why did mother come to her senses and want to go somewhere else?"

"Out of sight, out of mind. What do you know?" Tang was furious. "I used to be able to manage the household, but now I can't even touch them. I'm afraid those servants look down on me in private! I'm going to go out and relax. Don't make trouble. I'll find you a good wife in the future."

Tang had no choice, she could never defeat Yang Yanling and his wife.

Yang Yankang smiled and said, "That's great, mother, you can move in. I will come to visit you when I have time."

After all these things, Yang Yankang became much more honest. He at least knew that the entire marquisate depended on Yang Yanling, and without him, it would be nothing. He was not as ambitious as Yang Dongping, and he had no idea about the title of Marquis Wuding.

For him, in this life, as long as he has enough food and clothing, it is enough.

Tang sighed and went to the farm.

The mansion is now missing one more person. The two men are not at home during the day, so it's just her and Madam Yang. Fortunately, they still have a child.

"Look, can we not have more children?" Madam Yang laughed, "In the future, this mansion will have to rely on you two to fill it up."

Chen Ningyu looked at the tiny thing and thought that it would take decades, so it was still too early for this one.

When Yang Yanling came back, he also held Shi'er and played with him. Today he also praised Zhang Jiwan, saying that he worked very hard and it would not be difficult for him to get promoted in the future.

Chen Ningyu hurriedly said, "Don't shield him. Second cousin is not a stable person.

It won't be a good thing if he gets promoted. There are people who are young and proud, but how many of them are always good? He is prone to arrogance. He is young, so I think it's better for him to temper himself."

Yang Yanling laughed and said, "I just mentioned it, but you seem to understand it so well."

"Am I wrong?" Chen Ningyu raised her eyebrows.

"How could what my wife said be wrong? Cousin Zhang needs to endure more hardships. Don't worry, I will not give him a promotion in the next three to five years. Your husband will listen to you."

Chen Ningyu heard this and said angrily, "My Lord, you keep talking like this, and people just think I'm a tigress."

"Isn't that true, madam?" Yang Yanling teased.

Chen Ningyu gritted his teeth and slapped him with his hand.

Yang Yanling laughed out loud, this was not even a tickle.

After the two of them had enough fun, they hugged each other and talked sweetly.

That day, news came from the palace that Concubine Shu missed home and wanted to see her family, so Madam Yang and Chen Ningyu took Shi'er to the palace.

When Concubine Shu saw Madam Yang, she started crying and said she felt uncomfortable here and there.

Madam Yang comforted her, "It's not easy to give birth at your age. It's a little difficult. You have to bear with it. At least there are imperial doctors watching over you. If it falls on other families, it won't be so easy, right?"

Concubine Shu wiped her eyes and said, "Mother, please come to see me often in the future."

Now that she is pregnant, her temperament becomes younger and she thinks of herself as Madam Yang's youngest daughter.

Madam Yang smiled and said, "As long as the emperor allows, I will come."

Concubine Shu looked at Chen Ningyu again and said with a smile, "Show me Shi'er now."

In the blink of an eye, she even has nephews and grandchildren.

Chen Ningyu took Shi'er away.

"Oh, so good, he reaches out his hand when he sees me!" Concubine Shu said happily, "This child likes me."

She reached out and picked up Shi'er.

Sometimes she smiled, and her eyes were like black grapes.

"She's so beautiful! She might be even more handsome than Yanling in the future."

Concubine Shu asked someone to bring the golden lock. "It's just been tied."

When Chen Ningyu saw the golden lock, the corners of his mouth twitched.

It was so big, rich and golden. If it was hung up, it would definitely bend Shi'er's neck.

Madam Yang also said, "Why is it so big?"

Concubine Shu smiled and said, "Who knows? Let them make one. It's so big. Forget it, forget it. I'll wear it when it's bigger."

Chen Ningyu thanked him and accepted it.

After talking for a while, Chen Ninghua came and smiled when he saw Chen Ningyu: "Fourth sister, it's been a long time."

Chen Ningyu was stunned. She didn't expect to meet Chen Ninghua.

Concubine Shu smiled and said, "Chen Jieyu often comes here to accompany me. It is indeed rare for you two sisters to meet each other. Why don't you talk together?"

Chen Ninghua said, "I also want to ask my grandmother, where is my mother."

Chen Ningyu and Chen Ninghua went to sit in the side hall.

Chen Ninghua only kept Yulan as a palace maid.

After observing her for these few days, she felt that Yulan could be trusted, so she let go of everything else.

"Fourth sister seems to be doing really well and has gained weight." Chen Ninghua looked at Chen Ningyu and felt that she seemed to be more energetic and calmer than she was at home in the past. She no longer seemed difficult to approach like before.

Chen Ningyu said, "Third sister should be doing well, right?"

Chen Ninghua chose the path he wanted and got what he wanted.

Chen Ninghua said calmly: "It's nothing good or bad."

The emperor had so many concubines, and even if she was favored occasionally, it was nothing.

She asked about the lady.

Chen Ningyu said, "Grandmother is in good health, but Sixth Sister's matter made Grandmother sad, and it took a while for her to recover."

Chen Ningrou is still in the nunnery, and it is said that she has no regrets.

Chen Ninghua sighed: "Sixth sister is also stupid, but if the Fu family is willing, it is not a bad thing."

Chen Ningyu didn't respond.

Because neither the eldest princess nor Fu Chaoqing would agree.

Chen Ninghua lowered his head and drank tea for a while, then said after careful consideration: "I came here today to discuss something with you."

Chen Ningyu looked at her and saw that her expression was extremely serious and a little nervous.

That should be a big deal.

"Fourth sister, Concubine Ning wants me to poison Concubine Shu to death." She said slowly.

Chen Ningyu's eyes widened involuntarily.

"What? Is this true?" She was surprised.

"Is Concubine Ning crazy? She never acted like this even when the Third Prince was around."

Chen Ninghua sneered, "That's different. When the Second and Third Princes were almost grown up, it would have been fine if she didn't succeed then. But after the Third Prince was deposed, she must have thought that everything would go smoothly in the future, and the position of Crown Prince would definitely be in her pocket. But then Concubine Shu is going to give birth to a son. Isn't this interfering? I'm afraid she won't have the patience anymore."

This is absolutely true. Chen Ningyu nodded and said, "I guess that's the case. Is Concubine Shu really pregnant with a son?"

"Yes."

Chen Ningyu fell silent.

This matter is of no trivial importance.

Chen Ninghua was forced to discuss the matter with her, and he must have had no other choice.

She looked at Chen Ninghua and asked, "Does she have something on you?"

Chen Ninghua raised his eyebrows and immediately grasped the key point.

She sneered, "Whether it's true or not, I am nothing in front of her. It's easy for her to deal with me. But because of my friendship with Concubine Shu, I won't listen to her and really kill her. Besides, Concubine Shu is also your aunt, isn't she?"

The words sound nice, but I don't know if she really means it.

Chen Ningyu asked: "What are you going to do?"

"I can only delay it for now. If I want to poison you, there must be a chance, right?"

"What will happen if I tell the emperor?"

"There is no evidence or proof. If I say it, it's just my bad luck."

"Have you told Madam Shufei?"

"not yet."

Chen Ningyu fell into silence again, and this time it lasted for quite a while.

Chen Ninghua was also silent.

She was also tortured greatly because of this matter. If she didn't poison, she would die at the hands of Concubine Ning. If she poisoned, she would definitely die at the hands of the emperor. She didn't think she could get away with it after poisoning. After all, the emperor valued the child in Concubine Shu's belly very much.

Besides, if Concubine Ning succeeds, she will be killed by Concubine Ning sooner or later.

"Do you have poison in your hand?" Chen Ningyu suddenly raised his head and asked.

Chen Ninghua was shocked: "What?"

"Have you? Tell me the truth."

Chen Ninghua nodded: "Yes."

"The one who kills with blood?"

"Concubine Ning gave me several kinds of medicine, some of which are chronic and some of which will kill you if you take them." Chen Ninghua said, "What do you want to do?"

Chen Ningyu raised the corner of his mouth: "I was thinking, maybe you can poison yourself to death."

Chen Ninghua's heart was shocked.

Magnolia behind her also opened her mouth wide.

"You've done something cruel to me before." Chen Ningyu looked at her coldly, "Just consider this as atonement."

Chen Ninghua was stunned.

Half a month later, she really committed suicide by taking pills.

When Concubine Shu found out, she immediately sent someone to tell the emperor and at the same time detained everyone in the Heyu Palace.

Li Shiyu came in a hurry.

"What's going on?" he questioned Concubine Shu.

Concubine Shu looked pale: "I don't know either. Yulan came to ask for help, saying that Concubine Chen had taken poison and was about to die. I hurriedly asked the imperial physician to see her, but I didn't know either..." As she spoke, she gasped for air, extremely terrified, "Why is Concubine Chen like this? Not long ago, she often talked to me."

Li Shiyu hurriedly comforted her and said softly, "Don't worry, don't worry, I will ask someone to investigate thoroughly, go back and rest quickly, don't worry about it."

Concubine Shu said, "I don't know what to do, so I locked up everyone in Heyu Palace. I thought that Concubine Chen would not want to commit suicide for no reason."

Li Shiyu frowned.

Concubine Shu is absolutely right.

Chen Ninghua doesn't look like a weak person on normal days. She wouldn't be like this unless it was a big deal.

After persuading Concubine Shu to leave, Li Shiyu went to Heyu Palace.

The imperial physician had just examined Chen Ninghua and bowed, saying, "Fortunately it was timely, otherwise I'm afraid the life of the Concubine could not be saved."

Li Shiyu asked, "I really took poison."

"Indeed."

Li Shiyu asked again: "Are you awake?"

Before the doctor could answer, a scream was heard from inside.

Li Shiyu hurried in.

Chen Ninghua was sitting on the bed, crying in fear. When she saw Li Shiyu, she looked at him straight, tears streaming down her face.

"What's going on?" Li Shiyu asked, "Why would you take poison? Do you really want to die?"

Speaking of which, Chen Ninghua had a pretty good life in this palace. At least he often visited her.

Now, he is going to commit suicide.

Chen Ninghua cried, "I don't want to do

this either, but I can't help it."

Her voice was so sad that it made people feel uncomfortable.

Li Shiyu sat down at the table and lowered his voice: "What is it? Tell me."

Chen Ninghua shook her head: "I dare not say."

"You don't dare to do that even though I'm here?" Li Shiyu was annoyed. "Is there anyone who can force you to commit suicide?"

Chen Ninghua fell silent.

Li Shiyu stood up suddenly and shouted, "Is there really someone who dares to force you?"

Chen Ninghua cried out again, "Yes, it was Concubine Ning. I had no choice. Concubine Ning saw that I was in frequent contact with Concubine Shu, so she forced me to poison her. Of course I refused, but Concubine Ning could do something to my room at any time. I was really scared and could only die."

After listening to this, Li Shiyu didn't say anything for a long time.

He walked a few steps in the room and asked, "Are you telling the truth?"

"I dare not lie to the emperor. I originally wanted to die!" Chen Ninghua said, "I dare to swear to heaven. If I lie, I will be struck by lightning and never be reborn!"

This oath is very poisonous. Ordinary people would certainly not dare to speak out if they had done something wrong.

Chen Ninghua said: "There are also people from Concubine Ning in my room, so I dare not tell the emperor, for fear that Concubine Ning will know and frame me at any time, so..."

Li Shiyu interrupted her: "Forget it, stop talking!"

He is very confused now.

After all, Concubine Ning was the concubine who had lived with him for so many years.

The two also have a son named the Second Prince.

Seeing that Li Shiyu had not made a decision yet, Chen Ninghua added fuel to the fire and said, "The Concubine Ning forced me to poison her that day, but I refused. Then she said that the world would belong to her from now on, and told me to be aware of the current situation..."

"What?" Li Shiyu got furious when he mentioned the world.

As an emperor, what he cherished most was naturally the power in his hands.

Concubine Ning is just a woman, but she actually covets the throne. No wonder she is so scheming for the second prince.

Li Shiyu knew how excited Concubine Ning was after the third prince was deposed!

Although he treated Concubine Ning well, he could not say he doted on her. He just felt that she was not innocent enough. Now, in order to make the Second Prince the Crown Prince, Concubine Ning actually wanted to poison his unborn child. This was extremely vicious!

"Someone come here!" Li Shiyu shouted.

The guards at the door immediately stood at the door.

Li Shiyu strode out.

Chen Ninghua collapsed on the bed and spurted out a mouthful of blood.

She was really poisoned, so how could she recover so quickly? She just used all her strength to say those words, and now she was completely exhausted.

She closed her eyes and fell asleep.

Li Shiyu ordered his men to torture the palace maids in Heyu Palace.

He personally led people to Rui'an Palace.

Concubine Ning had also learned the news, but she was kept in the dark and had no idea that Chen Ninghua had already informed Concubine Shu and did not really commit suicide. She thought that Chen Ninghua was ungrateful and would rather die than poison Concubine Shu.

She found it strange. She had taken a liking to Chen Ninghua from the beginning and felt that she was full of ambitions, so she hoped to use her talents for her own benefit in the future.

But it turns out that I was wrong!

What great things can a person who doesn't even care about his own life accomplish?

Just when she despised what Chen Ninghua did, Li Shiyu came.

Concubine Ning hurried to greet him.

As a result, Li Shiyu had a gloomy face. When he saw her, he asked her directly: "You vicious woman, how dare you poison my child?"

Concubine Ning almost fainted.

how so······

She took a breath and said, "Your Majesty, I don't know what you are talking about. How could I be such a person?"

Li Shiyu sneered and ordered the imperial guards: "Arrest all the people in Rui'an Palace."

"Your Majesty!" Concubine Ning was so frightened that she knelt down with her legs bent. "Your Majesty, if you want to punish me, there must be a reason. What crime have I committed? Your Majesty said that I wanted to harm people, but what evidence do you have?"

"Evidence?" Li Shiyu said coldly, "There will be evidence soon."

Concubine Ning burst into tears: "Your Majesty, don't you know who I am?"

"It is said that you can know a person's face but not his heart." The Queen came late and bowed to the Emperor, saying, "I am incompetent, and such an unbearable thing happened in the palace. Please forgive me, Your Majesty!"

Concubine Ning hurriedly said, "Your Majesty, please speak a fair word."

Fair words?

The queen sneered. Ever since the third prince was defeated, Concubine Ning had always thought that she was the final winner and was often disrespectful to her as the queen. Although it was a small matter, how could she not see Concubine Ning's true character? If you think about it, Concubine Shu might be better.

How could the Queen not add insult to injury at this moment?

"Sister, whether you are innocent or not, we will know after we investigate. If you have done nothing wrong, why should you be afraid?" The Queen said slowly, "Sister, please get up quickly. You haven't investigated yet, but you seem to be a criminal."

Concubine Ning almost vomited blood.

There are so many dirty things in this palace. If anyone goes to investigate, he will surely find something.

She went to ask Li Shiyu for help again.

It's a pity that at this moment, there is no possibility for Li Shiyu to take back his order.

Concubine Ning's blood rushed to her heart and she passed out.

After Concubine Shu knew about this, she smiled and said, "If I had known this would happen, I wouldn't have done it in the first place."

Yuanniang agreed: "Yes, there is a saying that good and evil will be rewarded in the end. It's not that there will be no reward, it's just that the time has not come yet."

Concubine Shu glanced at her.

What's the point of revenge? If we really rely on God in this world, what can we accomplish?

Speaking of which, I still have to thank Chen Ningyu this time.

Concubine Shu thought that she would have to send a big gift after some time.

After a few days, the truth of Concubine Ning's case came to light. Some of the palace maids were loyal, while others were disloyal. Whoever could not withstand the torture would naturally tell the truth.

However, the emperor did not sentence Concubine Ning to death because of their old friendship and the second prince's sake. He only banished her to the cold palace.

But once she is sent to the cold palace, there is basically no chance of her coming out.

Peace returned to the palace.

When Shi'er was one year old, Shufei's child was also born, and it was indeed a boy.

The emperor was extremely happy and bestowed many gifts.

The Wuding Marquis Mansion was once again in prosperity.

Everyone knows that the Second Prince's position in the Emperor's mind may not be secure because of Concubine Ning, and this newborn will definitely become a strong competitor. When he grows up, he and the Second Prince will definitely end up in a life-and-death battle.

It's a cold winter day, but the sun is shining brightly today.

Chen Ningyu was sitting in the yard making shoes for Yang Yanling. Now all his shoes were made by her, whether they were cloth shoes or boots. She drew the patterns for the boots herself, selected the leather herself, and had them made to order.

Gu Qiu was by her side, holding her own son. Chen Ningyu suddenly heard a small, sweet "Mom".

The sole of the shoe in her hand fell to the ground with a thud.

"Shi'er, Shi'er, are you calling me?" She took Shi'er out of the wooden cradle next to her.

Shi'er put his two little hands to his mouth, staring at her steadily, but said nothing.

"Gu Qiu, Gu Qiu, did I hear you correctly just now?" she asked.

Gu Qiu smiled and said, "No, I heard it too."

"Shi'er, Shi'er, hurry up and call out again. Mother is waiting. Ah, if you call out, mother will ask the wet nurse to feed you milk. Otherwise, mother will take you out to play. The streets are very lively. Shi'er, do you want to go?" She tempted Shi'er in various ways.

Shi Er didn't know whether he understood or not. He blinked twice and suddenly said, "Mom, Mom!"

"He called me mom!" Chen Ningyu shouted,

"He called me mom!"

Gu Qiu was also happy for her: "Congratulations, ma'am."

Chen Ningyu happily kissed Shi'er all over the face.

When Madam Yang found out, she also hurried over and asked Shi'er to call her great-grandmother.

Chen Ningyu burst out laughing: "Grandma, it's hard to even call me mother, how can I call her great-grandma? That requires three words."

Madam Yang also laughed: "Look at my brain, I am also anxious. After all, Shi'er is still young, it's good enough that he can call mother now."

This kept them laughing till evening.

When Yang Yanling heard about it, he also lay in the cradle and refused to leave. He said the word "daddy" thousands of times in Shi'er's ear, but Shi'er just didn't say it. This made him very angry, but Chen Ningyu laughed.

It turns out that being a father and a mother feels the same.

At this time, news came from the palace that Chen Ninghua was pregnant.

Chen Ningyu's heart sank.

Things in this world are always one thing after another.

I wonder if the baby in Chen Ninghua's belly is a boy or a girl?

Yang Yanling saw that she was worried, so he came over and hugged her, saying, "It's too far away. There's no need to worry about it. Instead of thinking about this, it's better to think about what kind of wife we will marry in the future."

Chen Ningyu laughed: "Yeah, there's no way to avoid it, so we have to live in the present."

But there was still some sadness between her brows.

Yang Yanling turned his head and kissed her, then said leisurely, "I am satisfied with my life. I have a good wife, a son, and I have defeated the Mongolian soldiers. At worst, I can resign from my post and travel around the world with you."

Chen Ningyu was overjoyed: "Are you serious?"

"It all depends on whether you are willing or not." He is not greedy for power and can advance or retreat.

Chen Ningyu felt calm.

He is willing to give up everything to protect his family, and she can do the same. As long as we are together as a family, what can't be solved?

The two of them hugged each other and played together again.

Under the candlelight, the room was warm.

(End of full text)

Printed in Great Britain
by Amazon